Contemporary Drag Practices
and Performers

Methuen Drama Engage offers original reflections about key practitioners, movements and genres in the fields of modern theatre and performance. Each volume in the series seeks to challenge mainstream critical thought through original and interdisciplinary perspectives on the body of work under examination. By questioning existing critical paradigms, it is hoped that each volume will open up fresh approaches and suggest avenues for further exploration.

Series Editors
Mark Taylor-Batty
University of Leeds, UK

Enoch Brater
University of Michigan, USA

Titles
Authenticity in Contemporary Theatre and Performance
by Daniel Schulze
ISBN 978-1-3500-0096-4

Drama and Digital Arts Cultures
by David Cameron, Michael Anderson and Rebecca Wotzko
ISBN 978-1-472-59219-4

Social and Political Theatre in 21st-Century Britain: Staging Crisis
by Vicky Angelaki
ISBN 978-1-474-21316-5

Watching War on the Twenty-First-Century Stage:
Spectacles of Conflict
by Clare Finburgh
ISBN 978-1-472-59866-0

Fiery Temporalities in Theatre and Performance:
The Initiation of History
by Maurya Wickstrom
ISBN 978-1-4742-8169-0

Ecologies of Precarity in Twenty-First Century Theatre: Politics, Affect, Responsibility
by Marissia Fragkou
ISBN 978-1-4742-6714-4

Robert Lepage/Ex Machina: Revolutions in Theatrical Space
by James Reynolds
ISBN 978-1-4742-7609-2

Social Housing in Performance: The English Council Estate
on and off Stage
by Katie Beswick
ISBN 978-1-4742-8521-6

Postdramatic Theatre and Form
Edited by Michael Shane Boyle, Matt Cornish and Brandon Woolf
ISBN 978-1-3500-4316-9

Political Dramaturgies and Theatre Spectatorship
Liz Tomlin
ISBN 978-1-4742-9560-4

For a complete listing, please visit
https://www.bloomsbury.com/series/methuen-drama-engage/

Contemporary Drag Practices and Performers

Drag in a Changing Scene Volume 1

Edited by
Mark Edward and Stephen Farrier

Series Editors
Mark Taylor-Batty and Enoch Brater

methuen | drama

LONDON · NEW YORK · OXFORD · NEW DELHI · SYDNEY

METHUEN DRAMA
Bloomsbury Publishing Plc
50 Bedford Square, London, WC1B 3DP, UK
1385 Broadway, New York, NY 10018, USA
29 Earlsfort Terrace, Dublin 2, Ireland

BLOOMSBURY, METHUEN DRAMA and the Methuen Drama logo are trademarks of Bloomsbury Publishing Plc

First published in Great Britain 2020
This paperback edition published in 2021

Series design by Louise Dugdale
Cover artwork © Mark Wardel / Trademarkart.com

A catalogue record for this book is available from the British Library.

A catalog record for this book is available from the Library of Congress.

ISBN: HB: 978-1-3500-8294-6
         PB: 978-1-3503-1919-6
         epdf: 978-1-3500-8296-0
         ebook: 978-1-3500-8295-3

Series: Methuen Drama Engage

Typeset by Integra Software Services Pvt. Ltd.

To find out more about our authors and books visit www.bloomsbury.com and sign up for our newsletters.

This volume is dedicated to the drag warriors and the fabulous kings and queens of performance from the past and present. We salute the drag worker, butching, femming (or both), glamming or trashing on small stages throughout the world. We acknowledge the personal and transformative effort of your art form, which takes risk, investment and bravery. And heartfelt respect goes to those practising drag in places where there are legal restrictions, state laws and hostile, dangerous social environments; we admire and support you. Keep being dragulous! For those yet to experience the many landscapes of drag, welcome. Mind your step; the floor's probably sticky.

Contents

Illustrations

Contributors

Jae Basiliere is Assistant Professor of women, gender and sexuality studies at Grand Valley State University in West Michigan, USA. Their research sits at the intersections of LGBTQ+ performance art, social justice activism and rural queer studies. They are interested in the ways that LGBTQ+ performance artists interrupt the logics that correlate successful activism with inclusion in existing state and social structures. Jae's work has appeared in a number of places, including *Signs: Journal of Women in Culture and Society* and *GLQ: A Journal of Lesbian and Gay Studies*. They are currently one of the managing editors at *Feral Feminisms*, an independent, inter-media, peer-reviewed, open access online journal committed to destabilizing publishing hierarchies and uplifting underrepresented voices.

Olympia Bukkakis – Queen of the Heavens and of the Earth, Empress of Despair, and Architect of Your Eternal Suffering – began performing while completing a BA in social theory at Melbourne University in Australia and kick-started the local alternative drag scene with her party Pandora's Box. She also starred in Australian queer theatre company Sisters Grimm's *Summertime in the Garden of Eden*. Since moving to Berlin in 2012, she has organized, curated and hosted various queer performance nights, including Get Fucked, Fancy, and Apocalypse Tonight. Since 2015 she has organized and hosted Queens Against Borders, a performance event in solidarity with trans and queer refugees. In recent years she has begun to perform in contemporary dance and performance contexts, co-creating Jeremy Wade's 'Between Sirens', and in 2019 she completed a master's degree in solo dance authorship at the Inter-University Centre for Dance (HZT) in Berlin with her graduation piece, *Tales from a State of Shemergency*. *Gender Euphoria* has also been developed into a performance that premiered at Sophiensaele in Berlin as part of the Tanztage festival. She has a passion for the unholy marriage of queer utopianism and historical materialism and prefers darker shades of lipstick.

Nick Cherryman is an academic who works at the intersections between gender studies, feminist theory and queer theory. He holds an MA in gender, sexuality and culture from the University of Manchester, and a BA(Hons) in English literature and theatre studies from the University of Warwick. He has presented research at several international conferences and remains focused on developing his research for his PhD project at Warwick University. His primary interest is in theoretical readings of form and bodies in drag performance and how this reflects/inverts contemporary social trends. His research has covered subjects in popular culture and performance, structures of the graphic novel and theoretical analysis in queer film. He has a multidisciplinary approach that explores the broad fields of gender, media, visual culture, literary and cultural theory, and feminist/queer theory. He is influenced through his training as a transdisciplinary scholar where he felt the focus on a singular approach limited the scope of his research. He is also involved in creating and developing his own drag persona, Ibi Profane, for future research and his own personal amusement. Using an autoethnographic lens, he will explore how comedy and transgressive behaviour intersect and how this can be developed for creating social commentary in a world where boundaries of humour and politics are becoming more blurred. In his personal life he is an avid cook who enjoys SCUBA diving and spending time with his belligerent Jack Russell, The Miadog.

Mark Edward, PhD, is a pracademic and reader in dance and performance at Edge Hill University, UK. He is the author of *Mesearch and the Performing Body* (2018) with Palgrave and the co-editor of *Drag Histories, Herstories and Hairstories: Drag in a Changing Scene* (2021) with Bloomsbury. Mark has published in the areas of mental health and identity with Oxford University Press, risky ethics in autoethnographic and autobiographical performance research with Sage Publications, doing queer and LGBTQ+ research ethics with Springer, and writing on countercultural dance in the UK with Supernova Books. He has performed with the American performer and arts activist Penny Arcade in her work *Bad Reputation* (2004) and with the Australian performance maker and HIV/AIDS activist Jeremy Goldstein in his *Truth to Power Café* (2018). Mark has worked for Rambert Dance Company and toured his own dance theatre works. He is the writer and producer of the film and immersive installation *Council House Movie Star* (2012), featuring his drag persona, Gale Force. He is currently working on his autobiographical research work *What Have YOU Done to Deserve This?* and an autobiographical book and accompanying gallery exhibition titled *The Road to Wigan Queer*. In 1988 Mark was part of the UK acid house and ecstasy rave culture and the same year became involved in protests against Clause 28. He holds a PhD by practice research in mesearching and performance autoethnography, an MA in dance studies and a BA (Hons) in creative arts (specializing in live art, dance and drama). Mark is a lover of vintage clothing, especially velvet suits, and a collector of dolls designed by Jason Wu. In his spare time, he salvages Catholic religious chipped iconic statues from charity shops and queers them up into rejuvenated glittering art pieces. He practises mindfulness and dreams of migrating to warmer climates with a balcony overlooking the sea.

Stephen Farrier, PhD, is a reader in theatre and performance at the Royal Central School of Speech and Drama, University of London, where his work focuses on queer theory, performance, gender and the relations of theatre and performance to community. He has co-edited and written on a number of queer ideas, in particular he works on the relationship of temporalities to queer theatre-making and connects this work to community. He has written and presented on queer intergenerational work, the relation of temporalities to drag performance, queer histories and the playwright Joe Orton, drag performers and informal training, HIV and AIDS onstage, and queer research methodologies, in particular queer practice as research methodologies with Alyson Campbell. He has presented his work at conferences and by invitation across four continents. He co-edited with Alyson Campbell *Queer Dramaturgies: International Perspectives on Where Performance Leads Queer* (2016). He sits on the editorial board of the journal *Studies in Theatre and Performance* and on the advisory board of *Contemporary Theatre Review*. From 2009 to 2012, he co-chaired the Theatre and Performance Research Association's (TaPRA) Performance, Identity and Community working group. He regularly directs shows at Royal Central and elsewhere; he works in devised theatre and has directed work for festivals with well-received shows on cancer and queer identity and on growing up gay, and his co-devised show *Hetty the King (and Other Women I Have Loved)* was nominated for the LGBT prize at Brighton Fringe, UK, 2016.

Rosa Fong is a film-maker and academic. Her work has had an international reach across many formats such as documentary film, short films, film festivals, exhibitions, academic publications and through participation in public forums. Her films have won awards from the British Film Institute and Arts Council of England. She has directed programmes for both the BBC and Channel 4. Her television directing credits include *Chinese for Beginners*, *A Dream of Venus Butterfly* and *Red*. Rosa is also Senior Lecturer in film and television production. Her practice-as-research explores transcultural identities and displacement. Her recent research focuses on memory, displacement, identity and performativity. This is explored through her documentary called *Deconstructing Zoe* (2016), about a transgender actor; a multimedia exhibition called *Dragons of the Pool* (2018), on the forced repatriation of Chinese seamen in Liverpool in 1946; and a series of short films called BEAST (2019), which uses verbatim dialogue to explore the lack of screen representation of East Asians in Britain. Her focus on British Chinese representation on film and television has contributed to an increased awareness on the growing debate on British East Asian Identity and screen representation of British East Asians in the West. Rosa has also worked as an associate producer on the feature-length films *Cut Sleeve Boys* (2006) and *Front Cover* (2015) and *Suk Suk* (2019).

Chris Greenough, PhD, is Senior Lecturer in Theology and Religion at Edge Hill University, UK. His work explores the intersections of sexuality, gender, biography, living experiences and faith. He is author of *Undoing Theology: Life Stories from Non-normative Christians* (2018) and *Queer Theologies: The Basics* (2020). He has also published on the theme of methods in queer research.

Nina Kane, PhD, aka Jared, is a researcher, performer, dramaturg, fool, teacher and artistic director of Cast-Off Drama (www.castoffdrama.blogspot. com). She has nearly twenty years of experience in developing gender-based performance projects using gallery collections, and most recently delivered a programme for York Art Gallery on the Flesh exhibition (2016–17). She is a radical feminist and a gay trans* man, active in the trans* arts scenes of Manchester, Leeds and York. A fully professed Black Veil Sister with the Manchester Sisters of Perpetual Indulgence, she carries out queer community, activist and spiritual service as Sister Polly Amarosa of the Blessed Mercy Beau-Cul and Bona Aris. Dr Kane has an affiliation with the University of Huddersfield, has held associate lecturer posts at a number of UK universities, and is a specialist in the theories of Luce Irigaray. She is currently on long-term supply teaching in state secondary schools, covering English and drama classes and is 'out' as trans* in the classroom, inviting students to use 'Sir', 'Miss' or 'Dr' as they wish. Co-editor (with Jude Woods) of *Reflections on Female and Trans* Masculinities, and Other Queer Crossings* (2017), she is currently completing her first solo book for Routledge on the playwright Sarah Kane (due 2020).

Joe Parslow, PhD, is a researcher and lecturer working across the fields of drama, performance and queer studies. Their research focuses around drag and queer performance, and in particular the ways in which queer communities emerge around performance. They have published work on queer performance practices, with a particular focus on how modes of queer survival and resistance might be learned and passed on through drag. As a lecturer they have taught across the fields of applied theatre, performance research skills, queer methods and queer studies, and have been invited to present papers at national and international conferences exploring contemporary drag performance, queer histories, and politics. Alongside their research, Joe has worked extensively in LGBTQ+ nightlife settings as a producer and manager of drag, burlesque, cabaret and queer performance events, working with internationally renowned drag performers from the UK, European and US drag scenes to bring drag performance to stages in London and beyond.

Kieran Sellars is a doctoral researcher in performance studies and associate tutor in drama at De Montfort University, Leicester, UK. Kieran's doctoral thesis explores queer performances of masculinity in live art and how these performances reconfigure the dominant heteronormative gendered landscape. His research interests include gender and sexuality, feminist performance art and the male body in performance.

Kayte Stokoe, PhD, completed their doctoral thesis at the University of Warwick under the supervision of Dr Oliver Davis. Kayte's monograph, *Reframing Drag: Beyond Subversion and the Status Quo*, is published with Routledge. Their research interests include critical theory, comparative literature, drag, disability studies, transfeminism and trans embodiment. Their articles include 'Fucking the Body, Rewriting the Text: Proto-Queer Embodiment through Textual Drag in Virginia Woolf's *Orlando* (1928) and Monique Wittig's *Le Corps lesbien* (1973)' (2018). This is featured in *Queering the Second Wave*, a Paragraph Special Issue, edited by Lisa Downing and Lara Cox. Kayte is the author of 'Are Drag Kings Still Too Queer for London? From the Nineteenth-Century Impersonator to the Drag King of Today', which appears in *Sex, Time and Place: Queer Histories of London, c.1850 to the Present* (2016), edited by Simon Avery and Katherine M. Graham. Kayte has also written book reviews for *French Studies* and *Foundation*, and a bibliographical review article for Oxford Bibliographies.

Allan Taylor, PhD, is a London-based academic and practitioner working across media, performance and photography. His research interests centre on gender and performativity in popular and visual culture, particularly how citation and repetition underpin and solidify our idea of 'cultural reference', and he recently completed a practice-based PhD at Falmouth University entitled 'Performance, Photography, Performativity: What performance "does" in the still image'. As an artist, he has performed nationally and in 2016 became a Pride's Got Talent finalist with his drag act Lady Glamour Nouveau. He is currently Senior Lecturer at the University of East London.

Mark Wardel, aka TradeMark, is a contemporary artist whose work explores issues of identity, portraiture and the artificial self-created personae prevalent within the entertainment industry, club and urban LGBTQ+ subcultures. His distinctive hand-painted work draws on influences from traditional portraiture through post-punk graphics, New York urban art of the 1970s and 1980s, Soviet-era propaganda posters, 1950s physique photos, pop art and contemporary high-fashion imagery, and it has been exhibited in galleries and museums internationally, including London's V&A Museum, where he created an edition of 300 David Bowie life-mask sculptures as part of their record-breaking *David Bowie Is* exhibition in 2013. Clients include Soho House Films, Absolut Vodka, David Bowie Isolar New York, Homotopia Festival, *Dazed & Confused*, Boy George, EMI Records and Defected Records. He lives and works in London.

Raz Weiner, PhD, is a maker and researcher of performance. His PhD thesis at the Royal Holloway University of London is titled 'Out of Line: Performing Drag and Archive in Settler Culture', combining archival research, ethnography and autoethnography in the study of drag at the intersection of settler colonialism and queer theory. His work explores the phenomenological workings of drag and its implication in and extension to bodies other than human such as landscapes and architecture, where performance-making serves simultaneously as a methodology and a mode of contemplation. This study is informed by nearly two decades of intensive educational and cultural activism in Israel/Palestine. Raz was co-editor of *Platform: Journal of Theatre and Performing Arts*, based at the drama, theatre and dance department at Royal Holloway University of London (2016–18). His performance work presents in venues in Tel-Aviv, Jerusalem, London and Berlin, in the capacity of a performer, director and/or dramaturg. His drag persona, Tilda Death, is a life project, epistemic framework and activism all put in one short wig.

Kalle Westerling is a PhD candidate in theatre and performance at The Graduate Center, CUNY, working on a dissertation about the history and aesthetics of male-identified bodies in twentieth-century burlesque and twenty-first-century boylesque. He is currently an instructional technology fellow at Macaulay Honors College, CUNY.

Acknowledgements

The initial idea for this volume has been swirling around in both our heads for several years. After many late-night email discussions, early-hours rambling text messages, endless telephone conversations, Skype chats (while wearing 1960s camp and flowery house coats) and periods of hiding in faraway places, we have finally felt confident about letting our creative and critical work settle onto the page. We have taken a shimmy back from the labour of love that it has been and want to acknowledge the amount of generous support we have received, without which this project would not have been possible. It is difficult to know where to start and probably when to stop. In the words of Maria von Trapp, let us start at the very beginning with the largest amount of gratitude going to our contributors, without whom this volume would not be possible. We thank you for your patience and generosity, especially when we asked for changes and were perhaps pernickety and demanding. The volume is all the stronger for your contribution and forbearance.

We would like to thank the institutions who supported the project, Edge Hill University and the Royal Central School of Speech and Drama, University of London, for funding, teaching remission and much-valued support. In no order thereafter, we are most grateful particularly to Dr Nikki Craske, Professor George Talbot, Professor Kevern Verney, Dr Anastasia Konstantopoulou, Professor Steve Davismoon, Professor Victor Merriman, Professor Maria Delgado and Professor Simon Shepherd. We are thankful to Methuen Drama, especially the senior commissioning editor, Mark Dudgeon, for commissioning this and the second volume, *Drag Histories, Herstories and Hairstories: Drag in a Changing Scene* (2021). We extend grateful thanks to our editorial assistant at Methuen Drama, Meredith Benson, for the smoothness of the process and speedy replies to our questions and requests. We appreciate the time and effort given by the series editors, Professor Enoch Brater and Dr Mark Taylor-Batty; their positivity and helpful feedback suggestions have influenced what we have produced. We are equally appreciative to the artist Mark Wardel for providing such amazing artwork for the book covers. Our utmost gratitude goes to Mark Ravenhill for his enthusiastic foreword.

Mark has valued the support from his colleagues on the BA Hons dance degree at Edge Hill University – Elisa, June, Karen, Michelle, James, Julia, Debbie M, Debbie N, Gina, Vicky – and Edge Hill University's Arts Centre manager Dr Cathy Butterworth for acting as a wise springboard for Mark's daily tête-à-tête. Mark is most grateful to Dr Christiana Hadjidemetriou and Dr Louise Mercer for their ongoing support in his journey towards optimum well-being, and Pat for her spiritual wisdom. Respect goes to all those fabulous Wigan queens from the 1980s, especially the Clowns Bar and Henry Africa's posse, and to Chris D' Bray for his long-standing friendship, and to the late (and wonderfully fierce) Gary Bradshaw for his irreverence, queerness and bravery. During the research process for this volume, Mark's father, Joseph, died. He was rather proud that Mark and Stephen had secured a contract with Bloomsbury and even more proud of the fact it was going to be about drag. Joseph would have appreciated this book. Mark is fortunate to have a caring mother, Sylvia, who has shown Mark constant love and support throughout his life no matter how queer, crazy and unruly he may have been. Mark's siblings, Val, Liz and Barry, have been soul-building and enabled him to grow and understand (dys)functionality. In many respects, Mark's contributions to this volume pay homage to his late sister, Denise, who first introduced him to men in make-up and platform boots and encouraged his androgyny and glamour because of her love for David Bowie. Finally, Mark is eternally grateful to his partner Chris for his personal encouragement, unconditional love (until it comes to doing the housework and laundry!) and endless supply of cups of decaffeinated coffee.

Stephen thanks his colleagues at the Royal Central School of Speech and Drama, University of London, for their support in enabling him the time and space to take part in the project. It is too easy to forget that we rely on the understanding and flexible support of our colleagues for projects such as this. In particular, Stephen is grateful for the encouragement, support and guidance of Maria Delgado, Dan Hetherington and the team in the research office, as well as the contemporary performance practice degree team. Likewise, the open discussion with colleagues, PhD researchers, students and graduates working in drag and queer has been enriching for this project and Stephen's journey through it. And of course, thanks to Stephen's partner, George, for encouragement (and curtseying).

Mark would like to thank Stephen for his calmness and his ability to stick a soothing plaster over the sometimes-turbulent research process. Stephen would like to thank Mark for his impish ways and for ripping the plaster off, allowing the turmoil when needed.

Finally, we acknowledge previous drag scholarship and the range of performers that we write with and about. Their intellectual contributions, onstage effort, sweat, swagger and glamour pave the way for this book to be a valued neighbour on the shelf or on the hard drive. Move up! Make room. We are here.

Mark and Stephen

Foreword

Growing up in suburban Britain in the 1970s, my childhood was full of men in dresses. All of this on prime time television in the front room with Mum and Dad, my brother and I watching.

There was Dick Emery, who included amongst his range of characters the busty blonde Mandy. Her catch phrase 'ooh you are awful but I like you' was something we kids would regularly call out to each other in the school playground. Les Dawson played the northern housewife Ada Shufflebotham, who would mouth salacious gossip to her neighbour Cissie over the garden gate. Saturday night favourites *The Two Ronnies* would often perform 'female' characters.

There was Danny La Rue – still a big star, although starting to fade a little after his 1960s heyday. He billed himself sometimes as a 'female impersonator' and sometimes as a 'comic in a frock', with elaborately bejewelled costumes and lavish wigs.

And there were the genteel 'ladies' Hinge and Brackett, who had their own TV show and would pop up on others to sing light opera numbers with banter in between. A tiny proportion of the TV audience realized that their act had begun only a few years before in London's drag pub The Black Cap, with only the very filthiest of their double entendres removed for prime time television.

And it wasn't just on television. Down at the village hall, the local amateur theatre company would stage an annual pantomime. The local bank manager would wear a huge dress and wig to play the Dame. His wife, meanwhile, would wear thigh-high boots and adopt a butch swagger to play Dick Whittington or Aladdin.

This 'pantomime boy' was the last reminder of a music hall tradition. In the late nineteenth and early twentieth century, some of the famous and highly paid stars, such as Vesta Tilley, were women who impersonated men. By the 1970s in Britain, the traffic was almost all one way: white men, straight and gay, impersonating women – all of this rooted in a robust, popular tradition of working-class entertainment.

Representations of gay men on television at the time were negative. Dick Emery's cast of characters included Clarence, whose catchphrase 'hello honky tonks' was delivered in a camp sing-song. Emery was straight, but it was a caricature taken up by John 'I'm free' Inman and Larry 'Shut that door' Grayson, the most visible (if not entirely 'out') gay entertainers of the 1970s. With the wider public starting to be aware of the activities of the Gay Liberation Front, gay men in popular entertainment were shown as ridiculous but also frightening in their predatory sexuality.

As a child, I saw these gay characters as a warning of what not to be. A man in a dress seemed to me to be an altogether better role model.

When I was about four or five, my parents were happy to help me put together a dressing-up box. This consisted mostly of dresses, hats and costume jewellery, largely cast-offs from female family members. I would decide who I would be. Cinderella was a favourite, as was Maria from *The Sound of Music*. An audience wasn't necessary, although I would also 'perform' in frocks for the family and sometimes neighbours. I don't remember anyone being anything other than encouraging or at least indulgent of a boy in a dress.

Why then, I wonder, did I never step out of the house in my drag? Where had I understood that, although it was fine to dress and act like this inside, it would be unacceptable and even dangerous to do this in public and outside the frame of performance? At the age of five, and with no one explicitly stating the rules, I'd learnt the boundaries for my drag.

In 2009, to make the show 'A Life In Three Acts', I conducted a series of extensive interviews with Bette Bourne. Bette, the driving force behind the drag troupe Bloolips, opened up for me a history of drag in the 1970s and 1980s that was altogether different from my childhood experience of light entertainment.

It's a history with roots in radicalism and activism. In the late 1960s, Bette dropped out from a career in classical acting to join the Gay Liberation Front. Starting to wear a frock to discover a 'new way to be a man', he lived in a drag commune in Notting Hill (there were several in London at the time). 'I thought', Bette says, 'that I'd stopped acting. This was now about wearing frocks in the street as an out gay queen.' But eventually Bette combined drag activism with performing, founding the Bloolips as a theatre group of visible out gay men in drag.

Paul Shaw, a key member of the Bloolips, points out that in the 1970s there was a long-standing tradition of gay men referring to each other as 'she' and adopting female nicknames. But this had always been in private, a way of enforcing a code of secrecy. 'There were queens around', he says,

who would go to drag balls but never wore drag on the streets and only called each other by drag names amongst themselves. When I joined the Bloolips, Bette asked me what my drag name would be. I said that, amongst each other, my gay friends had called me Precious Pearl. So that's what I became in Bloolips. It felt quite illicit, naughty at first, showing off a femme-y queen side of myself that I'd had to supress. It was political because it was taking something that was hidden before and putting it out there.

Contemporary Drag Practices and Performers is a wonderful celebration of the diversity of contemporary drag. It's inspiring to read of the innovative and eclectic ways that contemporary performers are opening up new possibilities for identity and activism – and to see that in a globalized culture drag still maintains its power to challenge and surprise, that there are so many of us 'putting it out there'.

Mark Ravenhill (and interview with Bette Bourne and Paul Shaw), July 2019

Preface

Mark Edward and Stephen Farrier

It is remarkable to count the number of times, as drag performers and writers, we have been asked, 'Why do you want to do drag?', 'Why study drag?' or simply 'What is drag?'[1] Drag often attracts a continuum of questions, some of which can be directly answered, others not so straightforwardly (we come to answer a range of these questions in our joint contribution in Chapter 1). It is sufficient to say at this point that popular forms of drag have enjoyed immense success in the mainstream across the few years leading up to editing this volume. In part, this success and its impacts on the form and the communities that make drag are key drivers for our work on this project. We see this book as an example of both the beauty and chaos that result in combining in one place drag practices, the spaces in which it is made and plays, constructs of identity, reflective writing and academic engagement. In this volume, drag leaves the relatively safe space of its dressing room, performance spaces and air-brushed media settings in order to engage with performance analysis, narratives from makers and critical theory. Despite the messy chaos (mess is a resistive strategy in this context, more of which further on), the rich generativity of this exercise produces knowledge and constructive content and helps voice lesser-known practices.

Before we sketch out the insights from each of the contributors, first a note about terminology. Drag has reached popularity in the mainstream, its cultural influence mirrors contemporary discussions around gender and identity nomenclature. So often, such discussions of gender and identity terminology are loaded with anxieties, as their multiplicities are daunting to some while felt as restrictive to others. These debates can be experienced as happily radically revealing, positively purposeful and also injurious and harmful. Changing terminologies surrounding issues of gender and sexual identities are timely and necessary, especially in the mainstream and social media. As editors of this volume, we are sensitive to such issues and we see them as important. However, it is not our position here to offer an extensive explanation of definitions. This is partly because those definitions change so rapidly and the process of publishing cannot keep up, and also that we do not wish to express one form of identity description as 'right' or 'wrong'. Rather, in this volume we have encouraged contributors to self-identify as they please, and, where needed, asked some authors to point to sources where readers not familiar with the terms can find out more. More importantly, we have been keen not to expect or demand that any identification be justified by those who use it. Such calls for definitions fall inequitably to some members of the community more than others; as such it can be exhausting to continually explain a positionality or subjectivity. This editorial strategy is necessary, as this volume is not about specific debates in markers of identification. However, we understand that the constant call for defining oneself in relation to gender is generally only aimed at those who identify plurally or non-normatively. Demands for explanation can be felt as justifying an existence rather than defining it.[2] Therefore, definitions of the various gender positions in this volume are guided by the practices in which the contributors work. It is important to note, in any case, that all gender positions are plural, varied and context and historically specific, even where they appear fixed or transhistorical.

Despite this volume's desire to give room to a diverse set of drag practices, guided in part by gender discourses, there is an elephant in the room. At the time of writing, the power of *RuPaul's Drag Race* (Logo TV/VH1) in any discussion of drag, though resistible, is undeniable. The show has a gravitational pull on current discussions and serves as a popular touchstone for considerations of drag performance. Many of our contributors deal with its impact and unpick some of its problematics (we have done this ourselves in our joint chapter and connected popular drag practice beyond the historical timeframe of *RPDR*), yet, the show also has enabled a much wider consciousness of drag performance and has opened drag to a wider audience. Part of the challenge in a project like this is to pay attention to the power that *RPDR* has in discourses around drag and to balance that with making room at the table for other forms of drag to take a seat. As such, we have ordered the chapters in the book in a way that seeks to make space for voices and practices that are underrepresented in current discourses on drag.

On the note of dominant discourse in the area, there is another gravitational body around which many of the contributors orbit. The work of Judith Butler is resonantly powerful for many submissions, particularly her early work on gender performativity. Butler's work, however, does not form the core of the volume – that is taken up by performance – but her work does enact a profound influence on how drag is thought. We deal more fully with this in our joint chapter that follows, but we note here how the relatively small space Butler gave to drag in *Gender Trouble: Feminism and the Subversion of Identity* (1990) profoundly influenced discourses of drag and gender to the extent that discussions of them seem to go hand in glove. Yet, we notice that, although all performance is enmeshed with gender, this reflex is not stimulated in all performance analysis. So, for the volume in hand, we understand its influential power, but have also welcomed contributions that do not circulate these ideas, being open to polyphony as a key driver in our editorial choices.

The practices about which many of our contributors write might look the same, use similar tropes or embody performance in closely related ways. However, this similarity is not what coheres the voices in this volume; rather, it is their attention to work that is not part of the mainstream (at the time of writing) that ties the contributions. Though of course contributors connect to the mainstream in many ways, the strength of these combined voices in speaking to lesser-known practices (or the impact of dominant norms in drag) is less through an ideological togetherness, but more because of their joint focus on what drag can do or enact. We have not insisted that contributors agree about drag because we think there is strength in pluralism. Following a similar impulse present in queer theories, we position any attempt to cohere discussions around drag in performance as one that tends to have an ossifying effect and reproduces sameness. We are keen in this volume that we do not hold one form of drag as a yardstick for another because this kind of energy resists emergent forms, and we want the diverse set of practices circulating in drag performance to take up space in this volume. In the current context, a yardstick is first a means of measurement, but it can soon turn into a powerful tool with which to beat, or tempt, new work into a pre-recognized shape.

As a consequence of attempting to resist the ossifying effects of ordering performance practice – a task that some might think foolhardy – in this volume we have not clustered together forms of work that appear to be like one another. This may be a source of frustration to a reader who hopes that what follows will come to a singularity in relation to drag. Rather, the practice that we see and in which we are involved is plural; it can be clustered in any number of ways. Given that we think the essays presented in this volume, and the next, will provide focused narratives detailing drag performance, we acknowledge there is only room to reflect on a fraction of what is happening in drag. Thus, we see the whole volume as a cluster of work, a constellation that sits together by dint of its practice and location in this book. We have resisted, for example, separating out kinging from queening as happens in other works, in part because we do not feel that such separations are always obviously discernible in the performance work and because we want to emphasize connectedness, as Stephen has noted elsewhere:

Speaking of drag kings and queens together is the writing out of a political inclination, one that serves to look to what coheres these performances and performers in terms of a functioning community.

Although, as it has been noted, the audiences and traditions of kinging and queening are different and the effects in the performance room follow this difference, there are places where kings and queens speak similar languages.[3]

In this volume we emphasize that the work we look at is most often called drag practice, but these practices in themselves are diverse and connect to various histories, geographical locations and performance forms. Often, seeing a drag show is an experience of watching a number of short-form performances that are put in an order to make theatrical sense; they cohere because they are presented on the same bill. This is a kind of structure we wish to replicate in this book and, in so doing, offer readers a similar sense. Although we make the point that the chapters are connected by a kind of narrative thread, we also think that the following essays cohere because they are carefully put together in this volume in a way that emphasizes connectedness. And, like the experience of watching a drag show, there will be acts that some audience members are more interested in than others, and likewise with the chapters we present here, we expect that the bill of chapters will resonate in different ways for different readers.

Below we lay out our thinking when ordering the chapters. They are not ordered to move to a final conclusion, to make a specific point or to support a framework we have theorized. We resist this for the reasons above, that is, this strategy does not reflect the messiness of the form nor its diversity. But we do want to tell a story with the order of the chapters – as a broad map of a move from dealing with connections to mainstream work to indicating the distinctiveness of practices. We do not wish a coherent whole with the chapters; rather, the volume should be a starting-off, or springboard, from which a different journey might be taken through lesser-known, lesser-seen or lesser-understood practices (at least to a position only familiar with dominant representations of drag performance). This resistance to singularity is purposeful in that it follows the central shared ideas of queer theories of resistance to (homo)normativity and, more importantly for us as editors, often coming to a singular point, or even a series of points, means some practices are occluded, ignored or counted 'out' because they do not fit a particular formulation of what drag 'should' be.[4] Our gesture in this volume is to include a range of works, not all of which would be counted 'in' if we held to a fixed idea of drag. If we did this, we would be missing some vital work.

We kick off the discussion with a joint chapter dealing with the drivers for putting together a two-volume project on drag performance (the current volume deals with contemporary practices and the next, drag histories). We seek in Chapter 1 to lay out a case for the need to study drag and sketch it as a burgeoning field in the academy, help define some key issues, and emphasize the plurality of the form. This focus on the form's variety positions the discussion such that we see drag as a grouping of practices that have long roots and entangled histories. However, we do not want to forego looking to dominant forms, as they too are part of our field of study; as such, these dominant practices comprise the heart of the following two chapters and remain a touchstone for many others.

The next two chapters deal with the power of *RPDR*. Joe Parslow starts the conversation off in Chapter 2 by looking at the impact the programme has had on local drag practices in the UK. Their work speaks to ideas of drag and its journey across the Atlantic to the UK and what that enables performers to do in the other direction, from the UK to the US. The chapter lays out a complex relationship to dominant forms in a performance practice that is underpinned both by local traditions and an inbuilt resistance to being told what to do. Joe's chapter, then, seeks to balance the pull of the dominance in the form and the pushback (or, more accurately, the enfoldment) from local performers and forms.

Following this discussion is a look to what *RPDR* does to other local forms in the US. In Chapter 3, Kalle Westerling looks to the power the show has on the development of drag itself. Utilizing primary research, Kalle looks to the influence of the TV programme in relation to notions of success for drag performers and how those who do not appear on the show deal with their day-to-day material realities. The chapter notes that the influence of *RPDR* has been present across its ten seasons, and queens now come onto the scene in part because of it, so powerful is its pull. This has material consequences for established cultures of drag (in particular, the chapter looks to the 'trashy drag forms' in Brooklyn, New York), and Kalle unpicks how *RPDR* replicates itself in relation to its vision of what counts as success. Chapters 2 and 3 both seek to explore what we might call a colonization of drag through a dominant form.

Rosa Fong's chapter begins with a rather more established version of cultural colonization, that of the eighteenth-century European decorative style, chinoiserie. In the chapter Rosa, a film-maker, traces through the idea of chinoiserie drag, a hybrid of wide and inaccurate ideas about the East in eighteenth-century European contexts combined with embodied forms of performance about Asian subjectivity. By setting out a strategy for chinoiserie drag built from reading some early film, Rosa presents a reading of her film project *Deconstructing Zoe* (2016). Chinoiserie drag presents not only a way of thinking about issues of yellowface, but also a demonstration of how inherited narratives of gender and ethnicity might be transformed and examined when embodied in drag performance.

The idea of transformation follows through in Jae Basiliere's chapter, which focuses on how impactful drag work can be for individuals negotiating a number of identity markers, and also on how that might be enhanced by working with a collective or troupe. When this is combined with activist ideas, a strong cocktail is mixed. Jae's essay reflects on the work of the Gender Studs, a performance group in Indiana, USA, between 2011 and 2014, and traces how, alongside the development of an individual's journey with drag, there can be a concomitant political drive through fundraisers, protests and advocacy. At the heart of the analysis is a question of success, how it is conceived and lived by the troupe. This serves as a refreshing foil to dominant norms of success, as talked through in Chapters 2 and 3. The underpinning finding of the research is that success is related to an individual's perception of what is important, and Jae extends this as a challenge to a way of thinking about an individual's relationship to a community.

Raz Weiner's contribution picks up on the idea of the individual and their relation to community. He extends this to reflect on how history and memory might also function in this relationship by analysing his work as the performer Tilda Death, a drag character in a show performed for disabled veterans of the Israeli Army on Holocaust Memorial Day. Raz's autoethnographic account of the performance looks at how drag performance facilitated an intervention in the context. He makes a case for drag's undecidability and explores the idea that it opens up possibilities of interaction in the context. The chapter questions the truth of memory and the persistence of vision brought about by gendered expectations, while also honestly tracing his internal reflections and anxieties as he travels to the performance (a situation many performers booked for an extraordinary gig would understand). Central to his chapter is the image of movement and journey: to the character, the performance and the audience.

Kayte Stokoe's chapter also thinks through movement. Kayte's contribution looks to international practice across the US, France and the UK with a focus on bringing a transfeminist critique to the practices encountered in those contexts. The chapter returns us to the RuPaul touchstone to unpick its relation to specific sets of languages, images and embodiments that serve to highlight some of the sheer assortment of practices in these contexts, particularly in relation to trans identities and other non-cisgender positionalities. The chapter posits that the process of looking at the way in which the work is classified as either reactionary or subversive creates a malfunctioning binary, one which detracts from the complexity of the relationship between drag and its effects.

The idea that drag can be seen as almost always binary-resistant, while also using the binary it resists, is the basis for Stephen Farrier's chapter about the female drag queen Holestar. Holestar has been a mainstay on the London drag circuit (and other places in Europe) for about twenty years. The chapter looks to how the existence of female drag queen performance and performers manifests latent (and, at times, blatant) misogyny of the gay community, and examines how Holestar manages this. While looking at the performance work that Holestar makes, the chapter links an underlying energy in the work to popular performance, where drag has found a home for many years. Stephen looks to bond some techniques used by Holestar to drag histories embodied in performance, a performance that is marked by a passing-on of drag modes in and through live work.

Kieran Sellars' work for the volume also deals with the pressure of the past on the present. Sellars analyses a work of Harold Offeh, *Covers*, where the artist re-enacts poses present on influential record covers featuring black women. The chapter looks to articulate this as a form of drag, even when the artist is naked. Kieran packs Offeh's other work (particularly a discussion of a 'snapping workshop' as a way to think about nude drag) around a reading of the performance *Covers*. Kieran discusses how the work flirts with failure in that Offeh cannot hold impossible poses and thus constantly fails. By looking at *Covers* as a type of drag, Kieran accounts for how failure might work in the performances. In the analysis, chiming with Weiner's chapter in this collection, Kieran comes to articulate drag as a complex play of presence and absence and ends with a reminder that drag is hard work, and in Offeh's work, we see that effort laid bare.

Olympia Bukkakis also understands this material effort. In their analysis of the idea of gender euphoria (a counter to gender dysphoria), the discussion focuses on trans and non-binary drag performers. Through some much-needed primary research, Olympia traces the strategies and energies that trans and non-binary performers use to negotiate the places and spaces in which they work. Gender euphoria in the chapter serves as a key idea that looks to the drag space as a place where normative ideas of gender can be ignored, or sidestepped, thereby providing a way of articulating gender play without medicalizing the discourse. Olympia argues that this medicalizing discourse can be experienced as injurious for some people at specific moments. The chapter moves to close with a challenge that resists the trans and non-binary phobia existent in many drag spaces, presenting this challenge not as a nicety of inclusion, but as the opening up of spaces that make some forms of subjectivity possible and, importantly, comfortably welcome.

In terms of play, Nick Cherryman's contribution looks to forms of drag that attempt to undermine gender positions, or at least signal-jam any fixed reading of them. By looking at a small group calling themselves tranimals, the chapter examines the strategies the drag form employs to resist easy definition. Certainly, this kind of drag work makes moot any easy assumption of the gender or sex of the performer because often the performer appears somehow beyond human, in the realm of the animal or some other, fantastical world where drag exists on bodies not sharing all of our human morphology. Because of the indeterminacy of the representation, the chapter tussles with how gender does or does not function in the construction and reception of the tranimal. The idea of tranimal maintains clear links to drag tropes manifest in costume and make-up, which, although it appears slapped on, requires great skill to apply.

Mark Edward picks up this idea of skilfulness by reflecting on how people acquire skills as a drag performer. The chapter details and analyses the drag studies module in a university course developed by Mark. By way of his own large-scale immersive work, *Council House Movie Star*, Mark's reflections in the chapter highlight the importance of understanding the embodied practices of drag performance in concert with a consideration of the histories of the performance form (particularly with a focus on his context in the UK).[5] In the chapter Mark makes the case that, although university might be an unexpected place to drag up, the combination of both practice and knowledge is related and dynamically productive. He makes the point that, as the students explore the aesthetics of drag (wigs, make-up, padding), they also try on critical positions in order to make work intelligently but also make intelligent work.

Drag in unusual places is present in Allan Taylor's contribution, which describes a series of works of drag outside the usual spaces of the stage, bar or nightclub. In the chapter Allan analyses queerness as spectacle by playing with drag performance in parts of rural England to explore ideas of visibility, spectatorship and vulnerability, and drag as a mode of crossing personal and public personas. Allan's chapter provides a number of footholds for thinking through drag in public spaces. The discussion pays mind to the inherent vulnerability of public spaces and how drag signals queerness loudly in no uncertain terms. Certainly, the discussion deals with the function of shame in the context of the work, which resists an opening up of gender non-normativity (though when Allan drags up for a herd of cows in a field, that shame is perhaps in abeyance). At its core, the chapter traces an ethics of witnessing in relation to queerness as spectacle.

The volume closes with another consideration of drag in unusual places that links to an ethics of visibility, this time through religious identities and drag performance. Chris Greenough and Nina Kane explore the way that drag performance and/or drag identities have made use of religious images and positions. In the early part of the chapter, Chris lays out some primary research with drag performers in relation to their religious beliefs and thinks through how drag's reputation for subversion might sit with religion and its general emphasis on conservative normativity, noting the tension this creates for some performers. However, the chapter knits together drag and religion, finding commonalities and reading drag practice both theologically and as the embodiment of self-narrative. Building on this idea of life stories, Nina's narrative in the second half of the chapter takes centre stage as it describes a trans* journey in connection with religious ideas, in part through contact with the Sisters of Perpetual Indulgence and through performance works in a gallery. In these works, Nina uses a number of drag tropes – from costume to lip-synching – to think through ideas and embodiments in performance of rebirth and femininity, and the links possible between the past and the present in and through performance. Nina describes how the works in a gallery potentially re-orientated the gallery-goers while offering fruitful possibilities to engage with thinking of religion and plural selves. Nina's performance work embodies the context, in that the gallery is a space filled with pictures themselves fluidly plural as they encapsulate past visions of religious iconography and subjectivity.

Behind the (glitter) curtain

We are aware that, as we study and probe the performers whose work we watch and study, there is a gap in the process whereby the writer is only present through a kind of silence – this is replicated across academic work. We ask performers things we might not be so forthcoming about ourselves. Work in queer theory has taught us nothing if not that these kinds of silence are often indices of unacknowledged or under-acknowledged structural power. So, we understand that in a book such as this somehow providing a way of getting to know the authors through the writing is important. Thus, we want to join those writers in the area of gender and sexuality who offer a little bit about their background in relation to their experience of the world, of class, race, gender, sexuality and other markers of identity. Fully aware that stories offstage are as rich as the onstage narrative, we offer the following self-narratives that resulted in the collaboration for this book. We are two white, cisgender gay men who have a love of drag and performance. The current merging of the practice of drag with blazing new trails in its academic study is a context into which we have both ventured differently. Our collaboration emerged through our creative conversation, moments of hilarity and appreciation of queer performance, which resulted in friendship. Our histories reveal experiences of hardship, adversity, scholarship, grittiness and the messiness of life in research. We met in an academic setting at an international conference in Barcelona. Mark was sharing his latest practice-led film work, *Council House Movie Star* (2012), which focused on his immersive installation performance of an ageing drag queen, Gale Force. Stephen presented a paper on the issues and dilemmas of conducting queer research and engaged in debate and questions around how we do queer research when queer ultimately is slippery, silhouetted even. Both of us were allied through our backgrounds and narratives of survival, and both committed to similar areas of interest, such as ethics, equality, politics and integrity. This was all underscored with a working-class grit and the knowledge it brings. We found ourselves at places in our working lives where we had access to help set the stage for drag studies within the academy. This is not a wholly unusual story; in the process of coming together to edit this volume we were aware of the fact that we are not the only ones who have trodden this path as practitioners and academics, as makers, thinkers and researchers. What we have come to understand through our work and position, supported by our various privileges, is that we have an obligation both to support drag practice through our writing and performance work and to make sure that we engage critically with it where we feel it problematic. And, we are keen to make clear, our discourse in drag acknowledges that there are many perspectives, positions and attitudes that we do not represent by dint of our situation. Thus, we are of the opinion that when speaking about this kind of work, we do so with the understanding that this is contingent and acknowledge that, given the rapidity of the shifts in discourse around drag at the moment, some of what we say here might be out of date as soon as the ink dries on the page.

As a 1970s child, living in the suburbs of Wigan in the northwest of England, Mark used to play with his Bionic Man (a character called Steve Austin from the popular TV series *The Six Million Dollar Man*) and his Action Man figures by engaging them in deep-kissing scenarios, while his school friend and her Sindy doll looked on horrified.[6] He used to dress/drag up Steve Austin and Action Man by squeezing their muscular bodies into ill-fitting dresses and sticking white cotton wool on their heads to characterize huge blonde hair to resemble that of the film star Diana Dors, Agnetha Fältskog from the 1970s pop band ABBA, and the brassy and camp TV character Mandy played by the British comedy actor Dick Emery.[7] Mark used to firmly force their large feet into Sindy doll's red, stiletto-heel shoes. Creating a space where two male figures could kiss and wear dresses without fear of queer bashing was a display of Mark's childhood playfulness and innocence before the social and cultural structures and trappings of a working-class community in the northwest of England started to seep into his psyche as a developing gay teenager of the 1980s. This was an environment overly saturated with homophobia, where the terms 'gay' and 'homosexual' were unmentionable and drag not widely visible. Curiously though, drag and dragging up was acceptable if it was in the context (and confines) of the northern fun pubs and the person in drag could make people laugh.[8] Other acceptable dragging included fancy-dress parties and heterosexual male TV actors such as Emery, and those at the time who never revealed their sexuality (such as Danny La Rue) and remained largely presumed heterosexual by default, however absurd that might seem to us in the twenty-first century. Of course, the drag remained at a safe distance, a 'them' and 'us' divide. This was a world in which gay and drag were regulated and policed by a dominant northern working-class heteronormativity.

Stephen was born at the 'fag-end' of the 1960s and also comes from a similar background as Mark but based in the south of England, where his family had little money and lived in social housing and where he had experience of the UK care system. Both these contexts were rife with policing gender and sexuality; thus, much-needed survival tactics developed at a very young age. Like many others, as a young adult Stephen sofa-surfed while finding a sense of self and a place of refuge as a young gay man. He found a kinship among gay communities, where his narrow experience of the world was developed by others' kindness and tutelage. Unlike Mark as a boy, he did not have the foresight to redo Action Man's hairstyle with cotton wool; he would have enjoyed that.

These are not unusual stories (though their presence is rarer than we would like in our academic contexts). Many of the performers whose work is written about in this book will have similar experiences. To be clear here, we share these small narratives not to garner any specific affect, but rather to position ourselves as people who sometimes are in a place to understand, sympathize and empathize with the specific challenges of makers in the drag context – even when that is done from the relative comfort of our privileges. Thus, this volume has been fed and nourished by relationships, struggles, critical discourses, drag work and connections with makers, and it is fuelled by our insistence that less-recognized drag work deserves to step into the spotlight and take up its space.

Notes

1 To be clear here, Mark is a drag performer and academic; Stephen is a director and academic. For Mark, as a drag performer, these questions get more personal. Probing questions are not unusual in this situation, and he is asked on a regular basis: 'Where have you hidden your cock? I bet

you've shoved it up your arse!' and 'Do you want to be a woman?' and not
forgetting the obligatory 'Are those tits real?'

2 At the time of writing, the charity Stonewall offers a glossary of terms
online in relation to gender identity as they are commonly used. For more
academically informed definitions, the *Global Encyclopedia of Lesbian,
Gay, Bisexual, Transgender, and Queer (LGBTQ) History* offers a number of
sources and relates them to a global context.

3 Stephen Farrier (2017). 'International influences and drag: just a case of
tucking or binding?'. *Theatre, Dance and Performance Training*, vol. 8, no. 2,
pp. 171–87 (p. 185).

4 See Lisa Duggan (2002). 'The New Homonormativity: The Sexual Politics
of Neoliberalism'. In Castronovo, R. and Nelson, D. D. (eds), *Materializing
Democracy: Toward A Revitalized Cultural Politics* (Durham: Duke
University Press), pp. 175–94. Duggan uses the term to note the assimilation
of heteronormative ideals and constructs into LGBT culture.

5 In the UK context, 'council house' is a colloquialism for government social
housing. It has connotations of poverty and working-class identity.

6 Mark has been collecting vintage Sindy dolls for many years, partly
due to some form of rebellious act towards his parents for not being
allowed a Sindy doll as a child. It was not acceptable for a boy from a
northern working-class community to have a doll. His collection of vintage
(1966–86) Sindy dolls will be exhibited in the future as part of Mark's ongoing
autobiographical performance and exhibition work, *What Have YOU Done
To Deserve This?*

7 In 1971 (year of Mark's birth), Diana Dors visited Mark's hometown (Wigan,
UK) and gave a performance at the Queen's Methodist Mission Hall.

8 For an analysis of the northern fun pub scene of the 1970s and 1980s, see
C. D' Bray (2021). 'Camp and Drag in the Mainstream: A Critical
Study of the Phenomenon of the British Northern Fun Pub 1973–1993'. In
Edward, M. and Farrier, S. (eds), *Drag Histories, Herstories and Hairstories:
Drag in a Changing Scene*. London: Methuen Drama.

1

Drag

Applying Foundation and Setting the Scene

Mark Edward and Stephen Farrier

As we were editing this volume and writing this joint chapter between 2018 and into 2019, Mark performed alongside Otto Baxter in Jeremy Goldstein's *Truth to Power Café*. Baxter, whose drag name is Horrora Shebang, is a drag queen who has Down syndrome and performs in the UK with the east-London-based company Drag Syndrome.[1] Under the directorship of Daniel Vais, Drag Syndrome has started to garner mass recognition in the UK, overseas visibility and an international online media following. Vais's work with Drag Syndrome and his latest venture, *Radical Beauty Project*, in which photographic images are presented of models who have that 'something extra' (radiant beauty and an extra chromosome), are making strong waves in fashion, art, drag and photography. Both Drag Syndrome and *Radical Beauty Project*[2] present images and practices seldom seen in mainstream, or queer, contexts. These kinds of representations, images and people have mostly been situated as a discourse of the periphery (see Kuppers, 2003) but Vais's performances serve not only the community with whom he works but, for this book on contemporary drag practices, these projects also provide a prick to rupture ideas that saturate the way drag is so often seen. The Drag Syndrome project in particular exemplifies how we in this book, and the accompanying Volume 2 (Edward and Farrier, 2021) focusing on the histories of drag, identify drag in its broadest contexts.

For the project of writing a book about drag, Drag Syndrome opens much-needed discussions around the assumptions of drag visibility and the romanticized concept of what constitutes best drag practices, or drag practices per se. For example, Drag Syndrome's performance at Andrew Logan's 2018 Alternative Miss World (hosted at Shakespeare's Globe Theatre in London) smacks the audience with an array of drag personas dancing and strutting their drag to the sound of Divine's 1984 song 'I'm So Beautiful'. Here Horrora Shebang and others offensively gesture to the audience (by sticking two fingers up, which in the UK context is often offensive) while

Figure 1.1 Horrora Shebang (Otto Baxter) at Alternative Miss World, 2018. Photo: Damien Frost.

dragged up (see Figure 1.1). The performance is powerful and commands the space, resonant in part because the participants and performers occupy the high-profile Shakespeare's Globe, and via drag's aesthetics there is a demand to be seen through the obvious fakery of drag. This kind of drag performance resists boundaries constructed through a reductionist reading of stable identities in drag king and queen performance. Much of the kind of work presented at the Alternative Miss World is more regularly based at the margins and often positions itself as wanting no part of the normative.

Vais's works flows with those who challenge representations anchored in conventional glamour and perfection such as Rasso Bruckert's 2003 *Ganz Unvollkommen* (Completely Imperfect) in which Bruckert presents the viewer with imagery that explores the beauty of the nude and disabled body. Also noteworthy is Ashley Savage's ongoing exhibition and documentation work *Bodies of Difference* and Theo Chalmer's work for the charity Paul's Place, in which Chalmer documented various disabled people from the charity. Much of Robert Andy Coomb's work, particularly on disability and sexuality, is an archive of beauty: a celebration of difference. Earlier disabled artists, models and performers paved the way for others to take to the catwalk and theatrics, such as Debbie van der Putten, Viktoria Modesta, Aldon Plewuniska and Sarah Gordy.

However, our task is not to make an analysis of Drag Syndrome in terms of the visibility of disabled performers, though of course that is an important part of our work; rather, for this book the project and its performers embody one fabulous place on the wide gamut of drag performance. That is, in this volume and the next we are keen to open up the discussion of drag practice by consistently returning to a focus on the diversity of practices that constitute it. Thus, we examine drag's deep grass-roots and community connections and explore how drag for minority subjectivities and communities (mainly, historically, the LGBTQ+ community) in part provides a channel to articulate a voice and subject position, and/or a mechanism of access to speak in a certain way to a specific audience. Drag Syndrome also makes visible current trends in drag performance and can stand as a pathway to acknowledge countercultural drag performance, another long historical root that we explore in Volume 2. With, for example, the likes of the established drag performers/drag and trans activists Bette Bourne, Panti Bliss (discussed shortly), Marsha P. Johnson, Stormé DeLarverie and Sylvia Rivera, drag has powerful roots in subcultural contexts, and this position has fuelled its activist and political agendas. Though it is clear that not all those considered established drag follow an activist or political agenda, for example, Danny La Rue, Bunny Lewis, Lily Savage, Dame Edna Everage and Laverne Cummings are not known for fighting for their political beliefs. Understandably with the recent international rise of *RuPaul's Drag Race* (*RPDR*) (Logo TV/ VH1), much important attention has been turned to the way in which drag performance is constructed and represented for a mass audience; as film scholar Julia Yudelman understands, 'It is not surprising, then, that a vast amount of academic critique has surfaced surrounding RPDR phenomenon. Most of these analyses revolve around political questions of representing drag culture through mainstream media and, more often than not, ultimately argue for either a "yay" or "nay" position toward the reality show's representational accuracy' (2017: 16).

Even with the welcome energy *RPDR* has brought to drag, we are keen to see its representations as culturally and geographically specific, and historically positioned. Yudelman goes on to say:

As the most commercially successful queen in drag history, RuPaul Charles and his TV series have generated critique from scholars, critics, and fans alike. On the one hand, many accounts praise RPDR for its perceived fidelity in representing drag culture, championing the program … On the other hand, a plethora of critics have chastised the show for not accurately representing … drag culture progressively. (2017: 17)

In such a context we want to emphasize, contrary to popular discussions of drag at the time of writing, that not all roads lead to *RPDR* nor does *RPDR* represent drag's pinnacle. However, for good or ill, what stands is its contribution to the explosion of drag visibility in the recent past; it has stormed online and popular media and spawned chat shows such as *Hey Qween* (2018), films like *Hurricane Bianca: From Russia with Hate* (2018) and *Hurricane Bianca* (2016), and the fly-on-the-wall documentary series *Dancing Queen* (2018), which follows the life and everyday happenings of drag performer Alyssa Edwards/Justin Dwayne Lee Johnson's dance school; and the Brazilian cartoon series *Super Drags* (2018) turns drag queens into superheroes. (In addition, at the time of this book's production in the UK, *Drag SOS* (Channel 4), a drag makeover show, was aired and *RuPaul's Drag Race UK* was in production with BBC Three.) However, such visibility has not always been drag's comfortable home. Drag may find shelter or popularity in hegemonic, heteronormative settings, but in such settings, it tends to fall into the trap of repeating itself and appearing to solidify in a particular way, just as repetitions of gender performativity seem to stabilize sex. We note here performers like Dame Edna Everage and Danny La Rue (in the UK) made their living in mainstream entertainment (both received civil honours from Queen Elizabeth II). Important though these figures are, in this book lesser-known journeys are the fuel for the discussion, or at least we are interested in work that seeks, often explicitly, to make a difference to the contexts and communities in which it plays. Maintaining a focus on the mainstream risks our consideration of drag being cut off from its lifeline, which, when it is at its best in grass-roots contexts, pumps the life blood of disruption, perceptive anarchy and creativity into wonderfully crafted diverse forms of performance. However, we would not want to maintain a critical outlook that positions drag as only present in radical forms; historically it has a deep connection to mainstream audiences and performers. In addition, often performers like these did little publicly to change LGBTQ+ lives when working in the mainstream; indeed, La Rue often avoided discussions of gayness, and Everage reportedly expressed transphobic comments (see Glauert, 2019). Whatever their personal perspectives, developed in their historical and cultural contexts, these performers' works can be seen to solidify normativity. So, although these kinds of performers did little openly to question or uncorset gender norms, they remain part of the shape of the field of drag – and although we acknowledge their presence and success, for the volume in hand they will not form a major part. This position is so that we are able to give space to practices that are often overshadowed by the figures popularly known, and often, historically in any case, those figures who have survived and found success in the mainstream did so without much connection to queer or gay culture.[3]

At its roots, if those are possible to concretely know, or as part of its performance DNA, for this volume we are interested in addressing drag performance where it is anarchic, politically activist (as we discuss further in this chapter), questioning of current discourse, indecent, perverse, performatively disruptive, challenging, and socially and academically engaging. Yet we too would be falling into the trap of romanticization to think that all drag embodies this. On the contrary, lots of drag outside the mainstream reinforces normative positions and has a stake in the status quo, and we have both seen lots of work that is regressive, racist, misogynist, transphobic and homophobic, even. Thus, the position we might take in response to questions that drag reinforces binaries (see Taylor, Rupp and Gamson, 2004), or that it embodies misogyny (Berbary and Johnson, 2017), or that it might be a gender version of 'blackface' (Kleinman, 2000) is one that is balanced with the response: it depends when and what show/performer is being watched. There are plenty of practices across drag that reinforce what we would see as negative positions, but there are as many that challenge such assumptions – and complicatedly, there are practices that do both at the same time such that they require further discussion and analysis.

Drag visibility

Despite its chequered history, herstory and (t)hairstory, drag remains as current as ever on a local and international scale. Drag was once considered a subcultural form of 'impersonation' (Baker, 1968), yet to some extent it has made the transition from the periphery to mainstream culture within the Western world. As Kirk and Heath, in their 1984 publication of *Men in Frocks*, state, 'If you'd been living in Britain fifty years ago and wanted to see men in frocks, where would you have looked?' (1984: 7). The same could be said for women dragging up as kings. However, it does not take more than a glance around the globe to see drag's shift, mainly (though by no means only) in Western contexts, from underground and counterculture to mainstream culture. This has meant that others can see drag not only as a performance form exclusively embodied by drag queens, but what is revealed is the creative intelligence and diversity of contemporary drag: drag kings, sissies, bio-queens/kings, post/alt-drag, non-binary drag, animal-drag, for example – this list could go on. Drag is as multiple and creative as the forms are original, and it is in an ever-changing scene.

It is essential then to cast our net wider than the main player on the international scene at the time of writing (that is, *RPDR*). For instance, there are other cognate practices that have drawn our eye as we have been writing, including drag protests against US President Donald Trump's visit to the UK (2018); drag in challenging places, such as *The Fearless Drag Queens of Beirut* (BBC news); and Drag Syndrome, as noted above. Muslim drag performers have also been brought to prominence with the UK television documentary *Muslim Drag Queens*[4] (Channel 4, 2015), showing mainly Asian drag performers and their daily struggles with Islamo-, homo- and drag-phobia. There have been book projects ensuring or asking that young people do not forget the histories of drag performers such as *Mother Camp* (1972) and more recently *Drag Histories, Herstories and Hairstories: Drag in a Changing Scene Vol. 2* (2021), the companion volume to this edited collection. Likewise, social media debates include thought-provoking pieces about biologically female drag queens and cultural appropriation, drag as transphobic and children embracing drag performance.[5] The latter discussion is becoming more popular, with examples such as Montreal-based 9-year-old Nemis Quinn Melancon-Golden, who goes by the drag name Lactatia; in Boston (UK), 14-year-old Bailey Lewis goes by the drag name Athena Heart; and from Brooklyn, New York, 10-year-old Desmond Napoles, aka Desmond Is Amazing, has featured in RuPaul's videos and set up his own drag academy/club for children under the banner of Haus of Amazing.[6] These are self-affirming children who embrace the form as a source of creative self-expression.[7]

Drag is a messy business, in practice and in context. To attempt to see the patterns of activity in this mess, our aim is to begin to shift the focus of drag study to look at it as a performance form while considering the many threaded international narratives that make up the area. We are keen to make it clear that the emphasis of this work is not on the representation of drag as it may appear in plays and performance or as performers playing characters. Often this kind of work happens in what is traditionally known as 'straight theatre' (Campbell and Farrier, 2016) and as such mostly shows only the representation of drag in service of a larger narrative (some recent examples include *Priscilla, Queen of the Desert, the Musical,* and *Kinky Boots*). Frequently, the structure of works that represent drag serves to romanticize the form. The narrative often positions the drag performer as a function in a tale of redemption (of straight people in the case of *Kinky Boots*). Even in instances where this is not the case, drag characters in mainstage shows are rarely performed by drag performers themselves and lack authenticity as a result.[8] Of course, some works have a much clearer sense of being connected to the communities and contexts of drag: where queens' and kings' work appears on main stages and where writers occasionally invite queens onto the stage in straight plays to do segments of their acts or to play cross-cast characters (examples here would be Neil Bartlett's *A Vision of Love Revealed in Sleep* from 1987 and Mark Ravenhill's *A Life in Three Acts* from 2009).

Connected to this idea of 'in service of', we are also aware that drag is often used as an exemplar in discourses on gender, queer theory or politics, including performative theories of gender. This approach has been extensive, yet we aim to redress the balance and recentre discussions of drag exactly how it is lived and practised beyond, in spite of, or before this theory. In this sense, our focus is on drag practice. We highlight the importance of this sense of being historically and geographically specific, while simultaneously acknowledging that the form is inevitably and brilliantly intersectional. Although we may flirt with discourses of ethnography or sociology, such as those present in some contributions to Schacht's and Underwood's volume *The Drag Queen Anthology* (2004) and Esther Newton's foundational work *Mother Camp: Female Impersonators in America* (1972), our project here is neither systematically nor methodologically based in these discourses. Indeed, talking about drag in a way that tidies up the mess attempts to make neat and sanitary a form which is ambiguous, amorphous and tacit. We remain vigilant that any depiction or definition of drag we might produce is complex and contingent.

What is drag? Beyond what Butler saw

Drag is often researched in a certain light, and the well-trodden tracks of the field created by others speaking of drag often fall short of engaging with it as a form of performance. For example, King and Meyer take to task theorists who 'theorize drag, [in such a way that] shows a complete lack of knowledge of drag practice', and say that generally critics and theorists per se present an 'extremely 'skewed' reading of drag work because of a 'lack of field experience' (King and Meyer, 2010: 174). Much work that is available about the study of drag tends to see drag in relation to specific histories, for instance Lawrence Senelick's encyclopaedic and important book *The Changing Room, Sex, Drag and Theatre* (2000) focuses on cross-dressing and slides that into drag performance in a way that we would question. Added to this, some of the discussions on drag in Senelick's book are rather disparaging (particularly about the key drag performance technique of lip-synch), and it does not afford the same level of critical attention to drag as it offers to historical forms of cross-dressing.

Roger Baker's important 1968 (revised in 1994) work *Drag: A History of Female Impersonation on Stage* contains some of the foundational ideas with which we grapple. However, Baker's work has a tricky relationship with trans discourses and deserves updating. For instance, in the 1968 edition of the book, Baker starts by clearing up some of the terms associated with cross-dressing, which leads him to speak of 'transsexualism' in a way that is on one hand sympathetic in terms of the psychological challenge it presents, but on the other refers to any medical intervention as 'damaging'. This position, though quite radical in the 1960s because it understood gender fluidity and its relation to social context, certainly is offensive to a reader in the following century.[9] In the 1994 re-publication, Baker highlights the impact of contemporary lenses on history:

[s]o when my book appeared, in late 1968 I recall, it was a response to, as well as a product of, a particular time. And – like all books – it was the product of a particular person at that particular time ... Today, those years of the mid-to-late 1960s can be isolated quite clearly as a time of radical change in cultural, social and political attitudes, areas in which new approaches to, and different perceptions of, sexuality played an increasingly major role. (Baker, 1994: 4)

A position that fundamentally understands the contingent nature of drag – particularly in relation to historical depictions – allows us to embark on a journey of drag discovery that is not fixed in a specific aesthetic lineage of performers or performances. As such, we reflect fluidity and diversity, discounting rigid definition, taking note of the constantly shifting performance form in our definitions. Drag's pedigree is punctuated by constant crossings and unbecomings. Just as Dorothy Gale, in *The Wizard of Oz*, famously said, 'I've a feeling we're not in Kansas anymore', the same can be said when it comes to theorizing the performance of drag in contemporary culture. However, there are touchstones in the literature that help orientate discussions of drag.

Steven Schacht's and Lisa Underwood's *The Drag Queen Anthology* (2004) started life as a themed edition of the *Journal of Homosexuality* (vol. 46, nos 3–4). It is a collection of papers with some breadth. Yet, earlier than *The Drag Queen Anthology*, and hand in hand with it, is *The Drag King Anthology* (2004) by Donna Jean Troka, Kathleen LeBesco and Jean Bobby Noble, again published as an edition of *The Journal of Homosexuality* (vol. 43, nos 3–4). *The Drag King Anthology* successfully brings together voices from the academy, performers and cultural critics. Likewise, our vision of drag has developed in relation to the study of performance and pays less attention to the long arm of the social sciences, though as we have said, it is informed in relation to them. We engage with the research about drag as intimately part of a performance tradition and context within which the research takes place.

The work of Judith Butler (1990, 1993) is often used as a mobilizing factor to describe drag. It has connected a theory of gender to drag as a kind of reflex – to look at drag is to study gender – and we want to challenge this position. Primarily we want to be clear that although we see Butler's breakthrough ideas about gender as highly important to our understanding of gender intellectually and in our daily lives, her notion of gender performativity does not imply theatricality, a theatricality we are interested in pursuing with this volume. Drag, according to Butler, can serve to rupture the seeming stability of gender. In a much-needed turn away from theory, towards practice, Rupp and Taylor position '"drag-queenness" as a gender category outside femininity or masculinity' (2003: 5), noting how 'drag embodies ambiguity and ambivalence' (ibid.).

Rather than position Butler at the centre of drag theorizing, though recognizing her important position within it, we want to take time to seriously focus on the messy intersections of drag performance. We also want to resist a hegemonic theoretical centre of drag performance. So, to rupture the constant referencing of Butler in drag studies, we use her own words to bring her thoughts into perspective. Butler states how 'there were probably no more than five paragraphs in *Gender Trouble* devoted to drag [yet] readers often cite the description of drag as if it were the "example" which explains the meaning of performativity' (1993: 23). We understand that drag has been parodying, performing, creating, deconstructing and affirming long before queer theory opened its closets.

Where drag is debated and studied, it is often done so within terms of drag as parody or drag as queer resistance. Such discussion is at the level of representation and does not always engage in a very detailed way with the processes or the context of the community that produces it. Parody works because of its close relationship to the object of its activity. It can therefore be seen as a repetition with a critical difference: not a wholescale rupture of normative performativity. Nevertheless, like queer performance, drag frequently enacts rupture through parody, but oftentimes ambiguously or subversively so.

Drag's ambiguity and subversion lie in its openness to multiple interpretations. As a performance form, it does not primarily show gender as a construct; rather, it highlights the power of parody in tackling binary gender. Drag performance demonstrates the instability of all claimed identities on an intersectional basis: performers play with identity markers, including race, class, dis/ability and age. Therefore, to read drag solely or primarily as subversion of gender or sexuality is to miss, or ignore, its potency for intersectional critique grounded in live performance. Yet, we must be cautious to note that there is no drag utopia despite the intersectional focus we might encourage in its study – for every performer we have seen working cleverly unpicking intersectional issues, we remember a performer playing with the same markers of identity and reinforcing stereotypes.

Some drag practitioners not only throw shade, some throw rocks: Activist drag

As we have noted, drag is deeply related to protest and activism (though not exclusively so). Throughout the narratives of LGBTQ+ rights, the confrontational, oppositional and performance nature of drag has been at the forefront of politically charged arenas. Drag queens were famously present at the Stonewall riots in 1969 (McGraw, 2019), and as we have noted, drag protests marked the visit of US President Trump to the UK in 2018. Whereas the 1969 protest was one fight in many against injustice and discrimination against LGBTQ+ people by the police, the 2018 protest was against injustices and inhumane policies aimed at migrants entering the US, where families were separated, judged and deported.

Such resistance, while rarely the cause of radical change overnight, serves to solidify and empower communities. What is significant about the history of drag as protest is that across its history it is guided by a commitment to social justice. In its early demonstrations it was mainly concerned with issues faced by LGBTQ+ communities – hard-won battles for recognition and equality. Recent resistances have broader aims beyond issues that primarily hit the LGBTQ+ community. It may be that this further example of drag's relation to larger issues is associated with its surge in popularity and presence on a mainstream stage.

Even in spaces where drag has become commercialized, drag performers have used the spotlight to raise important issues. In one example of this, Panti Bliss mobilized drag activism to campaign for marriage equality in Ireland (see Walsh, 2016) and, more recently, as part of the vote on abortion. In the US, the 2014 Seattle Pride saw a confrontation between eloquent drag activist Mama Tits and fundamentalist Christian groups protesting against the expression of LGBTQ+ lifestyles at the event. Mama Tits's now-famous response was 'Not today, Satan, not today!' Similarly, but on an international scale, the Sisters of Perpetual Indulgence attire themselves as drag nuns to fundraise for LGBTQ+ groups and HIV/AIDS.[10] Their work has recognized importance to the social fabric of communities, with many organizations and people benefitting from the substantial amounts of money the sisters raise. Likewise, Asifa Lahore has raised awareness of issues facing the gaysian (gay Asian) community in the UK. As a Muslim drag queen, Asifa raises awareness of a double need for activism, being LGBTQ+ and Muslim. Sometimes performing in a rainbow headscarf, Asifa not only confronts the position of Muslim people in the West, but also questions the racism and anti-Muslim sentiments in gay communities.

Because of drag's bombast and fearlessness in the face of power, it lends itself to activism. Despite the acts of bravery, courage and commitment to issues of justice and equity, combined with the way that it fucks with gender and normative expectations, we must note that drag for some audiences and performers is primarily entertainment. Drag performers with an activist bent are acutely aware of the nuances of performing antagonism and understand it is a potent form of engagement and a catalyst for social change. And, of course, the drag performers protesting on the street are also gracing the stage and bringing some of the street with them into their acts; thus, they simultaneously occupy the position of being an entertaining drag performer as well as making a political point.

Drag and intersectionality

Despite activist agendas, drag has both complemented and clashed with issues of intersectionality. Some critics would argue that intersecting identity axes in drag culture reinforce inequalities, particularly in the area of race, class and ableism (Samek and Donofrio, 2013). However, Rupp and Taylor note how 'drag is an important strategy in the gay and lesbian movement's struggle' (2003: 5) and that 'drag can serve as a catalyst for a change in values, ideas and identities' (ibid.: 6). Although the image of the king or queen is immediately readable to those inside specific communities and serves to signal a welcome to minoritized sexualities and queer folk, this welcome is, indeed, ironic, given the often-acerbic put-downs used by drag performers on their audience members in what can constitute a 'read'. So, while its activist agenda has borne fruit in terms of drag's iconic visibility at equality and Pride events, we must not lose sight of the fact that drag is often politically *incorrect* through its parodic nature in a way that is for some in the audience uncomfortable in its ambiguity. In performance spaces, some drag performers mobilize elements of misogyny, homophobia, ageism, racism and disability discrimination to undermine these attitudes, some for the sake of cheap laughs. Some performers are proudly politically incorrect so as not to acknowledge intersectionality, seeing it as not important, demonstrating that getting the laugh is more valuable. Drag's playfulness need not work this way, but it often does. Parsing which kinds of performance and performers stray into this territory of misogyny, homophobia, ageism, racism and disability discrimination for serious examination or for cheap laughs is not always clear, however.

Indeed, the plethora of drag forms creates tensions between subdivisions; for example, in the UK the white expressions of drag culture exist in sharp contrast to the less visible drag performers of colour; similarly, slim queens versus fat drag performers. Whereas drag arguably can colour outside of normative expectations of gender and sexuality, it treads a fine line when it comes to issues of representation. In such a framework, it is often considered that drag queens who are biologically female (bioqueens/female drag queens/hyper queens) represent a form of gender presentation, albeit exaggerated, within expected social norms, yet we read them as subversive because they fuck the gendered norms of the cultures and spaces they inhabit.

Markers of race, fatness, thinness and ability/disability are all present in drag aesthetic presentations. Spectators of *RPDR* will be aware of how intersectional tensions are played out in the workrooms, rehearsals and performances. Diluted discrimination and microaggressions are seen mobilized against non-native English speakers, such as Puerto Rican contestants (McIntyre and Riggs, 2017). Bodies within such a culture are normalized, commodified and exceptionalized. The runner-up of Season 10, Eureka!, for instance, was encouraged to accentuate her non-normative, overweight body, and therefore she referred to herself as an 'elephant queen' as part of self-promotion and branding, using a message which embraces body positivity. Whether this was individual choice or competitive strategy remains unclear, but what this demonstrates is that normative cultures and power exist in drag domains (we might see her strategy as similar to the legendary performer Divine, who caricatured her fat embodiment as part of her presentation, in contrast to drag pageants popular in parts of the

US drag scenes). Issues of class are raised with reference to contestants' backgrounds: educational opportunities, jobs, geographic locations, experience of work. Contestants are able to showcase monetary status in the costumes and accessories they possess, all of which at points have been sites of strain.

RuPaul's famous tag line 'If you can't love yourself, how the hell ya gonna love someone else?' points to what can be read as a superficial ethos of self-love and self-care, yet throughout the competition, the judges reveal the deficiencies and exploit the vulnerabilities of the contestants. Although highlighting a person's shortcomings is not necessarily a negative impluse, in drag culture, pointing to an individual's deficits is part of the acerbic humour for which performers are renowned. The strategy of using sulphuric slurs against other performers or audience members has always punctuated the performance and culture of drag.

Drag norms as cultural hegemony is an issue for contemporary drag culture. There are concerns of bias, prejudice and injustice, which must remain pertinent questions for the community to consider as intersections of identity are negotiated and renegotiated within contemporary drag dialogues. In responding to the agenda of inclusivity with regards to gender and sexuality, drag culture has often been inconsiderate and guilty of exclusion itself. As we have noted, within the academic community, discourse rooted in drag must open its horizons beyond the consideration of gender theory and only local LGBTQ+ issues, and serve to critique and challenge issues of intersectionality and explicit and unconscious exclusionary thought and behaviour.

As such, the ground upon which we walk is diverse and plural. We are keen to make sure that the kinds of journeys we take through this field pay mind to this diversity. In part we want to make sure that the base of the practice of drag is shot through with numerous performance traditions, styles and genres. Thus, we note again, up front, that drag can be community-fuelling, political, liberal, inclusive and radically resistive to dominant norms; it can also embody misogyny, homophobia, transphobia and racism. Thus, we understand that drag as a performance form is presented both in service of a status quo and to question or attempt to radically alter it.

Conclusion

We acknowledge that this volume is not definitive and can never be. Indeed, the queerness of drag offers creative abundance and, therefore, is in constant creation. To offer a definition or claim a definitive guide misunderstands and rubs against what drag does. The discussions in this book give the reader an understanding of contemporary drag performers and practices, captured in words, but their essence offers much more than what can be written. We understand the wider complexities of drag forms to have a much broader narrative resonance than only in the area of performance and performing. This then challenges us with writing and presenting a range of chapters throughout this volume that ultimately present compact international droplets of significant and original work. Theorizing about and delving into drag goes beyond a thumbnail sketch of performance knowledge that has been committed to paper. As with any form of writing about performance, when researching and putting words onto a page, the capture is compromised. Fundamentally, the spotlight is on the living and breathing act of *doing* and *being* drag. We understand the challenge of extracting this from a living, breathing action onto a page, particularly the risk of the words being or becoming the sediments of performance(s) and the secondary remains of living drag narratives. We follow Piccini and Rye and acknowledge this as 'another telling' (2009: 46).

Just as the curious, or petulantly nosy, Alice in Wonderland discovered a creatively constructed and challenging playground when she fell down a rabbit hole, the contemporary relevance of drag provokes and challenges current thinking around culture, media, performance and performance making. It takes us down many holes, round winding loops and tricky bends, and it offers a position of the present, allowing us to critically examine contemporary theoretical frameworks. Writing about and producing drag is like knitting fog and herding cats in the sense that it is an impossibility to arrive at a final drag destination or solidity (indeed we have taken to using the phrase 'herding drag queens' for complex and difficult jobs!). We acknowledge that, as this book makes its way to press there will be new writings, which will follow on from this, that will complement and challenge the work here and further advance the knowledge and understanding of drag as it moves into its next changing scene.

Notes

1   *Drag Syndrome* involved five drag novice contestants and was a first of its kind in the UK. The creative director, Daniel Vais, intends to tour with the work and showcase it to a much wider audience. One of the drag participants featured in the project was Otto Baxter. Baxter is an award-winning film-maker and a noted Shakespearian actor.

2   Wendy Crawford and Gina Dixon have also explored disability and beauty (with women) with their *Raw Beauty Project*. The work premiered in New York at the ACA Galleries in 2014.

3   Though there are rare performers who have – perhaps because of a change
    in social attitudes – managed to be successful in the mainstream and still
    be a bit queer. In the UK context, Julian Clary for instance has at times
    bridged this divide, but his work emerged at a particular historical point
    where social attitudes changed in relation to performers being 'allowed' to
    make work shot through with queerness for a mainstream audience.

4   *Muslim Drag Queens* is a documentary that features, and highlights, the
    daily struggles of those who identify as Muslim and work in the genre
    of drag. The main drag narrative follows the life of Muslim drag queen
    Asif Quraishi and exposes the hatred towards Quraishi and other drag
    queen gay Asians. Quraishi has been subjected to death threats and daily
    homophobic abuse.

5   Scotland's unofficial Alternative Pride event in 2015 banned drag queens
    because they were reported to offend trans individuals. There was much
    online chatter about this, particularly in relation to the deep connections of
    the two communities. In the end, drag performers were allowed access to
    the stage.

6   Lewis Bailey was banned from entering his school's (Castle High) talent
    show in drag. Bailey defied this censorship and with drag pride attended his
    school in drag on a non-uniform day!

7   At the time of writing it seems that there are only drag queen children
    making the headlines; we have yet to see a child drag king appear in a
    similar way. It is worth noting that there is a range of online debates about
    children in drag – ranging from the celebratory to claims it is a form of
    child abuse. We would argue that for a child, engaging in drag can be part
    of their developing sense of self/selves in the world.

8   We understand 'authenticity' can be a tricky word. In this context we are
    referring to those who make a living from drag, have been reared on its
    form, and are embedded in their self-identifications and portrayals. Thus,
    for the discussion at hand it is the opposite of drag in service of a narrative,
    written and played by those who have no real experience of crafting and
    creating a look.

9   There are many trans people who perform as drag, for example Agnes
    Moore, Chiyo Gomes, Daphne Always, K.James and Stacy Layne Matthews.

10 The Sisters of Perpetual Indulgence (SPI) are a charitable organization that
    spans many regions, such as the UK, Europe, America, Canada, Australia etc.

References

Baker, Roger. (1968). *Drag: A History of Female Impersonation on Stage.*
    London: Triton.
Baker, Roger. (1994). *Drag: A History of Female Impersonation in the Performing
    Arts.* New York: New York University Press.

Berbary, Lisbeth A. and Johnson, Corey W. (2017). 'En/Activist Drag: Kings Reflect on Queerness, Queens, and Questionable Masculinities'. *Leisure Sciences*, vol. 39, no. 4, pp. 305–18.

Butler, Judith. (1990). *Gender Trouble*. London: Routledge.

Butler, Judith. (1993). *Bodies That Matter*. London: Routledge.

Campbell, Alyson and Farrier, Stephen. (2016). *Queer Dramaturgies*. London: Palgrave Macmillan.

Edward, Mark and Farrier, Stephen (eds). (2021). *Drag Histories, Herstories and Hairstories: Drag in a Changing Scene*. London: Methuen Drama.

Glauert, Rik. (2019). 'Dame Edna Everage Stands by Anti-Trans Comments'. *Gaystarnews*, 19 March. Available online: https://www.gaystarnews.com/ article/dame-edna-everage-stands-by-anti-trans-comments/#gs.g4hdwi (accessed 4 June 2019).

King, Thomas A. and Meyer, Moe. (2010). 'In Defense of Gay/Performance'. In M. Meyer (ed.), *An Archaeology of Posing: Essays on Camp, Drag, and Sexuality*, pp. 151–81. Madison, WI: University of Wisconsin Press-Macater Press.

Kirk, Kris and Heath, Ed. (1984). *Men in Frocks*. London: GMP.

Kleiman, Kelly. (2000). 'Drag = Blackface'. *Chicago-Kent Law Review*, vol. 75, no. 3, pp. 660–86.

Kuppers, Petra. (2003). *Disability and Contemporary Performance: Bodies on the Edge*. London: Routledge.

McGraw, Sean H. K. (2019). *The Gay Liberation Movement, Before and After Stonewall*. New York: Rosen Publishing.

McIntyre, Joanna and Riggs, Damien W. (2017). 'North American Universalism in *RuPaul's Drag Race*: Stereotypes, Linguicism, and the Construction of "Puerto Rican Queens"'. In Niall Brennan and David Gudelunas (eds), *RuPaul's Drag Race and the Shifting Visibility of Drag Culture: The Boundaries of Reality TV*. London: Palgrave.

Newton, Esther. (1972). *Mother Camp: Female Impersonators in America*. Chicago: University of Chicago Press.

Noble, Jean, Troka, Donna and LeBesco, Kathleen. (2004). *The Drag King Anthology*. New York: Harrington Park.

Piccini, Angela and Rye, Caroline. (2009). 'Of Fevered Archives and the Quest for Total Documentation'. In L. Allegue, S. Jones, B. Kershaw and A. Piccini (eds), *Practice-as-Research: In Performance and Screen*, 34–49. New York: Palgrave Macmillan.

Rupp, Leila J. and Taylor, Verta. (2003). *Drag Queens at the 801 Cabaret*. Chicago, IL: Chicago University Press.

Samek, Alyssa A. and Donofrio, Theresa A. (2013). '"Academic Drag" and the Performance of the Critical Personae: An Exchange on Sexuality, Politics, and Identity in the Academy'. *Women's Studies in Communication*, vol. 36, no.1, pp. 28–55.

Schacht, Steven and Underwood, Lisa. (2004). *The Drag Queen Anthology*. New York: Routledge.

Senelick, Laurence. (2000). *The Changing Room: Sex, Drag and Theatre*. New York: Routledge.

Taylor, Verta, Rupp, Leila J. and Gamson, Joshua. (2004). 'Performing Protest: Drag Shows as Tactical Repertoire of the Gay And Lesbian Movement.' In D. Myers and D. Cress (eds), *Authority in Contention*, pp. 105–37. Bingley: Emerald.

Walsh, Fintan. (2016). *Queer Performance and Contemporary Ireland: Dissent and Disorientation*. Basingstoke: Palgrave Macmillan.

Yudelman, Julia. (2017). 'The "RuPaulitics" of Subjectification in RuPaul's Drag Race'. In N. Brennan and D. Gudelunas (eds), *Rupaul's Drag Race and the Shifting Visibility of Drag Culture*. Basingstoke: Palgrave Macmillan.

2

Dragging the Mainstream

RuPaul's Drag Race and Moving Drag Practices between the USA and the UK

Joe Parslow

As a researcher and producer working in the UK's field of drag performance, I have a large number of conversations about RuPaul's Drag Race (RPDR). The ubiquity of the show, while sometimes frustrating, is testament to the mainstream reach it has garnered beyond the US. Given the show's prevalence in the contexts in which I work, it is important to account for such mainstream influence because it has a number of important effects on local performance.

This chapter explores the impact of drag travelling across international borders, particularly between the US and the UK. I examine two performers (Bianca Del Rio and Meth) as examples in order to begin a conversation about the mainstream influence that RPDR has on contemporary drag performance cultures. Using the image of the sequined gowns Bianca Del Rio and Meth wear, and the effect in performance of bright stage lights illuminating these begowned performers, this chapter explores the ways in which the movement of performers across the Atlantic Ocean in the wake of RPDR elicits the paradoxical erasure and exposure of drag performance, alongside discourses surrounding the politics of drag performance and queer identities.

Considering the relationship of local drag forms to RPDR, I follow Halberstam, who notes that 'subcultures do not simply fade away as soon as they have been mined and plundered for material' and that there is a 'utility in tracking precisely when, where and how a subculture is "beamed up" into the mainstream' (2005: 127). Halberstam, in the discussion, problematizes any unilateral flow of power, since subcultures influence the mainstream, and proposes that by paying attention to the intricacies of drag in its dominant forms, interesting and complex understandings of these performance forms can be exposed.[1]

Yet, *RPDR* pervasively impacts local drag cultures. As Stephen Farrier (2016) makes clear, 'some younger makers and audiences in the UK learn about drag, its culture and its construction, in ways that are transatlantic [...] which has implications for the stories that get told about the local community' (Farrier, 2016: 201), further asserting that 'if the work being watched by younger audiences has its form rooted in North America, then the communication of histories, temporalities, and culture will reflect a non-local historical experience [...] thus missing or obscuring local identities and performance narratives' (ibid.: 203).

However, Farrier goes on to propose that 'a position that maintains that North American forms are a dilution of local form does not take account of the agency and flexibility of the performers in rendering a North American form locally resonant' (ibid.: 204). In my discussion below I attend to the agency and flexibility of performers from both within and beyond *RPDR*. Before doing so, however, I move to foreground the contemporary context of a post-*RPDR* scene before exploring the effect of the mainstream on drag practices.

RPDR is a reality-based television competition where drag performers compete for the title of America's next drag superstar, and performers who appear on it are often able to perform internationally. In the UK, this touring started in around 2013, and at the time of writing there is a large quantity of individuals and groups of *RPDR* alumni (known colloquially as '*Drag Race* Girls' or 'RuGirls') performing to sell-out crowds in the thousands.

Contemporary commentators argue that one effect of *RPDR*'s presence is that it has sidelined local performers or taken audiences away from them (see Kelaides, 2018; Ling, 2018; Moylan, 2018; Oliver, 2018). They argue that the show regulates drag across a set of normativities that privilege certain forms of drag over others. This results in only certain forms of drag gaining mainstream attention – forms that are commercially and artistically viable within *RPDR* standards – thereby actively sidelining local differences.

In light of the announcement in late 2018 of a UK version of *RPDR*, discussions surrounding its negative impact re-emerged (see Levine, 2018; Jones, 2018). I challenge the idea that UK drag is simply being erased by US forms and performers, while noting that the show undoubtedly influences how drag is learned, regulated and understood. Here the implication is not just regarding the way drag performers learn drag, but that audiences watching *RPDR* come to understand and critique drag through standards limited to performers that succeed on the show. All of this contributes to an understanding of the globalizing force of *RPDR*.

In attempting to account for this globalization of drag practices, or an internationalization of drag, there is a corollary between these ideas and issues of globalization and sexuality. Key writers such as Denis Altman (1997), Jon Binnie (2004), David L. Eng (2010), Elizabeth A. Povinelli and George Chauncy (1999) and William Spurlin (2006), among others, account for the ways in which sexuality is perceived, produced and regulated in, across and through national and international borders. However, these discourses do not easily map onto a movement between the US and the UK, a boundary that reflects similarities in culture and heritage and, more importantly, this is not a simple movement (of bodies, ideas, practices) from a global power to a state perceived as less internationally powerful, as writers critiquing queer globalization and post-colonialism have noted. Thus, there is not a passive receiving of ideas of drag in a 'colonized' culture in the UK, much as there is not a passive receiving of colonized ideas of sexuality in many of the studies above. Consequently, I resist unproblematically transferring discourses of globalization, post-colonialism and sexuality onto these discussions of drag practices. It is still important, however, to account for the effects of a perceived 'Americanization' of drag in the UK post-*RPDR* and the effects this has had on UK drag, while paying attention to the local practices and resistances that emerge.

Moving beyond a circulation and regulation of performance forms, the show also circulates and regulates particular identities and identity formations. While there have been a number of trans-identifying performers on the show, RuPaul recently made problematic comments surrounding the inclusion of female, trans and/or non-binary performers. RuPaul suggested that 'Drag loses its sense of danger and its sense of irony once it's not men doing it' (Aitkenhead, 2018), later tweeting that 'You can take performance enhancing drugs and still be an athlete, just not in the Olympics' (see Fremke, 2018; McCague and Gerken, 2018), suggesting that medically transitioning would offer unfair advantages to trans-identifying performers who wanted to enter the competition. RuPaul's comments were misguided, relying on an understanding of trans and/or non-binary identities based on medical transition. Furthermore, this suggests she misunderstands the histories within which she places herself and her show (for example, the presence of trans identities in Jennie Livingstone's (1990) *Paris is Burning* or the figure of Marsha P. Johnson), as well as a contemporary moment in which there is an increasing visibility of drag performers who identify across a broad spectrum of gender and sexual identities.

While RuPaul went on to apologize for these comments, and it would be easy to dismiss them as being made from a place of ignorance, it is important to recognize the cultural significance her words have. Furthermore, while in certain venues in the UK female, trans and/or non-binary identifying performers and audiences are welcomed, it is important to note that this is not the case everywhere, and even within these venues performers who fall out of the apparently strict boundaries of men performing in drag may face discrimination and be made to feel unwelcome or unsafe. As such, RuPaul's comments are representative of forms of misogyny, transphobia and intolerance in the LGBTQ+ community.

Beyond the circulation and regulation of drag performance forms, *RPDR* also circulates and regulates queer identities in relation to drag performance. It would be too simple to suggest that the show functions as a globalizing and regulating force in relation to a diverse, local set of practices and performers, however. As indicated, transphobia and misogyny exist in local performance events. Furthermore, performance forms are regulated across different venues where, for example, performers who lip-synch rather than sing are less welcome in certain venues or enjoyed less by some audiences.

It is true that the show contributes to regulating forms of drag and identity; however, this regulation also happens at a local level. It is also true that the show contributes to the circulation of different identity forms in relation to drag since, despite RuPaul's comments, performers from a diversity of gender and identity positions achieve high levels of success, just as diverse performance forms happen in local venues regardless of and despite RuPaul's comments.

This discussion aims to challenge the simple assumption that *RPDR* is an always-already negative, globalizing influence on local drag performance forms and identity positions. I suggest that both this popular show and local performers contribute to the exposure and erasure of forms and identities. While it is important to note that the reach of the show means these *RPDR* circulations and regulations are more visible, to suggest it is only happening in the mainstream denies not only the agency and impact of local performance forms, but also the misogyny and transphobia that is present. Furthermore, while the commentators above lament the negative impact of *RPDR*, there is less discussion of what the mainstreamization might positively affect or produce. I argue that beyond the circulation and regulation of drag performance forms and identity positions, there is also a benefit from the bright lights of mainstream focus shining on drag performance.

The first positive impact is that when *RPDR* performers bring shows to the UK, they often work with UK-based performers as support acts. This means that local performers work in front of audiences numbering in the thousands. Secondly, the mainstream success of the show has also resulted in bigger audiences for drag in general. While commentators and performers would consider drag audiences to operate on a deficit model (if there is a *RPDR* performer bringing a show to London, for example, audiences will only attend this), I argue that the show has also opened up drag performances to audiences who may not usually see drag performance in local venues.[2] Finally, mainstream focus also exposes problematic and offensive local drag practices that perpetuate racist, misogynistic and transphobic narratives within drag performance, and it can potentially offer ways to challenge and resist these forms.

When engaging with discussions surrounding the effects of the mainstream on contemporary drag performance, it is vital to stage a discussion that pays attention to the ways in which both mainstream and local practices contribute to the circulation and regulation of diverse performance forms and identity positions, while being aware that the cultural (and economic) capital of *RPDR* and the performers who appear on it is clearly higher. It is important to pay attention to the effects of these mainstream movements without erasing the agency of local performers in challenging and contributing to these forces, while being fully aware that the ways in which performance forms and identity positions may be regulated can be exacerbated and challenged by this mainstream focus, as well as that local performers and performance events offer sites of resistance *and* facilitation to these mainstream moves.

I move now to consider two performers, Bianca Del Rio and Meth, in relation to these debates before returning to the image of their begowned bodies onstage as a productive metaphor to extend this discussion.

Bianca Del Rio

Bianca Del Rio, winner of the sixth season of *RPDR*, is arguably the most popular performer to emerge from the show. Known for her razor-sharp wit, offensive comedy and clown-like aesthetic, Bianca has toured the world performing stand-up comedy. She started her post-*RPDR* career in the usual circuit of clubs, before quickly moving to exclusively perform in theatre venues. At the time of writing, she is promoting a show at the SSE Arena, Wembley, in London in 2019, a high-capacity and renowned performance venue, 'delivering her politically-charged humour in a venue with a capacity of 12,500' (Baggs, 2018).

Prior to *RPDR*, Bianca had a long-standing career as a drag performer and comedian, and it was clear when she appeared on the show that she had carefully considered her role and how she would present herself. Of particular note was her relationship with fellow finalist Adore Delano, to whom she acted as a mother figure at certain points, undercutting her harsh comedy and biting one-liners by being maternal, caring and loving. Therefore, while Bianca's performances are often acerbic and offensive, this maternal side is known to the public and contributes to her success.

Bianca's performances recirculate the image of the drag queen as acerbic, quick witted and offensive. No social group is exempt from her scrutiny or, as she termed it during *RPDR*, her 'Rolodex of Hate'. This has not always been appreciated by audiences and, in particular, she came under public attack 'during a performance at Montreal Pride when she cracked a joke about a fellow contestant who had spoken on the show about being raped' (Baggs, 2018). While a discussion of discourses of offence in relation to drag performance constitutes an entire separate exploration, it is important to note that Bianca's comedy is often deemed 'too much' for certain audiences, and her performances have been both criticized and celebrated for this offensiveness. Therefore, Bianca recirculates the image of the 'offensive drag queen' as a desirable performance form, one which is desirable for many audiences considering her level of success.

While the form of performance she engages with reinforces certain drag architypes, her aesthetic both reifies and challenges assumptions. Self-described as a 'clown', Bianca does not conform to understandings of a drag performer trying to legitimately 'pass' as a woman. Bianca paints with heightened make-up and bold colours, describing herself as a 'drag clown' (her latest show is called 'It's Jester Joke' (Baggs, 2018)). Bianca's aesthetic subverts any idea of drag having to be believably female, an idea that is often expounded by the way performers are judged and regulated on *RPDR*.

These regulations of drag in relation to ideas of femaleness on the show are frequently misogynistic: "'Fishy", for instance, is regularly used on the program to refer to the legitimacy of drag queens' "womanly" presentation, but the term can, without doubt, also be read pejoratively to refer to the odour of female genitalia' (Brennan and Gudelunas, 2017: 4). These terms and regulations not only place illogical limits on drag, but also on the very idea of 'female', raising complex and problematic issues for both cis and trans performers and audiences. Bianca's aesthetic challenges these regulatory norms by presenting a heightened clown-like face – one which presents drag as a distinct performance form and aesthetic – rather than a presentation of imitable or ideal femaleness.[3] Here Bianca could be seen as resisting hierarchies of success based on misogyny that emerge from *RPDR*, circulating a heightened drag aesthetic that refuses to conform to misogynistic stereotypes of femaleness. Bianca's begowned presentation, however, may reinforce these norms and stereotypes, with her padded body (pads worn to accentuate her hips and chest) presenting a heightened version of an idealized female form. The form, however, in relation to her make-up, is deliberately exaggerated and challenges any assumption of 'female-illusion' that reinforces misogynist stereotypes.[4]

It is important to question whether these exaggerated forms of femininity resist or confirm problematic female stereotypes by returning to Judith Butler's (1990) early assertions that 'Parody by itself is not subversive, and there must be a way to understand what makes certain kinds of parodic repetitions effectively disruptive, truly troubling, and which repetitions become domesticated and recirculated as instruments of cultural hegemony' (Butler, 1990: 176–7). Butler's early formations surrounding drag's relationship to exposing the performativity of gender foregound contemporary drag discussions. Here, the importance of considering Bianca Del Rio as a drag performer who has performed in numerous mainstream settings across the world should be noted because it is possible to see how her performances might serve both to satirize and critique gendered normativities, as well as prop them up.

Moving beyond considering drag as only either subversive or hegemonic in its relation to gendered performance, Farrier (2016) insists on the need to '[see] drag as a queer performance form, rather than as an activity that exemplifies theorising around gender performativity' (Farrier, 2016: 182). While Butler's framework offers a useful discussion point in relation to Bianca's drag, considering her work more specifically in relation to drag as a performance form with its own set of discrete histories and practices offers a way of understanding how Bianca's drag inhabits a shifting position in relation to local drag forms. Furthermore, her drag and these local forms work to circulate identities that are both regulatory and liberating. It is crucial to consider the localized movements of these *RPDR* performers across stages, because Bianca Del Rio performing with Meth (discussed below) at The Black Cap, a now-closed LGBTQ+ venue in London, UK, is doing something very different to Bianca Del Rio performing at the Wembley Arena.

This consideration of the scale of venue is a simple formulation, but it is often lost in the polarizing debates about the impact of *RPDR* on local drag. In order to extend this discussion, I consider Bianca as a performer in relation to what her begowned body *does*. But before doing so, I want to consider another performer, Meth, as a critical example of a 'local queen' who adds useful nuance to these discussions.

Meth

Meth works primarily in London and is known as a lip-synch performer, who 'uses the technique in her work extensively [...] lip-synching to recorded singing and speech. For comic and political effect, Meth lip-synchs a juxtaposition of rock, heavy metal and rap-style music with the speech of well-known characters from television programmes' (Farrier, 2016: 201).[5] Known primarily for her lip-synching performance work, Meth is also an accomplished host, and she has appeared on a docu-drama following the lives of drag performers in London called *Drag Queens of London* (The Connected Set, 2014). Her profile is large because she produced a performance event called The Meth Lab, which ran between 2013 and 2015 and was known for being among the first shows to bring *RPDR* performers to the UK (including Bianca Del Rio). She is also known for curating and hosting her own drag competition, Not Another Drag Competition, throughout which she acted as a mentor to a large number of the most recent successful additions to the London drag performance scene.[6]

In part because of her role in producing and hosting drag, Meth garnered a strong following, with regular self-produced shows in London and one-off performances at other events across the UK, Europe and the USA. Meth's successes are linked to the successes of *RPDR*, both because she is known for working with RuGirls and because the general popularity of drag performance has increased in the wake of the show. She has achieved success because of *RPDR* and, arguably, despite it. Meth's work is interesting to note here because of her close relationship to the show and her aesthetic relationship with Bianca.

The phenomenon of being compared to various RuGirls is one that many UK performers experience, and Meth is regularly compared to Bianca. While often reductive, ironing out the differences between performers, the comparison is not baseless. Meth's make-up is as hyper-real and clown-like as Bianca's, although her make-up includes many more non-natural colours such as yellow, purple, pink and green, and she does not paint on eyebrows (her own eyebrows being shaved off when out of drag). Furthermore, while Meth is known for wearing gowns, her exaggerated padding is often more visible because of more tightly fitting looks. Meth's aesthetic is as complexly related to the norms and resistances of drag and identity forms as Bianca's, with her hyper-feminine, clown-like looks serving both to idolize these unachievable feminine forms and critique them. Arguably in Meth's work, her use of unnatural colours for hair and make-up make a more distinct critique visible in her aesthetic.

However, in shifting beyond the binary of idolization/critique (or regulation/liberation), I argue that Meth's work also operates as a celebration of forms (forms of femininity and forms of drag) and that this can be seen when considering her aesthetic and performance work together.[7] Considering Meth's use of spoken-word lip-synch performance and Bianca's comedy, I study moments of performance in their locality in order to pay attention to the ways in which stages, localities and performers all work in complex ways to contribute to the circulation of drag forms and identities.

Bianca Del Rio and Meth

In this section I want to consider two small moments from the same show in order to elaborate my arguments above. The performance event took place at The Black Cap in Camden, London, a legendary LGBTQ+ and drag venue that is now closed. It housed historic drag, cutting-edge performers from the London scene, and most recently RuGirls. The particular event, known as The Meth Lab, took place in July 2014, a few weeks after Bianca won Season Six of *RPDR*.

As Bianca enters to deafening applause and screams, it is clear she is adored by the fans. She walks onstage wearing a long black sequined gown, tall hair and bold make-up. As the noise subsides, she shouts: 'I aint got no album, I aint got a new song. But you know what I do have is one hundred thousand fucking dollars!' (Erenthae, 2014). Making reference not only to her recent victory and the prize money she received, but also to the growing tendency of drag performers to release albums after *RPDR*, Bianca exposes the mechanism of the competition as well as the expectations of her as a winner. Rather than fitting into the norms of a *Drag Race* winner, she continues doing what she would have been doing anyway, namely, stand-up comedy. While this is not a radical move, it does begin to challenge assumptions that all performers need to be able to sing, or dance, or lip-synch in order to succeed. It instead highlights a craft (both stand-up comedy and being able to work a room with a microphone) which is important in the drag performance scene but is often under-represented on the show.

More importantly, however, Bianca standing on that stage at that time means that on four separate dates in July 2014, nearly 300 people attended The Black Cap. These audiences also saw performances from Meth and other performers: Myra Dubois, Holestar and Dot Cotton. In the bright lights of mainstream focus, Bianca's begowned body is illuminated, and in the shining lights that reflect off the sequins, other performers are illuminated.

Meth's performance work differs from Bianca's as a lip-synch performer. Opening the same show, Meth is cheered on by hundreds of audience members who attend in order to see Bianca, although many know Meth already because they have attended other events with RuGirls. She lip-synchs the song "Bitch" by Meredith Brooks, the track intercut with acerbic, scathing and comic lines from film and television, including a long and well-known moment regarding the colour 'cerulean' from *The Devil Wears Prada* (2006).

In this moment and others like it, Meth's performance work is seen much more brightly and by many more people in the lights shining on her in part because of Bianca's presence in the show, and there is a communication of ideas, cultures and knowledges to audiences beyond a US and *Drag Race-*centric set of references, allowing an amalgam of complex contemporary and historic queer references. Beyond *The Devil Wears Prada* (2006), Meth also lip-synchs *Monty Python and The Holy Grail* (1975) and British political satire *The Thick of It* (2005), among others. This work puts a local spin on more generalized *RPDR* drag references, while also highlighting that acerbity, comedy and being scathing are as much part of UK drag culture as they are of US drag culture.

Conclusion

In the UK at the time of writing, drag performance has reached a critical moment; with regular shows in every major city starring RuGirls selling thousands of tickets, a critical mass of drag performers emerging on the scene, and the announcement of *RPDR UK*, the scene is shifting and will continue to shift.

While concerns surrounding the erasure of local forms is legitimate, this chapter begins to stage the need for a more careful exploration of what happens in the wake of *RPDR*. Mainstream attention is not neutral, and who gets to stand onstage is not meritocratic. However, in paying attention to the complex ways in which drag performers move across stages, and who and what gets to move with these performers, it is possible to uncover the complex hierarchies and institutions that regulate drag and, most importantly, *start to find ways to resist them*. In the bright lights of the stage and mainstream focus, the strategies of cultural reproduction are often made clear (as in Meth's act). Using these bright lights as performers, producers and academics, it is possible to expose problematic practices, challenge racist, misogynist and transphobic forms, unpick the complexities of drag in relation to queer forms of identity, culture and history, and celebrate and highlight diverse modes of drag and identity forms.

Having started with observations on global drag practices, I close with a local comment. After the closure of The Black Cap in 2015, during an informal conversation, Meth commented that queer and drag cultures are like 'glittery cockroaches' and that every time mainstream culture thinks queer culture has gone, it pops up elsewhere just as glittery as before. Drag performers have survived erasure and eradication in the past and, as the analyses in this chapter hope to show, drag performance and drag cultures are well placed in complexly and sensitively profiting from, playing within and resisting mainstream attention in the present and the future to come.

Notes

1   Halberstam discusses the mainstreamization of male impersonation and drag kinging. This chapter refers to drag queens almost exclusively, in part to pay attention to the important differences in practices and histories between drag queening and kinging (Farrier, 2016), but also because *RPDR* only features drag queens. While I underscore the importance different bodies and forms in contemporary drag scenes throughout this chapter, it is important to highlight that this discussion starts from drag queens to stage a broader discussion about drag.

2   These observations come from my experience as an event promoter working with RuGirls and local performers since 2012, witnessing rises in audience numbers from the LGBTQ+ community and beyond. It is important to note that this may not always be a positive thing. *RPDR* is also successful with non-queer viewers and, therefore, live performances may be populated with non-queer audiences (see Ling, 2018). If this translates into more audiences for non-*RPDR* shows in LGBTQ+ venues, these may be non-queer audiences that are part of a process of appropriation of drag as a queer form of entertainment, performance and even identity.

3   I refer to Bianca with she/her pronouns here since the use of these pronouns when a drag queen is in drag (and, often, out of drag) is an unofficially accepted rule in drag performance circles. While I argue Bianca's drag aesthetics might challenge drag representations of 'femaleness', they are still clearly bound up in female or feminine representations.

4   Bianca's speaking voice is also unchanged in her performance, with no attempt to present or parody a feminine vocal style but remaining the same in or out of drag.

5   Again, I use she/her pronouns for Meth as appropriate to her performance work as a drag queen.

6   It is important to state here that I am Meth's husband, and therefore am provided with insights to her work while being particularly implicated in the debates surrounding her work. Beyond our personal relationship, I also worked as co-producer of The Meth Lab and other drag events Meth produced or performed at, and therefore worked personally and professionally with a number of 'RuGirls' and saw first-hand the fandom

that the show produced and the impact of *RPDR* on the drag scene in London.

7   This is rarely done on *RPDR*, where the performers are judged on their performance (the task) and their aesthetic (their runway) separately. This extends beyond the show to the ways in which audiences engage with performers aesthetically on social media prior to seeing them live.

References

Aitkenead, Decca. (2018). 'RuPaul: "Drag is a big f-you to male-dominated culture"'. *The Guardian*, 3 March. Available online: https://www.theguardian.com/tv-and-radio/2018/mar/03/rupaul-drag-race-big-f-you-to-male-dominated-culture (accessed 10 Sept. 2018).

Altman, Dennis. (1997). 'Global Gaze/Global Gays'. *GLQ*, vol. 3, pp. 417–36.

Baggs, Michael. (2018). 'Bianca Del Rio: The first drag queen with a solo show at Wembley'. *BBC News*, 5 October. Available online: https://www.bbc.co.uk/news/newsbeat-45761536.

Binnie, Jon. (2004). *The Globalisation of Sexuality*. London: Sage Publications Ltd.

Brennan, Niall and Gudelunas, David. (eds) (2017). *RPDR and the Shifting Visibility of Drag Culture*. Champaign: Palgrave Macmillan.

Butler, Judith. (1990). *Gender Trouble: Feminism and the Subversion of Identity*. London: Routledge.

Eng, David. (2010). *The Feeling of Kinship: Queer Liberalism and the Racialization of Intimacy*. Durham: Duke University Press.

Erenthae. (2014). 'Bianca Del Rio Debut at Meth Lab, London pt 1'. *YouTube*. Available online: https://www.youtube.com/watch?v=ARKFjXZAHcc (accessed 2 Feb. 2019).

Farrier, Stephen. (2016). 'That Lip-Synching Feeling: Drag Performance as Digging the Past'. In A. Campbell and S. Farrier (eds), *Queer Dramaturgies: International Perspectives on Where performance Leads Queer*. Hampshire: Palgrave Macmillan.

Framke, Caroline. (2018). 'How RuPaul's comments on trans women led to a Drag Race revolt – and a rare apology'. *Vox*, 7 March. Available online: https://www.vox.com/culture/2018/3/6/17085244/rupaul-trans-women-drag-queens-interview-controversy (accessed 9 Oct. 2018).

Halberstam, Judith. (2005). *In A Queer Time And Place: Transgender Bodies, Subcultural Lives*. New York: New York University Press.

Jones, Charlie. (2018). 'Will RuPaul's Drag Race UK ruin the British drag scene?' *Pink News*, 13 December. Available online: https://www.pinknews.co.uk/2018/12/13/rupaul-drag-race-uk-scene/ (accessed 2 Feb. 2019).

Kelaides, Katie. (2018) 'RPDR Has Ruined Drag'. *The Daily Review*, 5 April. Available online: https://dailyreview.com.au/rupauls-drag-race-ruined-drag/73346/ (accessed 10 Sept. 2018).

Levine, Nick. (2018). 'What Do British Drag Queens Think About "Ru Paul's Drag Race" UK?'. *VICE*, 6 December. Available online: https://www.vice.com/en_uk/article/9k4z57/what-do-british-drag-queens-think-about-rupauls-drag-race-uk (accessed 2 Feb. 2019).

Ling, Thomas. (2018). 'Are Straight People "Stealing" RPDR'. *Radio Times*, 18 April. Available online: https://www.radiotimes.com/news/2018-05-04/are-straight-people-stealing-rupauls-drag-race/ (accessed 12 Oct. 2018).

McCague, Bernadette and Gerken, Tom. (2018) 'RuPaul apologises after trans drag queens comments'. *BBC UGC & Social News*, 6 March. Available online: https://www.bbc.co.uk/news/blogs-trending-43301583 (accessed 29 April 2019).

Moylan, Brian. (2018). 'RPDR Recap: Is Drag Race Ruining Drag?'. *VICE*, 25 May. Available online: https://www.vice.com/en_us/article/mbkbn4/rupauls-drag-race-recap-is-drag-race-ruining-drag-race (accessed 14 Oct. 2018).

Oliver, Isaac. (2018). 'Is This The Golden Age Of Drag? Yes. And No'. *New York Times*, 17 January. Available online: https://www.nytimes.com/2018/01/17/arts/drag-queens-rupaul-drag-race.html (accessed 12 Oct. 2018).

Povinelli, Elizabeth and Chauncey, George. (1999). 'Thinking Sexuality Transnationally: An Introduction'. *GLQ*, vol. 5, no. 4, pp. 439–49.

Spurlin, William. (2006). *Imperialism with the Margins: Queer Representation and the Politics of Culture in Southern Africa*. Hampshire: Palgrave Macmillan.

3

Race for the Money

The Influence of *RuPaul's Drag Race* on the Livelihood and Aesthetics of New York City's Drag Culture

Kalle Westerling

Introduction

In 1996, cultural critic Julian Fleischer described New York City's (NYC) drag scene as a unique cultural environment, different and distant from that of female impersonation prevalent in other parts of the country (Fleischer, 1996). In large parts, that culture had been shaped by RuPaul and her arrival in Manhattan's drag scene. With the increasing commercial and cultural success of the television show *RuPaul's Drag Race*, that environment reached an international audience. Over the past decade of *Drag Race* on television, I have seen drag shows several nights per week and had countless conversations with performers, witnessing first-hand a changing local culture. While previous studies of *Drag Race* have addressed how the show is an important aggregator around social issues and can sometimes be problematic, I wanted to understand specifically whether and how *Drag Race* has impacted NYC's local drag queen culture. This study is a partial response to the lack of studies, as Cory G. Collins has pointed out, on the 'range of inequalities [that] structures the political economy that [*Drag Race*] both produces and sustains' (2017: 131).

To find an answer to the question, I spent the autumn of 2017 listing 210 actively performing drag queens in any of the city's five boroughs. Approximately half of them (ninety-six) were asked to participate in any or both of the project's parts – a survey and semi-structured, in-depth anonymous interviews. Anyone who identified their performance as engaging with a drag queen aesthetic – regardless of their assigned gender at birth – could participate. None of the twenty-nine final participants had been cast on *Drag Race* at the time of the survey, which focused mostly on the financial aspects of NYC's drag queen performance culture before and since *Drag Race's* first airing in 2009. Approximately one-third of the participants in the survey started performing in drag between 2014 and 2017; another third started performing before *Drag Race* started airing.

To understand the survey results better, contextualize the changes that were addressed by many of the drag queens, and theorize any changes aesthetically to NYC's drag scene, I arranged for eleven interviews. The focus of the interviews concerned the performers' general sentiments towards the television show; whether *Drag Race* had anything to do with their start as drag queens; their desires to be cast on the show; important qualities in queens who get on the show; whether or not drag is becoming increasingly mainstream and whether that is a positive development; their relationship to venues and promoters; whether they are or were ever able to support themselves financially through their performance in drag; the importance of social media; whether they consider their art form their profession; whether the show represents the drag community in general and NYC's drag community in particular; and what they speculate will happen after *Drag Race* stops airing. All of the interviews were recorded, transcribed and coded, and in what follows, I have used grounded theory method to analyse the themes in the interviews in an attempt to generate a theory based on the performers thoughts and themes emerging in the interviews.

While speaking on those topics with performers, it became clear that *Drag Race* presents drag as a viable career option, which has led to an explosion of more performers. Meanwhile, the intelligent and savvy drag queens of NYC also acknowledged the paradox in the current situation: while the culture is growing with new performers, this has also led to decreasing financial reward per engagement. The television show also creates and perpetuates a culture of aesthetic 'feedback' between the show and live performers, where drag queens often perform *for* social media and the casting directors of the television show, following norms set by former contestants on the show, rather than building a deep interest in the artistic prospects of drag itself.

'If you're doing drag for the money, get out!': Drag as a career option

Many of the queens agreed that *Drag Race* has 'made drag into a viable option for a career' and that it has made drag 'more of a profession now' compared to when RuPaul started performing in NYC. All of them identified the show's unprecedented financial opportunity as the most important way that it creates careers. The winner receives $100,000 – a significant amount of money for performers who make between $50 and $100 at bar and nightclub engagements. However, the show also offers financial stability for all competitors who can 'get [their] fans and [...] forge a career that will be ongoing', as one queen expressed it. She continued: 'If you're smart, you can ride it for the rest of your life.' Another queen describes the television show as 'the beginning', where you can build 'a following' and 'become self-actualized and grow'.

When asked in the survey about their current financial situation, most of the queens indicated that they were struggling financially to be able to perform in drag and sustain the well-known and lively culture in NYC. The only group that diverged from this significant theme were the queens who started performing before the airing of *Drag Race*; their financial situations had either improved or remained the same. However, it is important to note that three-quarters of all the survey participants said that they were not entirely able to support themselves by performing in drag. Seven of those had been able to do so at some point in their lives. Only one of the participants in the survey was able to support themselves before and continued to do so after *Drag Race* started airing.

The survey's theme of balancing financial stability with an artistic career was mirrored in the interviews. One of the queens stated, 'You have to reach wherever you can to get gigs that pay very little. I don't know how other people do it if I'm honest!' Despite ten years of television success, still only a few performers in the capital of drag can support themselves from their art. They are regarded as examples of a combination of work ethic and luck: 'to support [myself] entirely from doing drag, I'd need to be able to ensure a source of income, but it doesn't right now, unless you're one of the top five queens in New York City [...] who work really hard.'

Thus, some queens express doubt in the depiction on *Drag Race* of drag as a possible career and disagree with drag currently being, or even considering drag, their 'career' or 'job'. One of them says, 'I would never see this as a job but only in the financial sense [...] I have to think about money as well as the thing that I love.' Still others point out that drag could not even, in the current financial setup of the performance culture, be considered a career. When asked whether they could currently support themselves entirely from doing drag, one queen remarked that 'it would be a total life-change to try to make drag into a full-time career', and added that 'it would be difficult.' She clarified that even if it 'were to actually be a real option for me [...] drag would have to be legitimized in a way that it is still not quite, in the way that professional musical theatre is legitimized with regulations, money and producers behind it.'

The queens agree that a drag performer's only possible financial stability from their art would come from being cast on *Drag Race*. One performer says poignantly, 'If you're doing drag for the money, get out!' She clarifies that 'the issue is that there is a track and it doesn't *necessarily* have to be the RuPaul track, but right now it's [the] only [...] track that people are going for. And when that's all there is, there is only a limited amount of slots there.' Another interviewed queen furthers the idea that drag as a 'career' depends on the existence of *Drag Race* in the first place:

> If you're performing locally, and part of the reason people see you is because they see drag on TV, and they want to see local drag because of it, then you're relevant. But if people stop remembering that drag is a thing that they can go to, then you're screwed. Maybe it's one of the reasons why I'm not so sure that going [into drag] full-time [...] is such a good idea because I think it's all so changeable. Taste is fickle, and [...] I don't want to give up every piece of security I have and then to have that total industry [...] disappear in a 'poof', when *Drag Race* stops airing.

The struggle to get paid in the city means that many of the performers have turned to touring outside it. Of the twenty-nine survey participants, twenty-three had performed outside NYC – most of them in the continental US. Seven of them said they had regular touring engagements. Four out of five queens who travelled to perform outside NYC claim they get paid more elsewhere compared to venues in the city. However, even with the higher pay rate outside the city, performers are not able to turn their art into a career. Even 'after doing this for six years', one of the city's well-known queens says that she could create a career out of doing drag but adds 'the way that the gigs are paying now, I cannot do that and take [my drag persona] in the direction I want to go'. The problem in NYC's drag culture today is that an increased number of performers pushes down booking fees as well as raises expectations on performers to come up with new routines, outfits and social media content. Those expectations mean that compared with a regular job, where 'you're making money on a regular basis', in the words of one queen, 'in drag, you're not and you're putting out all this money to do what you do.'

'It's not a lucrative business, so you have to get what you can': Increasing numbers of queens stiffen the competition

Queens strongly agree when asked whether there are more performers around today than when they started. Says one queen who started in 2004,

'Absolutely. It's amazing – and they keep refreshing at a faster pace. I used to see new queens every year; now you see new queens every three months.' When asked to consider reasons for the increased numbers of performers, some of the participants suggest that intermittent 'waves' of new performers are a 'natural' phenomenon. One performer has noticed them since she started performing in NYC in the early 2000s: 'I've seen a lot of them come up and I've seen a lot of them fall to the wayside because not everyone is going to continue in this. People evolve, change, leave, and die, you know?' Another queen agrees: 'There is this other wave [now] because we're all around thirty now. You know, there's a kind of a twenty-year-old wave.' Generally, most of the interviewees think *Drag Race* has brought around more performers, that it has 'strengthened the drag community; it has bolstered the community in giving people more courage to do it', in the words of one queen. Indeed, the survey indicates that many performers started because of *Drag Race*. Four out of five of the performers who started performing in drag since 2010 said that the show had somewhat or everything to do with their beginning to perform in drag: 'it's no secret at all – that girls get into drag because of *Drag Race*.' Some of them connect the rising number of queens to the fact that the television show makes the art of drag seem easy: 'I think that a lot of those girls don't realize at the start just exactly how much time, money, effort, and mental energy it requires to do drag.'

In this landscape of increasing numbers of queens and more competitors from NYC on *Drag Race*, one of the interviewed queens interestingly describes a recent introduction of a class differentiation: 'Now there has been enough queens in New York City to make a class of the New York City *Drag Race* girls, and it has become considered to be the highest level of [drag].' She continues: even someone 'who's fantastic and has been doing this for-fucking-ever, would probably by general consensus be listed lower than girls who have been doing it a lot less time but made it on *Drag Race*'.

When asked how the increasing number of performers in the city affect their livelihood in general, many of the interviewees speak about smaller booking fees. One of the queens explains that 'there are so many drag queens [...] that there's no reason to pay people more now'. The survey seems to affirm this statement: out of the total twenty-one participating queens who started performing in drag after *Drag Race* began airing, only two can support themselves entirely from their drag performances. One queen who has been performing since 2007 remembers 'back in the day, being paid more substantially'. She points out that more performers in the business also means that there will be performers who 'don't look to it as a career and as a business, and [say]: "I'll perform for free drinks."' She continues, people working for free drinks or fifty bucks makes it more difficult for performers that have been around for a long time that were getting paid a minimum of 500 bucks for a gig. It is hard to compete in that field because a small bar is not going to want to spend 500 bucks on a performer when they can spend 50 bucks on somebody who is just doing this as a hobby.

Faced with this changing financial situation, this particular queen is now looking to take on part-time or full-time employment.

The increasing number of queens in the city has also meant stiffer competition. Says one of the queens, 'there's a lot of that competitiveness because the coins are not there. [Drag] is not a lucrative business, so you have to get what you can.' Several queens bring up another example of the competition: bar competitions and mini-pageants, such as Miss Stonewall or Miss Hell's Kitchen. While competitions such as these are means for new queens to get visibility, many argue that they are bargains for the bars, allowing them to feature many drag performers in one night and only pay the 'winner' of the evening a cash prize of $50–100. Despite the low reward, some queens invest a lot of work and money in the competitions, and some speak about how they have gone into 'serious debt for a ten-week competition'.

'If you don't have a social media presence, you might as well not exist as an entertainer': The chore of social media fame

Another example of how competition has become stiffer in NYC's drag culture is found in the social media culture that has grown alongside *Drag Race*'s success. Over the past ten years, with the show's increasing numbers of viewers, Twitter, Facebook and Instagram have all become ubiquitous tools for communication. Many queens describe their relationship to social media as a double-edged sword: it is generally regarded as necessary to build and reach one's audience, but it is also what can disrupt an audience's deep engagement with the art form itself or something that 'flattens' a queen's live performance.

There's a general belief among the queens that social media builds an actual audience or 'fan base'. *Drag Race* may have contributed to establishing this belief, as television fame has led to larger numbers of followers and likes on the social media profiles of 'RuPaul's queens' compared to local performers. Of course, this belief may also have to do with the rise of social media marketing and branding more generally, where many of today's 'prosumers' believe that more followers equate to a higher success rate. It correlates with the idea that 'likes' and 'followers' on social media translate into real-life audience members at shows; none of the interviewed queens speak of inflated numbers of followers and likes through fake user profiles, for instance (c.f. De Cristofaro et al., 2014). Rather, almost every one of the interviewed queens thinks that a successful performer has a higher number of followers. Only one of the queens disagrees: 'On social media, you might have the likes, but that doesn't really mean anything. Same with Facebook events: You just get so many invites – who the fuck cares?'

When asked how the contestants' large numbers of followers affect her livelihood, one queen describes how 'a lot of places have had the experiences of hiring a *Drag Race* girl [...] for one night, and [while] she may be super-expensive, [...] they pack the place, and then they make in one night what they'd make in a month or so'. She continues, 'unless we're packed to the door, most of the venue owners or management or whoever booked me says, "Well, there weren't *that* many people."' Producers and promoters are generally less interested in the quality of their acts, and one queen specifies that producers are 'more interested in how much you're going to promote and what you look like'. Someone tells a story of another famous drag queen from NYC: 'She was trying to get a gig in Chicago, and they [...] said, "how many Instagram followers do you have?" She didn't have enough Instagram followers to get hired', and says with sadness in her voice: 'It was down to Instagram followers.'

While the promoters' sole focus on business concerns leads to fewer engagements for some of the queens, others speak of an added requirement besides performing: one queen describes her engagement with venues as 'less about the show and the art and more about being a party promoter'. She continues, 'as one person, putting on a show [...] and to add on top of that, being a party promoter – that takes a whole separate business; it takes a lot of time and energy'. This creates anxieties for many performers. One queen is concerned that she does not have 'the talent for short sound-bite meme-things', which is the reason she thinks the *Drag Race* 'social media stars' are successfully promoting themselves on social media platforms.

Participation in social media seems less a choice and more a chore. One of the interviewees says, 'it's sad to say but I think that it's very true that if you don't have a social media presence, you might as well not exist as an entertainer.' Many of them express a wish to 'be better' at social media. One of the queens is selective in which social media platforms she chooses: 'there are some [performers] who take *so many* videos and post so many Facebook Lives [...] it overwhelms me, and I shut off. [...] I can't handle that. I don't want to overexpose myself.' However, one of the queens thinks differently of social media than the other interviewees. For her, it is an extension of her stage, providing her access to a different audience: 'It's a way to reach people rather than just physically being at a show. And it's a way to put out more of your artistry than just being on a stage.' When asked to elaborate how she uses the platform, the same queen says:

> I partition them into different notions of myself: I'm such a visual person, so Instagram is a great way to put out different art and different processes and show different glimpses of *what I do*. I think Twitter is a great way to put out different notions of *who I am*, what I think about, and what I'm passionate about. YouTube is a great way to put out larger works and larger pieces of what I do. It's all tied to the same notion, but I put them in different boxes based on what I need to do. If I have a joke or something that pops into my head, that's great for Twitter. If I have something that I'm working on that I want to show other people, that's great for Instagram.

Feedback loop

Many of the interviewed queens expressed a concern that *Drag Race* and its 'social media stars' may portray only a 'slice' of drag culture and, as a corollary, may create or perpetuate the audience's expectation of seeing a certain type of look. Since the audience also consists of aspiring and popular queens who may shape their performances in relation to certain norms established on the show, this concern mirrors what Sarah Tucker Jenkins (2013) identifies as the 'policing' of drag occurring on *Drag Race*: the precise performance of just enough femininity, restricting androgynous types of drag, and maintaining a dichotomous performance of gender. While Collins has claimed that more recent seasons have changed and that the television show now permits for more varying 'modes of style ... within its boundaries' (2017: 133), many informants express that *Drag Race* has 'narrowed the scope' of styles performed in NYC. They fear that the television show 'ends up turning out automatons that all look alike, and people are copying those [performers] in the way they dress, in the way they do their make-up, in the way they have their hair, and the way they perform. That regimentation of looks is not great.' One queen said that she has 'had to learn how to adapt the powder look that all the RuPaul queens do', despite feeling like her face is not fit for that specific 'look'. Another queen addressed 'the obsession with *Drag Race* [which] aesthetically makes all the queens look the same now' and specifically how the trend using an 'overly aggressive contouring' is an example of how a trend 'has narrowed the bandwidth' of NYC drag: 'some people do it very well, but you don't need a fucking contoured nose. It looks stupid! A white stripe down the fucking middle of your nose. Like, no one was contouring like that back in the 90s; RuPaul wasn't contouring.' When asked to further develop her thoughts around this narrowing aesthetic, the queen explained that she thought 'the show has gone into a feedback loop with itself. As the show has found its audience, it starts to lean into that audience, which starts to expect certain things, which then the show delivers, in this feedback loop.'

Through the interviews, it is clear that a few themes emerged: *Drag Race* very explicitly presents drag as a viable career option, which has led, according to the queens who participated in the survey, to an explosion of more performers in recent years. Many of the queens argue that this explosion has led to many producers and party promoters paying less per engagement, because of increased access to performers (despite the fact that many performers also say that there are now more venues where they can perform). It thus is clear from the interviews, together with the survey results, that drag is hardly a career option yet, with the exception that one can get cast on *Drag Race*.

Many of the queens describe their performances, explicitly or implicitly, as participating in a feedback loop created and perpetuated by *Drag Race*. The television show seems to create a culture where, instead of building a deep interest in the artistic prospects of drag itself, queens now perform *for* social media and the casting directors of the television show. A recent full-length show by NYC drag queen Chelsea Piers, *Are you there, Ru? It's me, Chelsea!*, is a great example. The show's premise is that Chelsea has forgotten that the casting video for *Drag Race* is due today and she needs the audience to come along on her challenging path towards getting a video together. The meta-aspect of the show, thus, is that we learn that Chelsea has all the qualities needed to be a *Drag Race* girl. It also illustrates that, in order to book a mainstage production of a full-length show, complete with a band and video projections, Chelsea needs to use the shorthand of *Drag Race* to appeal to an audience and, importantly, approach producers of such full-length shows.

Conclusion

The central question of this study was whether NYC's drag queen scene has changed following *Drag Race*. While this is a complicated question, the survey and the in-depth interviews conducted for this survey provide a resounding answer: yes, the lives and aesthetics of NYC drag queens have undoubtedly changed following the first airing of *Drag Race*. Most importantly, from the sample in this study, the queens who started before *Drag Race* can generally support themselves from their drag despite rising numbers of performers. However, *Drag Race*'s promise that performing in drag can be a career seems exaggerated, especially for queens who started performing since the show's airing. Of the ones who say they are unable to support themselves from their drag, almost 86 per cent (eighteen) started performing in drag after the show started. In general, more performers seem able to support themselves *partially* from doing drag. Many of the performer's part-time or full-time jobs allow them to have a drag career on the side, and many of them are in creative industries.

Aesthetically, the show has dramatically changed the landscape of NYC's drag queens. Many of the informants speak of the homogenization of drag following *Drag Race*, especially in Manhattan – the borough with a long history of drag queens who spent many years developing their polished personalities. One queen says, 'Manhattan drag is [...] about the character, about who's in the dress.' While more queens are emerging every day, she adds 'you can be a great dancer, you can be funny, you can be a great performer, but if you can't show who you are, and you can't connect with the audience or with other queens and show that [...] person or the personality that's in the dress, then I think it's harder to make your way in Manhattan'. Hell's Kitchen, a neighbourhood in Manhattan near Times Square, is regarded the epitome of Manhattan drag, with 'a degree of cabaret-ness', but which can sometimes 'be very generic', one of the queens added. The focus of many of the shows is 'show tunes and chart toppers'.

In its creation of an explosion of drag queens all over the city, and decreasing salaries and booking fees, and with a simultaneous emergence of a strong sense of competitiveness, *Drag Race* has had an unexpected result in NYC's drag performance culture. In 2013, following the first iteration of the now-annual Bushwig festival, what is referred to as the 'Brooklyn scene' of drag materialized. In the second year of the festival, the number of performers had doubled and the organizers had inquiries for more than they could accept into the festival (Hoffman, 2013). Almost every interviewed queen in this study regarded the Brooklyn drag scene as particularly interesting in how it sets itself apart from the *Drag Race* aesthetic. Brooklyn's drag scene is more invested in drag as an artistic endeavour, with less focus on 'sequins and rhinestones', and the Hell's Kitchen queens' focus on theatre and cabaret is 'not reflected in the Brooklyn scene at all'.

The Brooklyn scene is shaped by a few individuals, especially Horrorchata and Babes Trust, who started Bushwig, and whose discourse marks Brooklyn performance as different from NYC's other neighbourhoods in the 'experimental and artistic nature of [its] performance' (Hoffman, 2013). One of the interviewees in this study says that when she got started, '[Brooklyn] drag was pretty pathetic and [...] the performance stuff was pretty pathetic'. But, she says, that the scene has 'certainly grown', and that 'the performances have gotten better' over recent years. However, the idea of Brooklyn as less refined still resonates with many queens who work mainly in Manhattan. Some of them think of Brooklyn as a place where queens can find a training ground to learn and practise their artistry.

While some queens point out that we risk oversimplifying when speaking about geographical differences, importantly, in my conversations it is clear that NYC is divided into two drag communities. Meanwhile, it is important to note that in the survey not *one single* performer who indicated that they perform in Brooklyn exclusively performs there. To varying degrees, they also perform in Manhattan, Queens, Long Island and Yonkers. The same cannot be said of those who indicated that they regularly perform in Manhattan, who exclusively perform there. Thus, it may be more appropriate to divide the city into smaller and more fragmented, local scenes. While it is not clear whether it is a direct consequence of *Drag Race*'s impact on the drag community in the city, the performers themselves consider the emergence of the Brooklyn scene a response to the increasingly untenable labour conditions of drag performers in Manhattan.

Confronted with the question of what will happen when *Drag Race* ends, many queens are hopeful that something else will materialize. They hope to see another television show or some opportunity for queens to maintain a career in drag: 'I think it has put drag out there as something that's entertainment for anybody and I think that a majority of the audience understands that now, rather than it being [...] just an LGBT-specific thing.' Others worry that 'there's like a dissonance [between] people who watch the show and [those who are] actually supporting live drag'. Their concern is that the audiences that *Drag Race* claims to have built for a more mainstream-oriented drag will not maintain their interest to see live, local drag performances once the show is no longer on the air. We can only speculate, of course, about what will happen. It is important to remember that drag culture is 'a bastion of experimentation and pushing the envelope' (Roschke, 2018). If we have learned anything from the history of drag, it is that it is a tenable and mutable art form, capable of resisting adversity and economic hardship and that it has captured audiences and performers alike who want to adopt a playful attitude towards gender in whichever way they desire (c.f. Senelick, 2000). While this study shows the adversity and economic hardship that the performers are living through, it should also be clear that NYC's drag culture is still healthy and vibrant, and that new and exciting local forms of drag are still emerging and waiting around the corner.

References

Collins, Cory G. (2017). 'Drag Race to the Bottom?: Updated Notes on the Aesthetic and Political Economy of *RuPaul's Drag Race*'. *TSQ: Transgender Studies Quarterly*, vol. 4, pp. 128–34.

De Cristofaro, Emiliano, Friedman, Arik, Jourjon, Guillaume, Ali Kaafar, Mohamed and Shafiq, Zubair (2014). 'Paying for Likes?: Understanding Facebook Like Fraud Using Honeypots'. In *Proceedings of the 2014 Conference on Internet Measurement Conference*. ACM, New York, pp. 129–36.

Fleischer, Julian. (1996). *The Drag Queens of New York: An Illustrated Field Guide*. New York: Riverhead Books.

Hoffman, Meredith. (2013). 'Bushwick's Second Annual Drag Fest So Popular It Turned Away Contestants'. *DNA Info*, 5 September. Available online: www.dnainfo.com/new-york/20130905/bushwick/bushwicks-second-annual-drag-fest-so-popular-it-turned-away-hopeful-queens/ (accessed 15 January 2018).

Jenkins, Sarah T. (2013). *Hegemonic "Realness"? An Intersectional Feminist Analysis of* RuPaul's Drag Race (MA Thesis). Florida Atlantic University.

Roschke, Ryan. (2018). 'Sashay Through the History of Drag Queen Culture— From Shakespeare to RuPaul'. *Popsugar*, 30 May. Available online: www.popsugar.com/news/History-Drag-Drag-Queen-Culture-44512387.

Senelick, Laurence. (2000). *The Changing Room: Sex, Drag, and Theatre*. London and New York: Routledge.

4

Chinoiserie Drag

Masquerading as the Oriental Other

Rosa Fong

Chinoiserie, a European decorative style made popular in the eighteenth century and inspired by art and design from China and East Asia, existed in the mind of the colonial imagination, invoking exotic, faraway places full of mystery. Anne Whitchard has called it a 'fanciful interpretation of Chineseness' (2017: 206). The exuberance of the rococo style of that period lent itself to the camp excess of, for example, the willow-patterned ceramics, opulent bird designs and pagoda-shaped pavilions of chinoiserie. Chinoiserie and such embellishment adorned European decorative arts, garden design, literature, theatre and music. In this chapter I demonstrate how chinoiserie was applied to the corporeal body, creating East Asian drag acts in the parodic performance of race. I identify chinoiserie drag as a performance which is a 'fanciful interpretation' of East Asian people. These performances appear in theatre, cinema and television. My focus here will be on what I term 'chinoiserie drag' in film. I will draw on the scholarship of Judith Butler and her exploration of gender and performativity; Katrin Sieg for her analysis of ethnic drag; and utilize a contrapuntal reading of the films analysed in this work. Contrapuntal analysis of a text was an approach developed by Edward Said where different perspectives are interpreted simultaneously to 'connect the structures of a narrative to the ideas, concepts, and experiences from which it draws support' (1993: 79).

Chinoiserie in the arts and crafts created a mythical image of Chinese culture and combined this with Western style to create something exotic and other. Although chinoiserie as a style more widely fell out of favour in the late nineteenth century, chinoiserie on stage and screen still persists in the form of drag acts.[1] For instance, the recent staging of *The Orphan of Zhao* (2012) and *In the Depth of Dead Love* (2017), both set in China but with a mainly white cast, were criticized for yellowface casting and erasure.[2] While yellowface refers specifically to the casting of (usually) white actors as East Asian characters, chinoiserie drag signifies the performance of ethnicity, which uses the physical stylistic expressions thought to be attributed to East Asian people. Chinoiserie drag is both a mimetic performance and an ethnic masquerade, which is devoid of any authentic source and thereby is often appropriated. The producers of *In the Depths of Dead Love* declared, 'While the characters have been given Chinese names, that is to reference the abstract and folkloric idea of the universal' (in Hewis, 2016). Such thinking creates a mythical and imagined idea of East Asia and has allowed for the formation of a racial performance that I call chinoiserie drag. In recent years, scholars have formulated an understanding of how race might be performed. Katrin Sieg, in *Ethnic Drag* (2009), borrows Judith Butler's (2006) use of the term drag as the parodic subversion of gender and applies it to race. Butler asserts that, far from being biological, gender identities are circumscribed and socially constituted. She theorizes that gender is thus performative because it produces a series of effects. In an online interview, she argues that 'we act and talk and speak in ways that consolidate an impression of being a woman or being a man ... ' (Butler, 2011). In Sieg's critique, ethnicity can likewise be perfomative as a kind of drag act. She writes, '[e]thnic drag includes not only cross-racial casting on stage, but more generally the performance of "race" as masquerade' (2009: 2). Sieg's analysis draws on Homi Bhabha's notions of mimicry and Butler's theory of performativity to describe the manifold possibilities of ethnic masquerade. Homi Bhabha's use of the word mimicry is central to his thesis on the ambivalence of colonial discourse. Bhabha adapted the term ambivalence, which was developed in psychoanalysis to describe contradictory feelings towards something that creates a love/hate relationship. In the context of a colonial discourse, this ambivalence produces tension because it decentres the relationship between the colonized and colonizer. The colonial master wants their subjects to mimic their habits and values. However, the mimicry produced is ambivalent because it is a pastiche bordering on mockery – it disrupts authority.

In this chapter, I hope to contribute to current scholarship on performing race by using textual analysis of films featuring East Asian characters. I also seek to broaden the debates on the screen identities of British East Asians and explore the complexities of negotiating agency within the social construction of race. Through the following discussion I interrogate the themes in the documentary film *Deconstructing Zoe* (2016) and demonstrate how, by performing a racialized gender, Zoe is able to enact her agency by authoring her own identity. I draw on two films featuring East Asian actors to illustrate how Zoe employs different aspects of chinoiserie drag to create her own identity. Looking at *Piccadilly* (1929), starring Anna May Wong, I explore the exoticization of Wong alongside the film's subversive elements that paradoxically challenge the exotification of race. Secondly, I give a textual analysis of Ray Yeung's short film *A Bridge to the Past* (1994), a dramatized documentary about the Chinese Hungry Ghost Festival, and I show how he successfully queers chinoiserie using mimesis and masquerade.

Both the long version of *Deconstructing Zoe* (52 minutes) and the short version, *Scent of an Orchid* (22 minutes), are documentary films about transgender actor Zoe/Chowee Leow. The film had its world premiere in May 2016 at *Translations Transgender* film festival in Seattle, USA, and went on to have international screenings across Asia and the UK. Both versions of the film have been used to inform debates on transgender identity and gender fluidity (*Being Human Festival*, 2016; *In Flux: The Queering of Race and Gender*, 2017).[3] The film captures Zoe's public and private performances of herself as a Chinese Malay trans woman living in London. The central themes in the documentary look at the fluidity of gender, sexuality and race. Some of these themes were developed in the collaborative film *Council House Movie Star* (2012) with dancemaker and academic Mark Edward. The underpinning research for *Council House Movie Star* looked at how identity is embodied through performance. My work on *Council House Movie Star* helped me articulate the approach I wanted to use when exploring the themes of gender, race and performativity in *Deconstructing Zoe*. The making of the documentary puts the theory of performativity into practice by capturing the conscious performance of the subjects in the film, thus allowing the audience to reflect on how we all perform our identities. *Deconstructing Zoe* explores the intersection between gender, race and sexuality, where Zoe plays out her identity in the postcolonial geographical spaces of her world stage. A review of *Deconstructing Zoe* highlighted how the film 'untangles the interconnections of Asian life in the diaspora and in the arts, exotification and imperialism, transmisogyny, gender and sexual fluidity, racism, and femininity' (3DollarBillCinema, 2016).

Deconstructing Zoe looks at the intersection of race and gender and poses this question: If gender is 'manufactured through a sustained set of acts, posited through the gendered stylization of the body' (Butler, 2006), then can the same also be said of race? Does Zoe act in ways that consolidate an impression of what it is to be Chinese, for example (Fong, 2018)? In this regard, Katrin Sieg's exploration in *Ethnic Drag* (2009) has proved fruitful, especially her argument that drag can uncover how race intersects with national identity and gender. I have written elsewhere that, while Sieg's study applies specifically to performing race and sexuality in West Germany, her analysis is a useful framework when applied to a broader notion of ethnic drag. In particular, her analysis of postcolonial theories of ambivalence and mimicry, and dramatic theories of mimesis and impersonation, have a direct relevance to Zoe's drag persona (Fong, 2018).

In his groundbreaking work, *Orientalism* (1978), Edward Said illustrates how Western colonialism constructed an idea of the Middle East. This Western construct of the East was endorsed through Western art, literature and academia, creating imagined geographies (Gregory, 1995), that is, an idea of the Orient. The Western colonial project further rationalized this experience by imagining the West as masculine and strong, and the Orient as feminine and weak (Hosford, 2010: 24). This shared rationalization has mapped itself onto contemporary notions of the East, where in Europe and America 'Orientals' include people from East Asia. This interplay creates an imaginative space in which chinoiserie drag can operate. Moreover, an enduring narrative of the imperialist project was often the depiction of Oriental women as highly sexualized, mysterious and full of erotic delights. Said's contrapuntal assessment of colonial art and literature traces the development of this representation, noting an 'almost *uniform association between the Orient and sex*' (Said, 1978: 188, italics in original). This association is mapped onto the Orient as a whole, creating a feminization and gendering of the East: 'Why the Orient seems still to suggest not only fecundity but sexual promise (and threat), untiring sensuality, unlimited desire, deep generative energies, is something on which one could speculate' (ibid.: 188).

Given that both come loaded with cultural discourse, how does Zoe create agency when performing gender and race? How does Zoe, as a transgender woman, deal with the social construction of identity such that she takes some ownership of that identity? A focus on the highly codified racial gendering of East Asian people in the West, where the women are fetishized and the men desexualized, is essential to answer these questions. Below I explore Zoe's brand of chinoiserie drag that empowers her to reveal her fluid-gendered self.

Speeding down the Westway: Invisibility of East Asian men and the hypervisibility of East Asian women

She [Zoe] goes, When I'm driving as a man nobody notices me, everybody goes Chink. But when I'm Zoe men are honking at me, they're tailing me. And she's like vroom, speeding down the Westway. (Ivan Heng quoting Zoe, in *Deconstructing Zoe*, 2016)

This vivid quote from *Deconstructing Zoe* serves to illustrate the contrasting ideas of East Asian gender. As an East Asian man in the West, Zoe feels she is rendered invisible – a 'Chink', a man who is despised – but as an East Asian woman she is desired and hypervisible. In this geographical space of a highly sexualized racism, I will demonstrate how Zoe is able to mediate her identity by deftly moving herself from a position of invisibility to visibility. Feminist anthropologist Ann Stoler (1989) asserts that the racialization of gender and sex was deeply ingrained in the colonial enterprise. Along the same vein, historian Claire Lowrie (2013) traces how the colonial master/servant narrative sought to infantilize Chinese male servants in order to assert white male potency. They were characterized as being passive, feminized, servile. Yet, as I will show, in the interwar years in Europe, Chinese men represented a sexual threat, with the potential to destabilize white superiority through miscegenation. The conceptual castration of Chinese men as feminine and eunuch-like underscored white men's fears of Chinese men (Lowrie, 2013: 52). This trope has since been perpetuated in numerous examples of East Asian characters and has led to their desexualization in Euro-American popular culture. In contrast, in the early literature of the European writers and missionaries, East Asian women were characterized as having a licentious libido, to be feared and desired in equal measure. This trope was played out throughout popular culture.

In E. A. Du Pont's silent film *Piccadilly* (1929), made for British Films International, Anna May Wong plays a lowly scullery maid thrust into stardom by becoming an exotic dancer in London's Piccadilly. Although Wong was a third-generation American-born Chinese, in her Hollywood films she always played the Oriental Other. She complained, 'I was so tired of the parts I had to play ... Why is it that the screen Chinese is nearly always the villain of the piece?' (Mackie, 1933: 11). To British audiences, Wong was the embodiment of the Orient. Her race was always foremost in the plot. The characters she played were personified by exoticness or deceit (Staszak, 2015: 9). This heightened performance of Chineseness was employed as self-exoticization by Wong; Yiman Wang calls it 'yellow yellowface' (2005: 325). There are many tropes of Orientalism at play in *Piccadilly*; one of the most enduring is the exoticization and feminization of the East. Jean-François Staszak observes how Anna May Wong's performances were rooted in Western imaginative geographies recreated in Euro-American film culture (Staszak, 2015). Here the interlacing discourse of sex, gender and race are tied in with her performances.

Although Anna May Wong was born in California, her screen identity was constructed through her perceived ethnicity and validated by her exoticization. When the audience first encounter Wong as Shosho, she is dancing seductively on the kitchen table, watched by night club owner Valentine. He watches her from afar, and the viewer is invited to share his vision of her uninhibited dance. Her nipples can be seen through her dress –

quite risqué for the time – and the camera tilts down her body to her legs, revealing laddered stockings. In fact, the film comes with a censor warning: for adults only. The hypervisibility of Shosho's body, and the subsequent exoticization of her ethnicity through Valentine's point-of-view shot, creates a subject/object relationship between them throughout the film.

The next time Valentine and Shosho meet is when he summons her to his office. Valentine sits at his desk drawing her likeness on a pad, eyeing her furtively. Again, the camera lingers on Shosho's legs. She tells Valentine that she danced once in Limehouse and reveals, 'They wouldn't let me dance again, sir – there was trouble between two men – knives, policemen'. This demonstrates Shosho's illicit appeal and is in keeping with the reputation of London's Limehouse at the time. Contemporary popular novels painted Chinese Limehouse as a place of vice and miscegenation, linking the two conceptually. Limehouse during the interwar years was seen as dark and exotic 'with hints of luxurious opium places hidden in the slums' (Whitchard, 2007). This dark charm appealed to the English society set looking for exotic delights. Bus trips ferried eager tourists to gawk at Chinamen in Limehouse. Shosho represents the promise of that Oriental excess. Miscegenation threatened the hierarchical structure of race upon which colonial rule was based.

It is Valentine who initiates the ethnic dragging of Shosho, declaring that she needs a Chinese costume to dance in. Therein the chinoiserie drag stage is set, through the exoticization and eroticization of Oriental femininity. Shosho convinces Valentine that the only place to buy an authentic Chinese costume is in Limehouse, except the Chinese costume Shosho chooses is reminiscent of a Thai or Myanmar dance costume. When Valentine asks her to try it on for him, she refuses him the pleasure and instead tells Jim, her Chinese boyfriend, to put it on. Valentine looks uncomfortable by the gender-bending charade, while Jim looks bored. Herein, this campy setup of gender and ethnicity is conflated to draw attention to the masquerade. In this swift turn of the narrative, Shosho highlights that Valentine's erotic pleasure has nothing to do with gender, but the imagined geography of race. Judith Butler theorized that drag acts can expose the performativity of sex and gender. Likewise, by lampooning ethnic stereotypes through estrangement and denaturalization, the performativity of race contests its mimetic logic (Sieg, 2009). In *Piccadilly*, Shosho and Valentine's interracial desire is challenged and damned. In the denouement the two Chinese characters Shosho and Jim die and Valentine is exonerated, ultimately restoring the (white) status quo.

In *Deconstructing Zoe* (2016), Zoe employs similar yellow yellowfacing tactics as Wong in *Piccadilly*. Utilizing the Butterfly myth, Zoe plays on the exoticization of Oriental femininity. The Butterfly myth is an enduring Western fantasy and construct, which evokes and reinforces the idea of the East as passive, submissive and childlike. This myth has been renewed throughout colonialism and postcolonialism. It has fascinated Italian, French and American writers, performers and audiences in equal measures. In France, the semi-autobiographical novel *Madame Chrysanthème* (Loti, 1888) describes the temporary 'marriage' between a French naval officer and Chrysanthème, a Japanese geisha. Loti's novel helped shape the way the West sees the East and is still in print today. In Italy, Puccini created the three-act opera *Madama Butterfly* (1904), which is based on Loti's novel. The French naval officer has been replaced by a US naval officer. In 1989, the myth was revived in *Miss Saigon*, relocating the story to Vietnam. The romance this time revolves around an American GI and a Vietnamese bargirl. The plot for each follows the same formula: a Western man journeys to East Asia, where he indulges his vision of the East by 'marrying' a local woman. The Western lover leaves the Asian woman, and she takes her own life in a final act of loyalty to him. In the Butterfly myth, the East is portrayed as a feminized, infantized, aesthetic construct (Wisenthal, 2006: 5), while the West is masculine and powerful. The central female character embodies the Western fantasy of the Orient as submissive, passive and childlike. In *Madame Chrysanthème*, the narrator imagines the real Japan as Japanoiserie, which he 'already knew in the paintings of lacquer and porcelains. It is so an exact a representation' (Wisenthal, 2006: 8).

In 1988, David Henry Hwang's play *M. Butterfly* opened on Broadway. The play was loosely based on the relationship between the French diplomat Bernard Boursicot and Beijing opera singer Shi Pei Pu. Boursicot had a twenty-year affair with his male lover, believing he was a woman who bore him a child. The play was a critique of the Butterfly myth, and was made into a feature film in 1993 by Cronenberg. *M. Butterfly* (1988) is a play within a play, which foregrounds the act of a stage performance. By performing multiple versions of Butterfly in *Deconstructing Zoe*, Zoe creates a construct within a construct, queering ideas of gender and ethnicity. In the documentary, Zoe performs two versions of the Butterfly myth. In the first, she is 'Butterfly', playing on chinoiserie drag. Ebonknee asks Zoe, 'So do you think you play the submissive Butterfly?' (*Deconstructing Zoe*, 2016) to which she replies, 'I think I project this image of a delicate oriental butterfly.' Zoe has explored this exotification of race in the stage play *An Occasional Orchid* (1996), which is restaged in the documentary. Together with the director Ivan Heng, they questioned why the orchid was prized as an exotic plant in the West, when in East Asia it was as commonplace as a rose. In *Deconstructing Zoe*, she shares her thoughts: 'The orchid is an exotification of a race or culture which is foreign to someone. I feel as Zoe there's this exotification of myself' (Zoe, in *Deconstructing Zoe*, 2016). Just like the narrator in *Madame Chrysanthème* (Loti, 1888), who imagines the real Japan as japanoiserie, what people choose to see in Zoe is chinoiserie – an idea of the East caught in a lacquered screen or a willow-pattern plate. In this version of Zoe's Butterfly, like chinoiserie, she is a pure invention.

Ray Yeung's short film *A Bridge to The Past* (1994) similarly uses racial masquerade and mimesis in the vein of chinoiserie drag. The film is billed as a stylized drama, incorporating elements of Peking opera (*sic*) and martial arts, which examine the beliefs underlying the Chinese Hungry Ghost Festival. In the vein of a docudrama, Yeung deliberately creates a pastiche, then a satire of the 'exoticized Oriental image' (Yeung, 2014). Costume and stylized acting are used in a deliberate attempt to add an other-worldly feeling to the setting and story. This, together with the presence of Mu Lan and mystical goddess Guan Yin, both in drag, is how Yeung lampoons the tropes of Orientalism. *A Bridge to the Past* uses both mimetic and masquerade as modes of address in order to usurp the hegemonic gaze. The opening scene of *A Bridge to the Past* immediately sets up the tropes of exoticness and mystery. Colette Koo, playing the part of the ghost mother of an older Chinese woman, is dressed in period cheongsam, holding a lantern and walking with trepidation towards an ornate wooden door.[4] Epic music, along with dry ice and red lighting, create a setting reminiscent of the films of the so-called Fifth Generation of Chinese filmmakers, such as Chen Kaige and Zhang Yimou. They set their stories in the past, often evoking a bygone era seen through the dramatic lens of sweeping vistas and a bold palette, serving to 'remythify Chinese culture and history' (Zhang, 2004: 237). Indeed, such films provided inspiration for neo-chinoiserie in contemporary fashion.[5] The opening scene in Yeung's film seems to reinforce the persistent configurations of colonial Other. But Yeung transforms the narrative. Colette Koo's performance as the ghost mother, and later as Mu Lan, employs ethnic drag using mimicry and mimesis as masquerade. Indeed, Koo's character employs 'sly civility' to complicate the reading of the docudrama.[6] In the opening, Koo plays the role of presenter, leading spectators through the story, teaching them about the Hungry Ghost Festival. In period cheongsam with hair in a demure bun, her bodily presentation is 'Oriental', but she speaks in English received pronunciation.[7] This configuration of bodily Oriental/English demeanour calls to mind V. S. Naipaul's mimic-men (1967) and Homi Bhabha's concept of colonial mimicry (Bhabha, 1994), where, in the discourse of post-Enlightenment English colonialism, the subject is Asian 'in blood and colour, but English in tastes, opinions, morals and intellect' (Macaulay, in Bhabha, 1994: 87). Bhabha argues that mimicry not only destroys the colonized person but also that 'the discourse of mimicry is constructed around ambivalence; in order to be effective, mimicry must continually produce its slippage, its excess, its difference' (Bhabha, 1994: 86). While Koo's ghost mother appears to uphold the image of 'colonial mimicry' and recalls the mimetic logic of racial identity by presenting a 'naturalistic' performance of race, other key characters in the docudrama throw this reading into doubt. In particular, the role of Chung played by Chowee Leow as a comic coolie Chinaman, played to camp excess, serves as a 'critical undoing of mimesis' (Sieg, 2009: 228). Chung fellating a saveloy sausage to a tune reminiscent of the breathless love ballad *Je t'aime* puts into check any misreading of this deliberate attempt at defamiliarization via excess. The ghost mother presenter tells Chung, 'It's a British delicacy... is it nice?' as he works the saveloy suggestively in and out of his mouth.

Zoe grew up in Malaysia, a former British colony, and she perhaps has experienced first-hand the legacy of colonial rhetoric. By masquerading as the Oriental Other, Zoe produces a similar effect as Koo's ghost mother in Yeung's film – that of mimicry. Zoe performs the enduring imperialist narrative of the Oriental woman with 'sly civility'. Bhabha hints at how mimicry can play a subversive role in postcolonial discourse (Bhabha, 1994), where the 'colonized subject' is able to shift and leak out of the constraints imposed on them. In *Deconstructing Zoe*, theatremaker and director Ivan Heng comments that Zoe plays the stereotype of the Oriental woman, 'playfully, knowingly, playing a game' (Heng, in *Deconstructing Zoe*, 2016). In acknowledgement of this, Zoe, proclaims she is a construct. This is not to say that Zoe is not her authentic self; rather, it is an acknowledgement that identity is produced and achieved and that it is not innate; rather, it is negotiated between people and relationships (Lawler, 2008). Therefore, for Zoe, taking ownership of that construct renders her visible. Zoe declares:

[I]t's fascinating for me when I walk down the street as a guy – how people perceive you as an Asian man and how that is different when you walk down the street as an Asian woman. You know you've got this energy and get looks and you know why that is? It's this exotification, because I'm this exotic Asian woman – this feminine creature which this big Western man wants to protect. The orchid represents this exoticness for me. (Zoe, in *Deconstructing Zoe*, 2016)

However, the success of Zoe's chinoiserie drag is dependent on Western perception. This is explained by Zoe's observation that when she is in England, people notice her race first, then her gender. While, back in Malaysia, it is her gender that people notice first and that the pass is less successful. Neil in *Deconstructing Zoe* comments that his idea of drag conjures up the idea of stage drag and that he does not see Zoe as drag, rather as transgender. However, Ebonknee tells Zoe that she sees her as glam drag. Rusty Barrett explains, 'the goal of glam drag is to produce an outward appearance indistinguishable from that of a "real" woman' (Barrett, 2017: 38).

The second version of Zoe's Butterfly is more nuanced. In this rendition, Zoe uses *M. Butterfly* to empower herself. In *Deconstructing Zoe* (2016), Zoe describes how she was a dancer in London's West End version of *M. Butterfly* (1988). Acting and performing in Hwang's play night after night must have left an impression on the young Zoe. Wearing a butterfly-themed shirt and sitting on the chaise longue Zoe says, 'The East has always been seen as something feminine, mystical [...] The West has always been seen as very masculine, very powerful, you know. And I think there is always this urge for the West to colonize the East because the woman needs to be protected' (Zoe, in *Deconstructing Zoe,* 2016).

This echo's Song's speech in *M. Butterfly*: 'As soon as a Western man comes into contact with the East – he's already confused. The West has sort of an international rape mentality towards the East [...] The West thinks of itself as masculine – big guns, big industry, big money – so the East is feminine – weak, delicate poor [...]' (Hwang, 1988: 83).

Elsewhere, Zoe tells Ebonknee, 'When I'm Zoe I think I project this image of a delicate oriental butterfly, because that in itself is powerful. But I think that's only powerful because I'm playing it from an Asian male perspective.'

Zoe's words are almost a direct quotation from *M. Butterfly* (1988) in the scene where Song reveals to Chin the nature of her power over Gallimard:

Song   Miss Chin, why in Peking opera are women roles played by men?

Chin   I don't know, maybe a reactionary element of male –

Song   No *(Beat)* Because only a man knows how a woman is supposed to act.

Lai Sai Acón Chan, in her analysis of this interaction in *M. Butterfly*, offers this insight: 'Song's strategy is playing the master's game and pretending to be what they think he is.' Within the logic of *M. Butterfly*, Hwang's commentary is that Asian men used their perceived femininity as a ploy to empower the subaltern (Lai, 2014: 14). In Sherrill Grace's reading, Gallimard (representative of the West), disappears further into his own fantasy, a 'vision of the Orient', until he becomes Butterfly, 'a woman created by a man' (Grace, 2006: 141).

As a film-maker of Chinese heritage, I have long been interested in exploring through my films how identity is fashioned through performance, and whether in the context of my projects what Butler says of gender can be said of race. In making my documentary, *Deconstructing Zoe* (2016), I investigated whether race can be performative, and whether we act out in ways that consolidate an impression of what it is to be Chinese (Fong, 2018).

To return to Zoe speeding down the Westway as a Chinese woman: this vivid image points to the power Zoe believes she is able to harness as an East Asian woman. She contrasts this image with the invisibility she has as a Chinese man in the West, who is metaphorically castrated of his power. By playing with an essentialized Western image of the Orientalized other, Zoe is able to destabilize the hegemonic order. Indeed it is her submission to the essentialized idea of Orientalized woman which helps her consolidate her power as an Oriental man. Zoe's refusal to conform to a fixed uniform racialized gendered identity enables her to shape her self-hood, creating manifold identities of contestation. By employing chinoiserie drag acts, Zoe makes her invisible self visible in the West.

Notes

1 *Orphan of Zhao*, RSC, 2012; *In the Depth of Dead Love*, Print Room, 2017; *Miss Saigon*, 2017–18, UK; *Sherlock Holmes, The Blind Banker*, BBC, 2010; *No Escape*, 2015, Dir. John Erick Dowdle.
2 See Fenton (2012).
3 A series of events and conferences to stimulate thought-provoking ideas and discussion.
4 Cheongsam is a traditional Chinese dress.
5 *China: Through the Looking Glass* exhibition 2015 at the Metropolitan Museum of Art, focusing on the impact of Chinese design on Western fashion over the centuries. For a critique of the exhibition, see Givhan (2015).
6 See Bhabha (1994: 99), 'Refusal to satisfy the colonizer's narrative demand'. Or a secretive means to defy the colonizing dominance while upholding a sense of civility.
7 Standard English pronunciation based on the educated speech of southern England.

References

A Bridge to the Past (1994). [film]. Dir. Raymond Yeung, UK: Force 8 Productions. Arts Council Black Arts Project.
An Occasional Orchid. (1996) [stage play]. Dir. Ivan Heng, UK: Ectectera Theatre.
Barrett, Rusty. (2017). *From Drag Queens to Leathermen: Language, Gender, and Gay Male Subcultures.* New York: Oxford University Press.

Bederman, Gail. (1995). *Manliness and Civilization: A Cultural History of Gender and Race in the United States, 1880–1917.* Chicago: University of Chicago Press Books.

Being Human Festival. (2016). 18 November. Available online: http://beinghumanfestival.org.

Bhabha, Homi. K. (1994). *The Location of Culture.* New York: Routledge.

Butler, Judith. (2006). *Gender Trouble.* New York: Routledge.

Butler, Judith. (2011). [Interview]. *The Big Think.* Available online: https://bigthink.com/videos/your-behavior-creates-your-gender

Deconstructing Zoe (2016) [film]. Dir. Rosa Fong, UK: Edge Hill University.

Fenton, James. (2012). 'The Orphan of Zhao at the RSC: a very modern massacre'. *Guardian*, 30 October. Available online: https://www.theguardian.com/stage/2012/oct/30/orphan-of-zhao-rsc.

Fong, Rosa. (2018). 'Deconstructing Zoe: Performing Race'. *Zapruder World International Journal for the History of Social Conflict*, vol. 4.

Fung, Richard. (1991). 'Looking for my Penis'. In Bad Object-choices (eds), *How Do I Look? Queer Film and Video.* pp. 145–68. Seattle: Bay Press. Available online: http://www.richardfung.ca/index.php?/articles/looking-for-my-penis-1991/ (accessed 14 July 2017).

Givhan, Robin. (2015). 'The fantasy of China: Why the new Met exhibition is a big, beautiful lie'. *Washington Post*, 5 May. Available online: https://www.washingtonpost.com/news/arts-and-entertainment/wp/2015/05/05/the-fantasy-of-china-why-the-new-met-exhibition-is-a-big-beautiful-lie/.

Grace, Sherrill. (2006). 'Playing Butterfly with David Henry Hwang and Robert Lepage'. In J. Wisenthal, S. Grace, M. Boyd, B. McIlroy and V. Micznik (eds), *A Vision of the Orient: Texts, Intertexts and Contexts of Madame Butterfly*, pp. 135–54. Toronto: University of Toronto Press.

Gregory, Derek. (1995). 'Imaginative Geographies'. *Progress in Human Geography*, vol. 19, no. 4, pp. 447–85.

Gregory, Derek. (2004). *The Colonial Present.* Malden: Blackwell Publishing United States.

Hosford, Desmond. (2010). 'Regnorum Ruina: Cleopatra and the Oriental Menace in Early French Tragedy'. In D. Hosford and C. J. Wojkowski (eds), *French Orientalism: Culture, Politics, and the Imagined Other.* Newcastle upon Tyne: Cambridge Scholars Publishing.

Hewis, Ben. (2016). 'The Print Room responds to yellowface casting claims'. *Whats On Stage.* Available online: https://www.whatsonstage.com/london-theatre/news/the-printroom-under-fire-for-yellowface-casting_42535.html (accessed 9 Aug. 2018).

Hwang, David H. (1988). *M. Butterfly.* New York: Penguin.

In Flux: The Queering of Race and Gender. (2017). Festival of Ideas, Edge Hill University. 21 June 2017. Available online: https://www.edgehill.ac.uk/events/2017/06/21/festival-ideas-screening-roundtable/.

In the Depth of Dead Love (2017) [stage play]. Dramatist Howard Barker, UK: Print Room.

Lai, Acón Chan. (2014). 'From Opera Queens to Rice Queens of Ethnic and Gender Identity'. https://www.academia.edu/4049604/From_Opera_Queens_to_Rice_Queens_Questions_of_Ethnic_and_Gender_Identity (accessed 13 May 2018).

Lawler, Steph. (2008). *Identity: Sociological Perspectives*. Polity Press, Cambridge.

Loti, Pierre. (1888). *Madame Chrysanthème*. Paris: Calmann Levy.

Lowrie, Claire. (2013). 'White "men" and their Chinese "boys": Sexuality, Masculinity and Colonial Power in Singapore and Darwin, 1880s–1930s'. *History Australia*, vol. 10, no. 1, pp. 35–57.

M. Butterfly (1993), [film]. Dir. David Cronenberg, USA: Warner Brothers.

Mackie, Doris. (1933). '"I Protest", by Anna May Wong; an interview with Doris Mackie'. *Film Weekly*, 18 August, p. 11.

Madame Butterfly (1904), [opera]. Giacomo Puccini.

Miss Saigon (1989), [stage musical]. Claude-Michel Schönberg. London: West End Theatre.

Piccadilly (1929), [film]. Dir. E. A. Du Pont, UK: British First International.

Said, Edward. (1978). *Orientalism: Western Conceptions of the Orient*. New York: Random House.

Said, Edward. (1993). *Culture and Imperialism*. London: Chatto & Windus.

Sieg, Katrin. (2009). *Ethnic Drag: Performing race, nation, sexuality in West Germany*. Ann Arbor: University of Michigan Press.

Staszak, Jean-François. (2015). 'Performing race and gender: the exoticization of Josephine Baker and Anna May Wong'. *Gender, Place & Culture*, vol. 22, no. 5, pp. 626–43.

Stoler, Ann L. (1989). 'Making the Empire Respectable'. *American Ethnologist*, vol. 16, no. 4, pp. 634–60.

The Orphan of Zhao (2012), [stage play]. Dir. Gregory Doran, UK: Royal Shakespere Company.

Wang, Yiman. (2005). 'The Art of Screen Passing: Anna May Wong's Yellow Yellowface Performance in the Art Deco Era'. *Camera Obscura Feminism Culture and Media Studies*, vol. 20, no. 3, pp. 159–91.

Whitchard, Anne V. (2007). 'A Threepenny Omnibus Ticket to "Limey-housey-Causey-way": Fictional Sojourns in Chinatown'. *Comparative Critical Studies*, vol. 4, no. 2, pp. 225–40. DOI: https://doi.org/10.1353/ccs.2007.0033.

Whitchard, Anne V. (2017). *Thomas Burke's Dark Chinoiserie*. Farnham: Ashgate Publishing.

Wisenthal, Jonathan, Grace, Sherrill E. and Boyd, Melinda. (2006). *A Vision of the Orient: Texts, Intertexts, and Contexts of Madame Butterfly*. Toronto: University of Toronto Press.

Yeung, Ray. (2014). Unpublished interview with Rosa Fong, New York/UK, June.

Zhang, Yingjin. (2004). *Chinese National Cinema*. Abingdon: Routledge.

5

'It's Always Better Performing with the Troupe'

Space, Place and Collective Activism

Jae Basiliere

Drag performances create a remarkable space where activism, community bonding and entertainment intersect. While drag shows may sometimes be perceived primarily as entertainment, as frivolous parodies or mindless shows, their presence also facilitates other types of community action and education that may not operate as seamlessly in other venues. This project centres the ways in which drag performance allows individual performers to cultivate nuanced relationships with their performance of gender within the particulars of their geographic location. This chapter explores these two themes while also considering the way that both gender diversity and geographical location generate activist opportunities for performers in their local communities. I argue that this effect is heightened in both non-metropolitan and rural spaces, where other opportunities for community bonding and activism may be more limited. While this sense of unity may originate from a desire for entertainment, it facilitates activism and education in a way that might not be possible without the presence of drag as an anchoring factor.

This chapter intervenes in conversations around drag activism using data collected from the Gender Studs, a collective (of which I was part) of drag performers based in Bloomington, Indiana, between 2011 and 2014. Using a combination of participant observation, autoethnography and semi-structured interviews, I investigate how my research participants understand what it means to be successful. I engage with existing literature that considers the possibilities of drag performance as activist, primarily through raising awareness, personal validation and social commentary. In addition to these modes of performance, my participants enact activism by using drag as a venue for advocacy, fundraising and outreach education. I contend that drag provides an exceptional platform for this type of social justice work because of the ways in which entertainment culture creates community.

This chapter suggests that a notion of success rooted in individual experience does not have to remain centred on the individual. My participants use an individualized set of criteria to shape the lens through which they read success. However, every participant in this project simultaneously factors their larger community into their success model. The non-metropolitan drag performers who participated in my research do not separate their broader social impact from their reading of their own success – whether that is through an investment in pleasing the audience, fundraising or advocacy outreach.

Drag as activism

Scholars interested in the link between drag and activism have often focused on either the educational possibilities of drag performance or the unique type of public culture that is formed around places where drag performances occur. Early work on drag king culture identified an effect on the gender awareness of the (primarily) female consumers of drag king performance. In a discussion of Diane Torr's New York City–based Drag-King-for-a-Day workshop, Halberstam asserts that '[m]any women described their experiences of Torr's workshop as mind-blowing or earth-shaking; Torr receives many letters attesting to the drastic and permanent transformations in gender consciousness that her workshop participants undergo' (Volcano and Halberstam, 1999: 79). In this context, the activist work of Torr's drag workshop comes in the form of raising gender awareness. Torr allows woman-identified females to understand that 'maleness is not sacred' (ibid.). Halberstam classifies this type of activist work as distinctive from the type of education that happens in the traditional nightclub performance space, but it nonetheless suggests an important intervention that drag king performance facilitates. Halberstam's reading of Torr's workshop suggests that those same transformative effects of a drag performance on lived gender performance may occur in a variety of contexts.

In another discussion of New York City–based drag activism, Amy Jo Goddard suggests that public performances that interrogate the stability of identity categories may have a transformative effect on the audiences who consume those performances. Goddard argues that 'the artists' position as cultural workers allow them to bridge activist movements and communities that might not otherwise form alliances. Besides the creative work itself, their activism extends to the creative processes in their work, touring with their work, as well as other aspects of their lives' (Goddard, 2007: 97–8). She marks performance art as a bridge – a venue through which otherwise disparate entities can come together and collaborate. In a discussion of Imani Henry's performance art, Goddard considers the way this influence plays out on college campuses. She claims that Imani Henry's performance operates as an activist commodity – student groups form coalitions to bring Henry to campus; this in and of itself is activism (103–4). The educational nature of Henry's performance creates another type of activist space, one where education and entertainment meet in a way that generates student interest. Goddard ties this type of educational activism specifically to drag performance in an interview with drag king Dred Scott. Scott positions drag as a venue where performers can simultaneously entertain and educate – in this context, the education comes in the form of awareness raising. The message that diversity is not only acceptable but desirable comes through in Scott's performances because of the way that his very visible deviance from established gender norms interacts with the value assigned to his performances.

In both of these examples, the activist intentions of drag performances come from the pairing of entertainment with a direct challenge to the hegemonic norms of masculinity. In the case of Torr's Drag-King-for-a-Day workshop, the challenge to masculine norms comes from allowing feminine-presenting individuals to embody those norms for themselves, and in the case of Scott this challenge comes through the act of translating a largely Western form of masculine performance into a transnational context. In addition to this type of activism, which explicitly undermines masculine norms and social codes, drag performers can also enact change through more direct community interventions. Leslie Grey argues that drag kings, by nature of the way they engage with gender and sexual fluidity, have something to offer individuals who work in sexuality education and community sexual health outreach. According to Grey, 'Drag kings' narratives serve as a point of entry by which to delve into the multiple ways in which selves – and knowledges – are constructed. Therefore, these narratives have significant pedagogical value for sexuality education in examining the relationships between subjectivities and knowledges' (Grey, 2011: 180–1).

In other words, Grey contends that drag kings are simultaneously occupying multiple contingent subject positions, a social location that gives them a situated perspective on the process of creating embodied knowledge. The activist potential of drag kinging comes in the ways in which it makes explicit the possibility for rejecting a singular definition of gender or sexuality. Grey's contribution to the conversation about drag kings and activism comes in the way she reveals the possibilities of using drag performance in a classroom education context.

In conjunction with education and awareness, drag performance also possesses the possibility to enact change on the state and social level. In their discussion of California activist efforts to combat gay marriage bans, Taylor et al. argue that public culture has a profound ability to enact social change: 'the lesbian and gay movement historically has been more likely than other social movements to deploy cultural performances and repertoires to assert identity claims and to promote particular goals... Our findings raise questions about how contentious cultural performances in less public venues might be connected to larger campaigns' (Taylor et al., 2009: 886). This intervention, in particular the claim that performances do not need to manifest on a national stage to impact activist campaigns, is the basis for my analysis of drag performance moving forward.

Advocacy, fundraising and outreach education

Many performers enact activism by using drag as a venue for advocacy, fundraising and outreach education. I contend that drag provides an exceptional venue for this type of social justice work because of the ways in which entertainment culture creates community. Thus, individuals who use drag for activism have a double investment in participation, as both the performance and the cause create appeal.

In February 2013, the Gender Studs were asked to participate in an outreach event as part of Condom Fashion Week. This week consisted of a series of events, sponsored by Illumenate Bloomington, designed to raise awareness about safer sex practices in the community.[1] The show that the Gender Studs were asked to participate in was of particular significance because it was performing double duty as both an outreach event and a fundraiser. Illumenate Bloomington had recently lost its state funding. Without a significant exogenous investment, the Illumenate coordinators were likely going to have to discontinue their programming. The show's $5 cover, in addition to any tips received by the performers over the course of the performance, would all go into a fund to help save Illumenate's programming.

The event itself deviated from a traditional drag performance. The show was a drag retelling of *Snow White and the Seven Dwarves*, intent on discovering 'what happens when you take a classic fairy tale and infuse it with all the genderfucking your heart could desire, an awesome soundtrack, and hilarious dialogue'. The character representing the Evil Queen was played by a drag queen (Argenta Perón); the characters representing Snow White and Prince Charming were played by Misters (Titanium Perón and Charming);[2] and the characters representing the Huntsman and the dwarves were played by drag kings and members of the Gender Studs (BJ Brinker, Max Powers and Jameson). The show was a combination of dialogue interspersed with drag performances. The overall effect was a narrative performance, a show that told a story beyond what a traditional drag show is able to accomplish.

In a modification of the traditional Snow White narrative, the show told the story of a love triangle between Titanium, Charming and Argenta Perón. At the beginning of the show, Titanium and Argenta are represented as lovers, but Titanium quickly dumps Argenta when the younger, masculine Charming enters the bar. The Huntsman (Jameson) comes to function as the genderqueer father figure in the show, rather than the queen's servant. In line with the traditional narrative, the Gender Studs (dwarves) serve as the show's comic relief.

Based on audience reactions, one of the most favoured segments of the show was the scene where Snow White (Titanium Perón) eats the poisoned apple. After Argenta gives Titanium the poisoned apple (in this case, a spiked apple martini), Titanium performs to Ke$ha's song 'Die Young'. As the song draws to an end, Titanium begins to appear more intoxicated, and his dancing becomes less precise. During the final chorus of the song, Titanium staggers across the stage and falls into my (Jameson's) arms:

I hear your heart beat to the beat of the drums
Oh what a shame that you came here with someone
So while you're here in my arms
Let's make the most of the night like we're gonna die young
(Kesha, 2012)

As the last line of the song fades out, Titanium's body has become limp in my arms. I gently lay him down on the ground, centre stage, as the remaining Gender Studs enter from stage left to the opening lines of Alice Cooper's song 'Poison'. We (BJ, Max and I) begin to dance in a circle around Titanium, taking turns acting as lead vocalist. Periodically, during the song's chorus, Argenta peers in from offstage to remind the audience that she's the poisonous woman in question:

I wanna love you, but I better not touch (don't touch)
I wanna hold you, but my senses tell me to stop
I wanna kiss you, but I want it too much (too much)
I wanna taste you, but your lips are venomous poison
(Cooper, 1989)

This interplay between story and performance resonated well with the audience, who responded by donating additional tip dollars to the cause.

At the end of the show, several members of Illumenate Bloomington came onstage to talk about their experiences with the MPowerment programme, and several community members made additional donations to the cause. The net effect of this show was to raise a significant portion of the funding that Illumenate needed, as well as raise awareness about the function of Illumenate's programming within the community. This particular event highlights the interplay between activism, community bonding and entertainment – a relationship that is common in drag performances. In this singular event, audience members were entertained, gained awareness about a social organization in their community, and helped support said organization's continued existence. Ultimately, this event's success came from the relationship that Illumenate was able to form with the rest of the community.

Following this benefit show, BJ Brinker, Max Powers and I all maintained our relationship with Illumenate Bloomington by participating in a monthly event called 'Testing, Trivia, and Tiaras'. This event was held on the first Tuesday of every month, at Uncle Elizabeth's nightclub in Bloomington, Indiana. It combined drag performances, rounds of bar trivia (with questions that focused primarily, but not exclusively, on public health and LGBTQ+ history), and free HIV testing for anyone interested in receiving that service. Periodically throughout the night, the trivia host for the evening would talk about the available testing services and share information about why knowing your HIV status is important. While receiving HIV testing was not required of event attendees, most people chose to take advantage of the service after hearing the justifications for such a practice.

The use of drag as a catalyst for advocacy, fundraising and/or education is not universal. Certainly, not all drag performers choose to donate their time or energy to outreach causes, particularly because such a decision often means performing for free. There are several factors that may contribute to a performer's decision regarding outreach drag performances: the individual performer's level of investment in the cause being supported, the performer's available time and resources, and the model of performance success that the performer in question utilizes in evaluating a performance. BJ Brinker explains his view on the relationship between drag and activism: 'it's [performing in benefit shows] different. Sometimes I spend more time getting ready for a show if I'm passionate about the cause [laughs]'. Rather than feeling put out by performing for free in a benefit show, BJ ascribes a positive value to the experience. This sentiment was echoed by other members of the Gender Studs – including Max Powers, Damien Masters and Jimmy Tool – who all affirmed the emotional and activist benefits of performing in benefit shows. This approach to drag, which divorces performance success from monetary gain, likely lends itself to an increase in activist-oriented drag performances.

When performers choose to combine drag and activism, it also strengthens their connection with their community. On the troupe level, for performers who belong to troupes, the act of working together towards a common goal can act as a bonding experience, and ultimately has the effect of bringing the troupe closer together. On the community level, this can serve to create lasting relationships between troupe members and community organizations. In the anecdote discussed above, BJ, Max and I all developed and maintained a relationship with Illumenate Bloomington in part because of our participation in the Condom Fashion Week benefit show. Each of us had experienced social interactions with members of the organization prior to that show, but participation in the benefit solidified the relationship between our performer identities and the group's leadership.

Drag as a community-building space

In addition to activism outreach projects, drag performers can also enact positive social change through community relationships and education. In her discussion of ethnographic work conducted with the Disposable Boy Toys (DBT), a Santa Barbara–based troupe of drag performers, Eve Shapiro identifies a three-part activist approach embedded directly within the troupe's structure. DBT supported its troupe members who were actively exploring their own gender identities by offering information and sharing experiences. In addition to informative support, DBT allowed members to explore or try on new gendered expressions through the venue of public performance. And finally, DBT provided its members social support through the creation of a community that positively reinforced variant gendered expressions (Shapiro, 2009: 262–6). For Shapiro, these three converging strategies indicate that 'doing drag in a group context with an oppositional collective identity, feminist political commitment, and collective organizational practices can harness drag's disruptive power' (266–7). This particular strain of gender activism is not universal to drag, but rather 'organization and context and ideology that contains the potential for challenging gender on the individual and social level' (268). Shapiro's work highlights the potential for activist work originating from within the structure of a drag troupe. This possibility is likely amplified by existing connections between drag king culture and feminist activist traditions. Katie Horowitz (2013) suggests that there are significant differences between drag king and drag queen culture which, while outside the scope of this work, warrant mention. In particular, she highlights the ways that drag kings are more likely to centre care and community engagement than their drag queen counterparts.

Alana Kumbier describes this experience of using drag as a means for exploring multiple gendered expressions as such: '[t]hrough my experiences as a drag performer (and avid drag king fan), I have learned a great deal about my own gendered subjectivity, my desire, and my relationship to my body' (Kumbier, 2002: 192). I argue that this is activist work. While, as many have been careful to point out, drag performance is not inherently subversive, there is social potential inherent in the possibility for exploration and experimentation that drag provides. Further, this type of activism also allows for the creation of communities of like-minded individuals. Many of my participants claim that they began doing drag after seeing a performance and being drawn in by the possibilities of what they saw onstage. This appeal, this recruitment process, can make the site of drag performance a catalyst for what are ultimately fruitful community relationships.

The potential for drag performance to educate about, or positively affirm, variant gender expressions extends outside the performer, to the spectator as well. In her discussion of the Chaos Kings, based in Washington, DC, Jennifer Lyn Patterson argues that 'drag kings fulfilled an emotional and social need for themselves and for their lesbian audience' (Patterson, 2002: 120). The space of the drag show itself, and the outlet it provides its audience, is the most significant contribution of drag king culture. She goes on to elaborate that for the performers she works with, 'the illusion of male realness is either secondary or unimportant to their performance. Their primary goal is to please the audience' (ibid.). This sentiment that audience satisfaction is a major factor in evaluating a performance's success is mirrored by many of my participants. Rock Ruffergood describes this experience:

> I think what defines a good show, to me, is the extent to which I feel like the audience is responding to me in the way that I want them to. They seem like they're having a good time, or they play along with me [...] Do I start onstage and they immediately all turn to their drinks, or do I come onto stage and then they look up from their drinks?

In line with Patterson's discussion of the Chaos Kings, Rock privileges audience engagement with his performance. Returning to Patterson's commentary about the 'rambunctious' nature of a drag king audience, we can see that this interpretation of audience enjoyment is shared by both entertainer and spectator. This focus on audience investment creates a relationship between audience member and performer that contributes to the development of community around drag king culture.

Activism and community in non-metropolitan spaces

Thomas Piontek draws attention to the possibilities embedded within drag king communities in his work with the H.I.S. Kings, a performance collective based in Columbus, Ohio. While Eve Shapiro's work, discussed above, focuses on the potentials of gender fluidity from an interpersonal context, Piontek considers this type of gendered activism as a staged phenomenon. He notes that members of H.I.S. perform types of drag that differ from Halberstam's canonical definition of a drag king as a female who 'dresses up in a recognizably male costume and performs theatrically in that costume' (Halberstam, 1998: 232). Rather, Piontek contends that 'H.I.S. Kings make visible not only the part that masculine women have played in the construction of modern masculinity but also the part that lesbians and butch women have played in the construction of femininity' (Piontek, 2002: 139). Interestingly, Piontek marks this fluidity as a function of H.I.S. Kings' location in the Midwest, arguing that '[k]inging in the heartland is not a limitation. Quite the opposite. It is precisely H.I.S. Kings' location on the margins of national queer culture that allows them to push the boundaries of drag, most noticeably when it comes to the issues of race and gender' (140). Piontek ascribes the transgressive possibilities of the H.I.S. Kings' performances to their distance from the regional conventions of drag found in cities considered to be major queer epicentres. He argues that the performance work the H.I.S. Kings do challenges hegemonic masculinity, honours non-traditional or queer masculinities, and undermines the notion that there is a singular way to be masculine. All of this social work, according to Piontek, infuses 'the drag king performance with theoretical reflection and political commentary' (140) in a way that is particular to its Midwestern context.

Following Piontek, I contend that the types of communities that form around drag king culture are distinct in non-metropolitan areas in the United States. The fundraising relationship that formed between members of the Gender Studs and Illumenate Bloomington, discussed earlier, grew out of necessity. The series of circumstances that prompted that situation – Illumenate's sudden and unexpected dearth of funding, the existing social relationships between members of the Gender Studs and the leadership of Illumenate, and the ability to plan and house a show on short notice – were all made possible in part because of our location in Bloomington, Indiana. Our presence in Indiana, a state that is notoriously stingy with its funding for safer-sex education, prompted the need for a fundraiser to begin with, while our location in a college town with a relatively small queer community certainly facilitated the existing relationships that made organizing a production such as *Titanium Perón and the Gender Studs* possible on short notice. This is not to say that such an arrangement could not have existed in a more urban setting, but our social positioning played a role in how events evolved. Certainly, in a more metropolitan area it would have been nearly impossible to book stage time at a gay bar on less than one month's notice.

Community interaction as celebration and outreach

Shortly after the formation of the Gender Studs, the troupe began the tradition of performing at the Bloomington PRIDE Film Festival (Pride). This festival is an annual celebration of LGBTQ+ film, and a moment of community gathering for individuals in Bloomington. The closest traditional gay pride celebration takes place an hour away in Indianapolis, Indiana, so the Pride film fest stands in as Bloomington's version of a pride celebration. The festival takes place over four days, with film screenings on Thursday and Friday evenings, in the afternoon and in the evening on Saturday, and in the afternoon on Sunday. Each screening session is broken down into three parts: a series of short films, a 10–15-minute live performance by a community group and a feature-length film.

The Gender Studs began preparing to perform at Pride nearly a month in advance of the show. Roughly four weeks out, a few members of the troupe would pick the songs that accompanied our performance and would begin the labour of mixing them into an appropriate-length montage. Once the music was completed, that same group of individuals would begin blocking out choreography and preparing a list of prop and costume needs to distribute to the troupe. Approximately two weeks before the show, the troupe would gather for rehearsals. We generally met five or six times to rehearse, and each rehearsal would last two or three hours.

The Gender Studs' performances at Pride told a narrative, usually compatible with the festival's guiding theme. In 2011, the theme of the film festival was 'family', and we crafted our performance narrative around the story of a young man looking for a family of his own. The performance opened with an excerpt from the song 'Little Boxes' by Malvina Reynolds. BJ Brinker and Richie played the role of adoring parents, with Damien Masters as the outcast queer child who could not find a way to fit in. The music then shifted to 'Bohemian Rhapsody' by Queen, and found young Damien on the streets surrounded by a hostile world and unsure of how to proceed. Excerpts from 'Who Wouldn't Wanna Be Me' by Keith Urban and 'Father Figure' by George Michael took Damien through a cowboy and leather bar respectively, and 'Proud' by Heather Smalls closed out the performance with a celebration of families both chosen and found.

After that performance, we were approached by a representative from the Great Lakes Leather Alliance, who invited us to come perform at their annual event in Indianapolis the following summer. This interaction after the show cultivated a relationship between the Gender Studs and GLLA, such that the members of the troupe who were willing and able continued to perform at their event for the next three years. This is just one example of the ways that the Gender Studs' participation in Bloomington Pride facilitated greater connections with the community. Several members of the troupe sat on the festival's steering committee during their time in Bloomington, a further illustration of the ways in which drag kings may form symbiotic or mutually beneficial relationships with members of their community.

Ultimately, it is these relationships that were most appealing to members of the Gender Studs. While it is undeniable that the thrill of using a stage as large as the one the film festival offered and the thrill of performing in front of such large audiences were alluring, it was largely the opportunity to participate in this community celebration that continued to draw us back to the festival. Members of the troupe framed their participation in terms of giving to or celebrating with their community. This, again, demonstrates the possibilities for a vision of success that is rooted in the individual but not isolated to the individual. Even though each member of the Gender Studs had an individualized model for assessing the success of their performance at Pride, they all tagged their assessment of success back to the community in some manner.

Conclusion

The forms of community I discuss here all centre on questions of education, advocacy and outreach. This attention to community is rooted in the ideas that experiences of gender diversity and relationship to location create possibilities for particular types of advocacy and outreach. The manifestations of this can be either internal, in the form of troupes providing support for members thinking through gender, or external, in the form of drag kings reaching out in to their communities. In both cases, the act of outreach is driven by both individual and collective desires.

The data discussed in this chapter illustrates that a notion of success rooted in individual experience does not have to remain centred in the individual. My participants use an individualized set of criteria to shape the lens through which they read success. However, they also factor their larger community into their success model. Whether that is through an investment in pleasing the audience or outreach, the drag performers who participated in this project do not separate their broader social impact from their reading of their own success.

This linking of the individual and the community could have huge implications for thinking about LGBTQ+ political activism more broadly. By reimagining the relationship between individual and community needs in our assessment of success, we could create a space that allows for individual celebration, while still acknowledging that there is yet significant work to be done in buttressing other members of the community. A more expansive understanding of community, then, can lead to a more expansive understanding of success.

Notes

1 Illumenate Bloomington was part of the MPowerment Project – a national project geared towards gay and bisexual men between the ages of 18 and 29 years. The project's biggest goal is to bring community among young gay and bisexual men while educating them on safer sex practices and HIV. For more information, see the organization's website: http://mpowerment.org/.
2 Misters are masculine, generally male-identified entertainers who perform masculinities on stage.

References

Cooper, Alice. (1989). 'Poison' [song]. *Trash*. US: Epic.
Goddard, Amy J. (2007). 'Staging Justice: New York City Performing Artists as Cultural Workers'. *Social Justice*, vol. 34, no. 1, pp. 97–116.
Grey, Leslee. (2011). 'Chapter 12: Sexuality Education: Lessons from Drag Kings'. *Counterpoints*, vol. 392, no. 1, pp. 171–85.
Halberstam, Judith. (1998). *Female Masculinity*. Durham: Duke University Press.
Horowitz, Katie, R. (2013). 'The Trouble with "Queerness": Drag and the Making of Two Cultures'. *Signs*, vol. 38, no. 2, pp. 303–26.
Kesha. (2012). 'Die Young' [song]. *Warrior*. US: RCA Records.
Kumbier, Alana. (2002). 'One Body, Some Genders: Drag Performances and Technologies'. In D. Troka, K. Lebesco and J. Noble (eds), *The Drag King Anthology*, pp. 191–200. New York: Harrington Park Press.
Patterson, Jenifer L. (2002). 'Capital Drag: Kinging in Washington, DC'. In D. Troka, K. Lebesco and J. Noble (eds), *The Drag King Anthology*, pp. 99–124. New York: Harrington Park Press.

Piontek, Thomas. (2002). 'Kinging in the Heartland; or, the Power of Marginality'. In D. Troka, K. Lebesco and J. Noble (eds), *The Drag King Anthology*, pp. 125–44. New York: Harrington Park Press.

Shapiro, Eve. (2009). 'Drag Kinging and the Transformation of Gender Identities'. *Gender and Society*, vol. 21, no. 2, pp. 250–71.

Taylor, Verta, Kimport, Katrina, Dyke, Nella V. and Andersen, Ellen A. (2009). 'Culture and Mobilization: Tactical Repertoires, Same-Sex Weddings, and the Impact on Gay Activism'. *American Sociological Review*, vol. 74, no. 6, pp. 865–90.

Volcano, Del L. and Halberstam, Judith 'Jack'. (1999). *The Drag King Book*. London: Serpent's Tail.

6

Of Hills and Wheels

Tilda Death Drags Memory

Raz Weiner

In May 2016, I performed the drag monodrama *Life and Times of Tilda Death* in an unusual venue – Beit Halochem (Hebrew: House of the Warrior), a culture and leisure centre catering for disabled veterans of the Israeli army (IDF), on Holocaust Memorial Day. I use this experience to interrogate drag's political effects. Due to the unusual circumstances, the auto-ethnographic account of this experience serves more as an observation in an acentric case study that heightens what otherwise might have been covert, rather than an example to be followed or replicated. Building on Sara Ahmed's *Queer Phenomenology* (2006) and others, I unpack several moments from my day in Beit Halochem to demonstrate how the confusion of categories inherent to the act of drag was utilized for political intervention, facilitating a momentary 'surpass [of] the limitations of an alienating presentness' (Muñoz, 2009: 5).

The way

Saturday morning. I drive with Shir, my producer and stage manager, from Tel Aviv to Haifa, travelling north along the eastern coast of the Mediterranean. We are about to perform my drag-mockumentary, Life and Times of Tilda Death, *which I created with my brother, Neta Weiner, in 2013.*[1]

Appropriating aesthetics typical of testimony-events of Holocaust survivors in Israel as its generic framework, this monodrama relates a fable of a Jewish girl from a small Hasidic community in Poland who became a partisan fighter, musician and rap artist. Tilda's biography not only goes beyond her activities in the Second World War, but also includes chapters in the Civil Rights Movement of 1960s New York, the Mizrahi Black Panthers' struggle for equality and recognition in 1970s Jerusalem, and contemporary artistic collaborations with Palestinian musicians in the West Bank. The show oscillates between first-person narrative, spoken word and rap numbers. Tilda continuously references a wide range of political and cultural figures, from the Red Army commander Gregory Zhukov, Israeli Prime Minister Golda Meir and Mizrahi Black Panther activist Ruven Abergil, to Nina Simone, Mick Jagger and the Mizrahi soul diva Margol (Margalit Tzan'ani). All these are woven through her fantastical biography along two parallel trajectories that (along with politics) dominate her life, music and antiracist struggle. In this way Tilda offers an alignment (or alliance) between her experience as a Jewish woman during the Holocaust, black women in the USA and Mizrahi and Palestinian women in Israel/Palestine. She embodies what the literary scholar Michel Rothberg terms multidirectional memory, one that 'encourages us to think of the public sphere as a malleable discursive space in which groups... actually come into being through their dialogical interaction with others' (2009: 5). Being a drag persona, Tilda reframes the malleability of collective memory as well as that of gender performativity.

The show consciously appropriates aesthetics and norms of a testimony-event, especially the way it is performed in educational settings in Israel, and exports it to the realms of drag and performance art.[2] By testimony-event I refer to the occasion of the retelling of personal histories by Holocaust survivors, most commonly in schools around the time of Holocaust Memorial Day. In conceptualizing testimony-event as a genre of performance, I build on the performance studies scholar Marvin Carlson, who identifies 'performative attributes of mourning, memorialization, and the operations of historical trauma' (2004: 55).[3] As these public narrations of testimonies are ritualized as part of the collective culture of memory, they come to bear standardized language, tone and structure, familiar to most graduates of the Israeli educational system. The show draws attention to these ritualized, indeed iconized, aesthetics which normally are neutralized and thus invisible in a usual testimony-event. Tilda wears an elegant black suit and sunglasses; her face is pale with bold red lipstick, and she walks with a slight limp on her left foot, the reminder of an injury from the days of the war. Her accent is deliberately untraceable, commingling mannerisms from Yiddish, German, Polish and Russian. Evocative of, yet somewhat exaggerated in comparison to, a woman speaker in a testimony-event, these aesthetic devices constitute Tilda as an icon, a reference, and not as mimetic representation. This distance is of course significantly enhanced by the drag.

Today's show was commissioned by Beit Halochem, a culture and leisure centre catering for disabled veterans of the Israeli army (IDF). The

cultural events programmer of the institute chose Tilda for the annual
commemoration event of the Israeli Holocaust Memorial Day. I haven't
performed this show in several months, so while dusting up lines and
trying some new puns on Shir, gulping coffee and trying to simultaneously
wake up and warm up, I contemplate the very unusual circumstances we
have got ourselves into.

The Israeli national-historical narrative binds together the commemoration of the Holocaust and Zionism, and the relation between them is fixed in the Israeli calendar. Operating through an implied metaphor of a (collective) journey, the Zionist semi-secular liturgical cycle begins with the festival of Passover and its traditional retelling of the story of Exodus. Holocaust Memorial Day takes place one week after Passover and one week before Remembrance Day for the IDF's Fallen Soldiers, and Independence Day, which is celebrated on the following day. The anthropologist Jackie Feldman summarizes this dramatic process thus: 'World/exilic Jewry [defined through the story of Exodus and is likened to it] is rescued from utter chaos and death (Holocaust Memorial Day), and through self-sacrifice (Fallen Soldiers Memorial Day), raised to the order and life of the State of Israel (Independence Day)' (2010: 49). The individual events are 'lied-up', naturalized by repetitions which blur and invisiblize their conditions of arrival (Ahmed, 2006: 38–9). Their alignment becomes the line that orientates spaces of memory and commemoration. Therefore, a critique of the nationalized memory of the Holocaust, for example, is easily labelled a critique of Zionism at large, and of Israel's current policies and actions of the IDF, as well as degrading the memory of fallen IDF Soldiers. Tilda's show in Beit Halochem is scheduled for the Saturday between the two memorial days, right at the heart of the cycle. The challenge of her multidirectional politics of memory and struggle to the hegemonic nationalist narrative is potentially contentious at any day of the year, and with this particular timing she is clearly out of line.

It is hard to conceive of a site further removed from the context, discourse and politics that Tilda embodies and in which the show was created than Beit Halochem. Opened in 1985, the impressive six-storey complex is one of four health, sport and culture centres operated by the Zahal Disabled Veterans Organization (ZDVO). With around 50,000 members, ZDVO receives new members to its ranks annually, which include ex-soldiers who 'became disabled as a result of or during their activity in the IDF, [as well as] civilian victims of terror' and their family members (ZDVO's website). Regarding itself as a complementary institute to the Israeli Ministry of Defence (ibid.), the ZDVO is generously funded by both the government and private philanthropists. As expressed by the tone and content of its website, the organization's centres and their communities are openly aligned with Israel's national, militarized, patriarchal and heteronormative state ideology (*The Zahal Disabled Veterans Organization Website*, 2018).[4]

IDF disabled veterans are somewhat of a paradox within the Zionist able-body- and reproduction-favouring attitude, described by the culture studies scholar Meira Weiss as 'the ideology of the chosen body' (2004). Despite being glorified as war heroes, as disabled people, IDF disabled veterans are marginalized by a dominant culture that defines itself through idealized notions of able-bodied agency and constructs its social as well as its physical environments accordingly (ibid.). The luxurious facilities of Beit Halochem are thus perceived as the just and exclusive reward for those who sacrificed their bodies – a crucial aspect of their normativity – to the national cause. A fictional figure set up to undermine nationalistic sentiments, heteronormativity and hegemonic discourses of national security, Tilda is engineered as the persistent negation of all that is normative: a queer, unaffiliated, non-Zionist, single artist, whose major lesson from her life experience is to always stand opposite to hegemonic power (usually embodied as national army or police). She is positioned in stark opposition to much of what ZDVO and its underlying ideology of glorified national sacrifice may connote. For this reason, the fact that it is Tilda, and Tilda alone, who earned me an entrée into this fortified club is all the more bewildering.

The opportunity to acquaint Tilda with an audience unlikely to have attended any of my usual performances is both exciting and nerve-wracking. When Shir forwarded me Beit Halochem's invitation email, my first response was to rewrite the brief of the performance, making sure they fully understand what Tilda is all about. As this much more direct, even crude, description of the drag show and its contents did not seem to deter their programmer, I felt compelled to inquire into their vested interest in Tilda. I found out that one of the central activists in Beit Halochem had seen my performance the previous year in Haifa Theatre. She insisted on it being booked for Holocaust Memorial Day and her judgement was trusted unquestioningly. I did not know the woman nor what her motivations were. This thought did not make me any calmer as the southern neighbourhoods of Haifa came into view through the car window.

It is the first time I've performed this drag-mockumentary so early in the morning, and on a Saturday too. So far, Tilda has performed in different fringe venues, in several galleries, and participated in an outdoor music festival. All these stage appearances occurred between 8.00 and 11.00 pm, customary for fringe performances and drag nights. The bright daylight of the late-spring coastal plain road seems almost blasphemous to the idea of a drag show. Despite the annual midday appearances of drag queens atop trucks in gay pride parades in different major cities, bright light is counterintuitive to the practice of drag. Bright light tends to disturb and expose illusions, stitches and tricks, and drag's modern history in the global north is mainly associated with dark nightclubs, side alleys and nightlife (Newton, 1979; Senelick, 2000; Greer, 2012).[5] Even before beginning to address the unusual setting (site, audience, social context) of the show we are about to perform, the requirement to 'drag-up' in broad daylight clearly indicates that both Tilda and I are out of our comfort zones.

A parallel movement from darkness to bright light, from the margins to centre stage, is observed in the mainstreaming of drag globally in recent years. While drag personas such as Lily Savage (Paul O'Grady), Dame Edna Everage (Barry Humphries), Divine (Harris Glenn Milstead) and Madea (Tyler Perry), however different from one another in style and politics, have featured widely in Anglophone film and television for several decades, RuPaul's drag reality shows have achieved unprecedented heights of mainstream popularity (Logo TV, VH1; Daems, 2014). Digital broadcasting platforms, such as Netflix, contribute to the global dissemination of the drag queen trend to both queer and heteronormative audiences, far beyond the USA. The growing demand for television drag queens, however, does not imply the embrace of drag as a practice or politics of subversion or transgression, characteristics with which founding queer theorists have linked it (Butler, 1993; Muñoz, 1998). The proliferation of popular representation of drag indicates the need for a careful interrogation as to which elements of drag are being embraced and circulated on prime time television and Instagram, and which are edited out.[6] Through reconstructing key moments of my experience with Tilda in Beit Halochem, I will frame a few areas in which drag can become a vehicle for political performance-intervention.

The space

Upon arrival to the gate of Beit Halochem, further incompatibilities present themselves. I feel a certain embarrassment and reluctance while passing through the gates and into the nearly empty massive building of brutalist architecture; this passage for me resonates with drag's crossing of categories as well as with acts of trespassing or infiltrating, breaking in. After a long interrogation by the guards, who did not anticipate our arrival nor seem to understand how the two of us could fulfil the annual slot for the Holocaust Memorial Day event, we are let in. Once inside we find it very hard to orientate ourselves. Our able-bodied logic of stairs and corridors seems to

fail us in an alternative topography that privileges wheelchairs, and some
time passes before we manage to find our way around.

'If orientation is about making the strange familiar through the extension of
bodies in space', proposes feminist and queer studies scholar Sara Ahmed,
'then disorientation occurs when that extension fails... Some spaces extend
certain bodies and simply do not leave room for others' (Ahmed, 2006: 11).
Ahmed's queer phenomenology initially addresses the incompatibility of
queer bodies in heterosexual hegemonic spaces. In this context, privilege,
inclusion and exclusion – whose bodies' extension prevails and whose
fails – is most heightened though not as neatly organized in binaries or finite
opposites. Along with the increasing daylight and Tilda's incompatibility
with the ideology of the site, the sensation of the movement through its space
amounts to what Ahmed terms 'oblique', where 'disorientation itself becomes
worldly or becomes what is given' (159).

The technical manager of the institute's performance space continuously
misgenders Shir, insisting on addressing her as a man. His suspicion of us
does not seem to allow any negotiation on the matter, and so Shir's identity
remains invisible – in Ahmed's terms, it fails to find room. At the same
time, in other ways Beit Halochem has anticipated our arrival beyond our
expectations. When we enter the space of the intended performance and
are about to lay out the minimal set of the show – a national flag and a
memorial candle – we discover that the stage was already set for us, with
more or less the same items.

In the show, the flag and the candle reference the genre of the testimony-
event, situating the audience in its context even before Tilda goes onstage.
Once there, she is interacting with and commenting on them, thus creating
a referential distance between the trope of the testimony-event and herself.
Now, the stage of Beit Halochem is all set for Tilda's testimony-event precisely
because there was no theatricality intended on the behalf of the organizers.
They have followed protocol and prepared the stage for a standard Holocaust
Memorial Day event with its ritualistic objects (i.e. flag and candle).
Dramaturgically, this coalescence risks compromising the very difference
that sustained the performance as I knew it, the ironic distance between
a source and its representation. As a maker and performer, this situation
compels me to rethink the entire premise of the show. While taking Tilda's
wig out of its box and brushing it, in my head I try to re-situate the work,
which bears no small measure of parody and allusion, into a space prepared

to perceive it simply as testimony-event, a thing in itself, at face value and in broad daylight.

Alliance

Right when I am done adjusting Tilda's bra, a woman enters the dressing room. She introduces herself as Maya, the person responsible for commissioning Tilda in Beit Halochem.[7] I learn from her that she is a teacher, and that she is linked to the centre through her husband, who was wounded in military service. Maya is also the daughter of a Holocaust survivor, and it was the similarities that she found between Tilda and her mother that moved her the most when she watched the show the previous year. Maya said she was tired of the 'hackneyed repertoire' of testimonies that were being commissioned every year by the institute and that Tilda was an opportunity for her to challenge the norm 'in her own home'. She told me that, like Tilda, her mother always rejected the title of 'survivor', contending that she never felt 'survived', recovered or compensated. Maya referred to one of Tilda's lines in the show:

I am not Me. Me was left there, in the pit.
Now only partly here, the bare requisite, mere tool.
A parasite on the back of the bull that
crosses a cool river full of horrors and loneliness-ghouls

Initially, I articulated the standing of the rejection of the trope of survival intuitively, through Tilda's personality and without any predetermined theoretical agenda. As with the rest of the show's text, we wrote it as something Tilda 'would say'. Through Maya's comparison of this verse to the things her mother says about herself, I understand Tilda on a vitally deeper political level. That Tilda should foster such powerful identification, and trust, to the extent that Maya chose her as a representative of her views, and the voice of her mother, in the ideological fort of Beit Halochem on a contentious occasion such as Holocaust Memorial Day is to me a profound reassurance of the political workings of this project.

In her book, the education and literature scholar Lilach Naishtat Bornstein discusses the 'right and wrong in Holocaust testimonies' (2016). She contends that even among the survivors 'the right to speak about the Holocaust is not granted equally, some are allowed more than others ... first are those who went through the hardest suffering and were heroes' (Naishtat

Bornstein, 2016: 7). A testimony is not perceived nor heard just on the merit of being a subjective experience of a survivor, but rather is expected to confirm and reaffirm the wider ideological structure in which it is featured (i.e. a national narrative of victory, heroism and salvation). The historian Susan Hillman warns against the popular tendency to construct the Holocaust 'mythologically', whereby it is 'staged in terms of a morality play, with survivor-heroes ultimately triumphing over evil' (Hillman, 2015: 216). As the drag persona that she is, and with the mediation and agency of Maya, Tilda sounds unheroic aspects of testimonies, which are being silenced or overshadowed within nationalized memory culture.

Onstage

From backstage, I can hear the members of the audience entering the performance space. As part of the sponsored cultural programme of the centre, the performance is free of charge; the audience of Beit Halochem probably do not perceive themselves to be guests, as theatre spectators often do. It is me, and Tilda, who are the guests here, performing in their symbolic collective living room. This seems to alter the economies of power I am accustomed to with this show, as Tilda's command over her audience,

Figure 6.1 Tilda Death in performance. Clipa Theatre, 2018. Image by Eli Katz.

both conceptually and emotionally, usually relies on the premise of them being guests in her testimony-event, her symbolic living room. I can hear them talking loudly, announcing reserved seats for latecomers. This sense of ownership on behalf of the audience is new and foreign to me. I find myself worried that Tilda will receive neither the courtesy of suspension of disbelief as a fictional character, nor tolerance as a drag performer. When I register the atmosphere of gravitas typical of an audience anticipating a Holocaust memorial event, my pre-performance worry turns to a full-blown anxiety.

Once onstage, the primary audience reaction I encounter is one of attentive confusion: a reluctant willingness to follow through albeit the inability to fully decipher, comprehend or classify. I am alert to various acts of resistance from the audience. Several people leave halfway through, but the clear majority stays and, in varying degrees, delves into Tilda's stories and spoken-word numbers, laughs at her jokes and engages when she asks questions. One audience member who occupies a seat very close to the stage expresses disapproval and dismay in several parts of the show. As Tilda concludes a story about her injury from a battle against Nazis, by drawing out of her purse a couple of hand-grenades, this audience member shouts at her that she is 'out of line' and that she 'can't do such things in here'.[8] I have to agree with him that the use of such graphic imagery in front of an audience with a high likelihood to suffer from battle-related PTSD is not very well thought through. Having said that, I cannot dismiss the fact that even in such a direct, and justified, conflict between Tilda and the audience (over the use of seemingly real hand grenades), the fiction of drag is preserved. Furthermore, it is enhanced through it (see Figure 6.1).

Following the philosopher Ernest Bloch, José Esteban Muñoz advises astonishment as an 'important philosophical mode of contemplation' (Muñoz, 2009: 5). He theorizes astonishment as a mode from which relational queer critique can be reclaimed and a queer utopia can emerge: 'astonishment helps one surpass the limitations of an alienating presentness and allows one to see a different time and place' (ibid.). While to Muñoz astonishment pertains to awe, surprise and admiration, I suggest confusion as a related yet distinguished mode in which the fixation of presentness and, with it, judgement is suspended: not necessarily, or solely, by constructing a counter-narrative or by dazzling the audience with fabulousness, as by shuffling the very means by which hegemonic memory is signified, expressed and discussed. Confusion of the kind I wish to entertain here is one that targets the audience's, as well as the maker's, well-rehearsed mechanism of making (political) sense, and therefore, to judge, classify and align. Thinking with Sara Ahmed, it is a state of disorientation, where the horizontal and vertical lines of phenomenological space are questioned.

In spite of voicing doubts of the need for a performer to enact a role of a survivor in place of a real one (as Shir told me some audience members did), not once during the show was my identity as a woman challenged. As Tilda's drag is intertwined with her politics of multidirectional memory and anti-racism, through her (fictional) biography, by reproaching her rather than me, the audience member reinforced Tilda's independent fictional existence and, with it, her political argument, or rather, the political argument she embodies. Based on my experience as both a performer and educator in similarly ideologically charged spaces, I speculate that if it was me performing as myself that morning on the stage of Beit Halochem, with the same ideas that are expressed freely, even flauntingly, by Tilda, it would not have been long before I was stopped and taken off the stage, regardless if I was a man or woman. Tilda, a drag persona, was confusing enough to be allowed a voice that 'authentic' agents such as myself, or Maya, or Maya's mother, were not.

After the show

One of the few audience members who waited in the space to talk to me after the show was a woman who complimented different aspects of the performance before inquiring, 'Why does it have to be a woman? Wouldn't it have been as good if it was a fictional man in Tilda's stead?'

At first, I did not find a satisfying answer. Right from her early beginnings, Tilda was conceived as a woman. Beyond foregrounding the association of patriarchy and fascism, what is the significance of the technique of drag in a performance that aims to contemplate alternative legacies of memory and solidarity? Ahmed observes that 'the etymology of "direct" relates to "being straight" or getting straight to the point. To go directly is to follow a line without a detour, without mediation' (2006: 16). By confusing her audience, leading them indirectly to a point, Tilda Death capitalizes on gender ambiguity in securing them time for meditation on the way to 'the point'.

In a time of solidifying nationalistic positions, in Israel and globally, where historical narratives are being essentialized and co-opted, performance of confusion proposes an act of resistance. Tilda's experience retold in this chapter foregrounds means by which drag can be a vehicle and an ally to subversive multidirectional interventions in hegemonic discourses of memory. This, I find, is not only due to drag's well-theorized (conditional) potential to subvert categories of gender, but also in its capacity to astonish and, after Muñoz, to facilitate encounters with the utopic, to allow for public imagining that is beyond the present.

Notes

1 *Life and Times of Tilda Death* is the English translation of the original Hebrew title על החיים ועל המוות (*Al HaChaim VeAl HaMavet*). The protagonist of the show's Hebrew name is עדה המוות (Ada Mavet). Unlike its English translation, the name Ada resonates the Hebrew word עדה (Eda), the feminine form of the noun 'witness'. For the sake of clarity, I use the English translation throughout the text, although the show in discussion was performed in its Hebrew original.

2 I wish to distinguish here the testimony-event from the broad literature on the trope of testimony championed by literary scholars and psychoanalysts such as Shoshana Felman, Dori Laub and others. After the philosopher Theodor Adorno and with much reliance on the writing of the survivors Elie Wiesel and Primo Levi, they theorize the Holocaust as the crises of witnessing and testimony as a universal performative jest of a ceaseless struggle to utter the unutterable (79). This view has been criticized by a number of scholars, some highlighting that 'testimony is not authentic, egalitarian and universal as it may seem. It is, rather, traversed by power relations, constructed by the government as a spectacle and is abused by it' (Naishtat Bornstein, 2016: 159. See also Hillman, 2015; Givoni, 2011; Trezise, 2012; Shenker, 2015). Although the scope of this text does not allow the due explication of the relevance of this discussion to my work, it is significant to qualify that despite the reliance on video-testimonies in the making of *Life and Times of Tilda Death,* the work is discussed as testimony only to the extent of its generic frame, indeed its form as an event of performance, and not as a survivor's testimony.

3 As a point of comparison, in his work on the Holocaust and postmodernism, the literary scholar Robert Eaglestone theorized testimony as a genre (Eaglestone, 2008: 6, 37).

4 The complete majority of disabled members are men and the membership model is based on heteronormative family structure, by which a spouse and children are the only non-disabled beneficiaries.

5 A similar dynamic is pointed out by the theatre and performance scholar Bryce Lease in relation to *RuPaul's Drag Race*: 'in certain challenges, contestants are asked to walk around on the street, which is

positioned – even if implicitly – as the major obstacle of the challenge. Here, drag is framed exclusively as an indoor practice in private or at least privatized spaces intended for performance or performative labour' (Lease, 2017: 139).

6 Several scholars have heavily criticized the drag-queen style of RuPaul as heteronormative, misogynistic and oppressively neoliberal (LeMaster, 2015; González and Cavazos, 2016; Chernoff, 2014; Norris, 2014).

7 Maya is a pseudonym.

8 I use the empty cans of tear gas used by the IDF against Palestinian demonstrators in the West Bank as prop hand grenades. As Hebrew is a highly gendered language, every direct address of Tilda in the feminine-form resonates and reaffirms her authentic presence.

References

Ahmed, Sara. (2006). *Queer Phenomenology: Orientations, Objects, Others.* Durham: Duke University Press.

Butler, Judith. (1993). *Bodies that Matter: On the Discursive Limits of 'Sex'.* Abingdon: Routledge.

Carlson, Marvin. (2004). *Performance: A Critical Introduction.* 2nd edition. Abingdon: Routledge.

Chernoff, Carolyn. (2014). 'Of Women and Queens: Gendered Realities and Re-Education in RuPaul's Drag Empire'. In J. Daems (ed.), *The Makeup of RuPaul's Drag Race: Essays on the Queen of Reality Shows*, pp. 148–67. Jefferson: McFarland.

Daems, Jim. (2014). *The Makeup of RuPaul's Drag Race: Essays on the Queen of Reality Shows.* Jefferson: McFarland.

Eaglestone, Robert. (2008). *The Holocaust and the Postmodern.* New York: Oxford University Press.

Feldman, Jackie. (2010). *Above the Death Pits, Beneath the Flag: Youth Voyages to Poland and the Performance of Israeli National Identity.* Reprint edition. Berghahn Books, 2010.

Givoni, Michal. (2011). 'Witnessing/Testimony'. *Mafte'akh*, vol. 2, pp. 147–69.

González, Jorge C. and Cavazos, Kameron C. (2016). 'Serving Fishy Realness: Representations of Gender Equity on *RuPaul's Drag Race'. Continuum*, vol. 30, no. 6, pp. 659–69.

Greer, Stephen. (2012). *Contemporary British Queer Performance.* Palgrave Macmillan.

Hillman, Susanne. (2015). '"Not Living, but Going": Unheroic Survival, Trauma Performance, and Video Testimony'. *Holocaust Studies*, vol. 21, no. 4, Oct., pp. 215–35.

Lease, Bryce. (2017). 'Dragging Rights, Queering Publics: Realness, Self-Fashioning and the Miss Gay Western Cape Pageant'. *Safundi*, vol. 18, no. 2, Apr., pp. 131–46.

LeMaster, Benny. (2015). 'Discontents of Being and Becoming Fabulous on *RuPaul's Drag U*: Queer Criticism in Neoliberal Times'. *Women's Studies in Communication*, vol. 38, no. 2, Apr., pp. 167–86.

Muñoz, José Esteban. (1998) *Disidentifications: Queers of Color and the Performance of Politics*. Minneapolis: University of Minnesota Press.

Muñoz, José Esteban. (2009). *Cruising Utopia: The Then and There of Queer Futurity*. New York: NYU Press.

Naishtat Bornstein, Lilach. (2016). *Their Jew: Right and Wrong in Holocaust Testimonies*. 1st ed. The MOFET Institute, The Hebrew University of Jerusalem.

Newton, Esther. (1979). *Mother Camp: Female Impersonators in America*. 1st ed. Chicago: University of Chicago Press.

Norris, Laurie. (2014). 'Of Fish and Feminists: Homonormative Misogyny and the Trans*Queen'. In J. Daems (ed.), *The Makeup of Rupaul's Drag Race: Essays on the Queen of Reality Shows*. Jefferson: McFarland.

Reynolds, R. M. (2008). *Moving Targets: Political Theatre in a Post-Political Age*. VDM Verlag Dr Müller.

Rothberg, Michael. (2009). *Multidirectional Memory: Remembering the Holocaust in the Age of Decolonization*. 1st ed. Stanford: Stanford University Press.

Senelick, Laurence. (2000). *The Changing Room: Sex, Drag and Theatre*. Abingdon: Routledge.

Shenker, Noah. (2015). *Reframing Holocaust Testimony*. Bloomington: Indiana University Press.

The Zahal Disabled Veterans Organization. http://www.zdvo.org/HOME/about.asp?id=123 (accessed 25 Jan. 2018).

Trezise, Thomas. (2012). *Witnessing Witnessing: On the Reception of Holocaust Survivor Testimony*. New York: Fordham University Press. *Project MUSE*, https://muse.jhu.edu/book/29253.

Weiss, Meira. (2004). *The Chosen Body: The Politics of the Body in Israeli Society*. New ed. Stanford: Stanford University Press.

7

A Transfeminist Critique of Drag Discourses and Performance Styles in Three National Contexts (US, France and UK)

From *RuPaul's Drag Race* to Bar Wotever

Kayte Stokoe

Employing an intersectional, transfeminist approach, this chapter will critique presumptive discourses of cissexism, appropriation and binarism as they permeate the popular series *RuPaul's Drag Race*, before analysing certain French performers' use of language on social media. The chapter will then examine the drive to create performances and spaces which challenge racism, misogyny, transphobia and other forms of oppression. In order to analyse the discourses at work in various drag contexts, this chapter will scrutinize the impact of different forms of language. My examination of *RuPaul's Drag Race* will explore three points: Harlem drag ball idiom, the positioning of languages other than English, and RuPaul's doctrine on the practice of drag. Having examined the hierarchies created in these contexts, the chapter will then scrutinize the language employed by French drag queens on Instagram, using this to explore the perception of French as a 'very gendered language' (Wittig, 1992: 76).

In general, transfeminist approaches combine intersectional feminism with trans theory (Enke, 2012: 3) and seek to extend the insights garnered in both fields. My transfeminist approach will build on the work of Julia Serano and Sam Bourcier and will reject the commonplace definition of drag as 'performing as the opposite sex' – a definition which automatically situates drag within a binary model. This transfeminist approach to drag will be discussed at length in my forthcoming volume, *Reframing Drag: Beyond Subversion and the Status Quo*.[1] This chapter will characterize drag as a performance of femininity, of masculinity or of a combination of gendered attributes, thereby breaking with the cissexist logic which positions manhood and womanhood as the two sole genders, naturally opposing one another. This chapter will equally challenge the positioning of drag as either subversive or reactionary, as these approaches have a tendency to overlook the diversity present within different drag subcultures. The interrogation of discourses, attitudes and performance styles in this discussion will enable me to achieve its three aims. First, to elucidate the latent and surface discourses at work in *Drag Race*, thereby clarifying the impact of these discourses on other drag cultures. Second, to expose the flaws in the classification of drag as subversive or reactionary, and to demonstrate how to theorize drag outside this paradigm. Finally, this chapter will show how drag can be theorized in a transfeminist manner, thereby demonstrating the value of this approach.

Cissexism in *RuPaul's Drag Race*

As Kai Kohlsdorf and Mary Marcel have stressed, *Drag Race* contestants must be assigned male at birth and, for eight seasons, contestants were not permitted to be in the process of transitioning hormonally or surgically (Marcel, 2014: 28–9). Although some trans people do not transition medically, either through choice or circumstances, these regulations indicate a level of hostility towards trans people and created barriers for trans applicants to bypass. The argument that candidates who transitioned medically would have an unfair advantage seems less convincing when we consider that male-identified candidates who had undergone plastic surgery could compete freely (Kohlsdorf, 2014: 85). Equally, although some trans women, such as Carmen Carrera, Monica Beverly Hillz and Kenya Michaels, competed on *Drag Race* prior to Season 9, these women were not 'out' during casting. As yet, it is unclear whether the restrictions regarding transition have been lifted. In an interview with *The Guardian*, RuPaul asserted that drag queen performance is most powerful when undertaken by men, and intimated that he would be unwilling for contestants who had transitioned medically to participate in *Drag Race*.[2] In addition to creating barriers to participation, this comment suggests that RuPaul differentiates between women who have transitioned medically and women who have not. Although the participation of Peppermint, an out, trans woman, in Season 9 suggests that *Drag Race* has become more inclusive, gender binarism continues to pervade the series.

This is particularly obvious in the catchphrase 'may the best woman win', which appears in the theme tune and prior to the catwalk section of each episode (*RuPaul's Drag Race*, 2017). This catchphrase arguably delimits drag, suggesting that the series will reward the most 'convincing imitation' of womanhood, rather than judging contestants on the basis of talent or innovation. When combined with 'gentlemen start your engines', this catchphrase positions drag queens as 'men performing as women', which overlooks other, more inclusive, definitions. In addition, to frame a catwalk performance with the line 'may the best woman win' when there is only one woman performing seems at best insensitive and, at worst, markedly cissexist. From a transfeminist perspective, the failure to distinguish Peppermint's womanhood from the performance of femininity undertaken by other candidates echoes the transmisogynistic positioning of trans womanhood as necessarily artificial, which Julia Serano critiques in 'Reclaiming Femininity' (2012: 172).

Drag Race, language and linguistic hierarchies

In what follows, I interrogate three discursive forms which pervade *Drag Race*: Harlem drag ball idiom, accented English and RuPaul's doctrine on drag, its definition and its practice. Although *Drag Race* features contestants from diverse ethnic groups and backgrounds, audiences who are not watching in translation hear only English and Spanish. Many contestants exhibit close ties to their local scenes, their heritage, and their dialect or native language, although the manifestations of this differ between candidates. In her insightful analysis of the impact of language and accents in *Drag Race,* Libby Anthony has argued that aspects of the series operate according to a 'Standard English ideology', in which standard English is positioned as 'a better fit for communication' (2014: 59) than other spoken forms of English, while speakers with accents can be dismissed due to their perceived linguistic capacity (ibid.). In my view, Season 9 is generally less prone to this tendency than earlier seasons: previously, candidates with heavier accents, especially those who did not appear completely fluent in English, often received demeaning and patronizing comments from judges and other candidates (Anthony, 2014: 59–63). Nevertheless, the concept of a 'Standard English ideology' remains useful when exploring Season 9. In particular, Libby Anthony's observation that Latinx contestants with pronounced accents are those who are most likely to be penalized for their speech patterns (ibid.: 63–7) remains applicable in this season. In Season 9's 'Snatch Game' episode, Cynthia Lee Fontaine receives two sniping comments about her accent and its supposed impact on her performance. When RuPaul approaches Cynthia in the workroom, Cynthia's brief characterization of Sofia Vergara, a Latina performer with a strong accent, receives a scathing 'So when are you going to start doing Sofia?' from RuPaul (09 minutes, 47 seconds). In addition to demeaning Cynthia's acting, this comment suggests that, despite Cynthia's exaggerated tone and use of gesture, RuPaul is unable or unwilling to differentiate Cynthia's vision of Sofia Vergara from her usual persona, simply because both have pronounced accents. This subtle insinuation that an accent is likely to detract from a performance is underscored in the judges' responses to the game show, when Cynthia is told 'I didn't understand what was going on, and it wasn't the accent' (30 minutes, 51 seconds). Although Cynthia's mode of speech is not openly under attack here, the underlying assumptions present in this statement, such as the positioning of an accent as a barrier to understanding, arguably typify the Standard English ideology.

Drag Race and Harlem drag ball idiom

I now address the mobilization of Harlem drag ball idiom on Drag Race. When I refer to Harlem drag ball idiom, I include phrases such as 'banjee', 'reading', 'realness', 'sickening', 'throwing shade' and 'werk'. This idiom developed in Black and Latinx drag ball communities in Harlem and elsewhere (Levitt, 2013: n.p.) and is connected to African-American Vernacular English. This vocabulary was catapulted into the white cisheteronormative mainstream by Jenny Livingston's Paris Is Burning, which arguably exoticized it by defining certain terms on screen. It seems that the New York club scene, in which RuPaul began performing, shared certain features with the ball scene, making it natural for RuPaul to incorporate ball culture idiom in his vocabulary.[3] Equally, RuPaul's frequent references to ball culture can be perceived as an homage to the LGBTQIA+ artists who have performed in these contexts. However, the contestants' use of this idiom merits attention on three levels. First, as in ball culture and other drag cultures, contestants frequently refer to each other with female pronouns and with feminine epithets, such as 'girl'. I suggest that this use of language can create a sense of community and shared experience among performers. Equally, this terminology can be gender affirming for those who use female pronouns outside performance contexts. However, using this idiom does not necessarily indicate respect for trans individuals, as can be seen from the example of Margo, of the '801 Girls', who used this idiom alongside transmisogynistic remarks (Rupp and Taylor, 2004: 122–3). The second use of ball culture idiom that I want to highlight occurs during mini challenges. The phrase 'the library is open' precedes one reoccurring challenge, in which contestants 'read' one another – offer a biting critique of another's performance style – meaning that contestants need to be familiar with ball culture idiom in order to participate. This specialist knowledge may be acquired through an awareness of drag ball cultures, by watching *Paris Is Burning* or by watching previous seasons of *Drag Race* itself. Significantly, however, familiarity with this idiom creates access to a community based in shared history. Finally, *Drag Race* contestants frequently deploy drag ball idiom on social media. While this usage can have a commercial motivation, as it enables performers to advertise their work, it makes performers' work accessible to those who are just discovering drag, which might enable them to experience a sense of community that they are unable to access elsewhere.

RuPaul's doctrine on the practice and definition of drag

I contend that aspects of RuPaul's doctrine on the practice and definition of drag can be discerned from an analysis of series footage and of interview material. RuPaul has previously been criticized for his public stances, particularly in relation to the use of transmisogynistic language. In a 2016 interview with E Alex Jung, RuPaul distanced himself from Logo TV's decision to remove the phrase 'You've got she-mail' from future episodes of the series, affirming that certain activists take the use of language too seriously and that this attitude can stem from a desire to 'reinforce [one's] own victimhood' (2016: n.p.).⁴ In this interview, RuPaul declined to discuss the relationship between drag and the trans community, labelling this as a 'boring' subject before asserting 'It's so topical but they're complete opposites. We mock identity. They take identity very seriously' (ibid.). This declaration of a marked opposition between drag performers and trans people, which overlooks or erases trans performers, differs starkly from the attitude held by RuPaul and Michelle Visage in the extract of the 'What's the Tee' podcast which was included in Episode 12 of Season 9. During this extract, Peppermint discusses the discrimination she has experienced as a trans women in drag culture, and her initial fear that her identity was incompatible with her performance career (7 minutes, 57 seconds). In response, Michelle Visage passionately states, 'You don't ever need to be one or another. Nobody has to put anybody in any kind of box' (8 minutes, 16 seconds). RuPaul then thanks Peppermint for her honesty and remarks 'You is a marvel!' (8 minutes 32 seconds) which might suggest that his attitude has developed since his interview with Jung. However, this interview contains remarks which echo comments that RuPaul has made elsewhere. In particular, RuPaul suggests that drag is about 'mocking identity' (2017: n.p) or 'making fun of identity' (Abramovitch, 2017: n.p.).⁵ Such remarks resonate with the definition of drag as engaging with gender archetypes, or as challenging expectations regarding gender expression.

This aspect of RuPaul's understanding of drag – the emphasis on creativity, fluidity and play – will appeal to people of all genders and is likely to have a positive impact on future seasons of Drag Race. However, RuPaul's rejection of what he regards as 'taking life too seriously' (D'Addario, 2017: n.p.) means that he is fundamentally unwilling to consider certain perspectives, such as the idea that misgendering people is unacceptable (ibid.).[6]

Drawing attention to problematic dimensions of Drag Race and of RuPaul's attitude can facilitate a fuller understanding of the series and of its influence on other drag subcultures. However, I want to clarify that I am not suggesting that Drag Race is necessarily reactionary. For example, Season 9 showcased a range of talented performers, some of whom promoted inclusive attitudes both on and offstage. Moreover, I contend that dismissing a given scene or subculture as necessarily reactionary is counterproductive, as it can mean that diversity within a scene is not recognized or that certain problematic behaviours are not interrogated when they appear outside of that context.

French drag queens and linguistic cultures

Continuing my analysis of language use in drag subcultures, this section examines the use of English and ball culture idiom by certain French drag queens on social media. Kimberlé Crenshaw's intersectionality theory (1991: 1244) and Libby Anthony's work on the Standard English ideology (2014: 58–9) provide a nuanced approach to these language uses. I first focus on the Instagram profiles of two French performers, Rebecca Show Transformiste and Holly White. These performers appear to be white, gay, cisgender and slim, with no visible disabilities. Consequently, although they may experience discrimination as gay men, they do not face the intersecting forms of marginalization experienced by many of the performers in American ball culture, which is a predominantly black and minority ethnic subculture. While the use of English hashtags such as 'dragqueen' and ball culture terms such as 'realness' might represent these performers' desire to participate in English-speaking drag communities, these hashtags may also have a commercial motivation, as English hashtags seemingly receive more traffic than French ones. Although a commercial motivation is unsurprising in itself, it is arguably problematic that those with a certain degree of privilege appropriate ball culture idiom for financial gain when members of that culture experience high rates of poverty and homelessness (Jones, 2013: n.p.).[7] The question of appropriation becomes even more pressing when performers such as Holly White and Rebecca Show Transformiste juxtapose

English hashtags such as 'dragqueen' or ball culture idiom such as 'realness' with transmisogynistic language[8] or with imagery featuring cultural appropriation.[9] From my intersectional, transfeminist perspective, the use of culturally appropriative imagery and transphobic language is unacceptable, irrespective of its motivation. However, I equally suggest that the extensive use of English hashtags by French performers merits further consideration.

While commercial motivation may be at play here, this use of English hashtags also resonates with Libby Anthony's description of a Standard English ideology, in which Standard English is positioned as a 'better fit for communication' (59) than other languages or forms of English. These linguistic habits, then, might point towards a perception of English as *the* language for communicating matters of LGBTQIA+ identity and performance, and/or of a perception of French as inappropriate for this usage. Such a view of French may be connected to the perception of French as a 'very gendered language' (Wittig, 1992: 77). For Monique Wittig, the perception of English as an 'almost genderless' language (ibid.: 76) is erroneous, as both English and French require speakers to employ gender 'in the dimension of the person' (ibid.). While Wittig perceives the linguistic gendering of nouns in French as 'relatively harmless' (ibid.), she argues that a person's gender is particularly visible in French as a result of agreement with adjectives and past participles (ibid., 79). Although the French equalities council has issued guidelines for language use, which are intended to challenge sexist formulations, the recommended forms have not yet been widely adopted.[10] Equally, as Caitlin Field has demonstrated, certain French-speaking genderqueer people experience erasure as a result of linguistic gendering.[11] While Luca Greco's valuable article 'Un soi pluriel: la présentation de soi dans les ateliers Drag King. Enjeux interactionnels, catégoriels et politiques' (2012)[12] shows how French-speaking activists have moulded existing language to make space for diverse identities (2012: 74), these terms are unfortunately yet to come into wider use. French-speaking LGBTQIA+ activists have developed the pronoun 'iel' (they) to refer to people who would prefer not to be gendered as 'il' (he) or 'elle' (she). While this is a positive step, 'iel' is currently used only in certain contexts. (More information about 'iel', its usage, and what its creation suggests about binarism in French language can be found in Swamy and Mackenzie, 2019.)

Before turning away from the use of English hashtags by French drag performers, I want to emphasize the point that this usage is not unique to performers who deploy transphobic language or culturally appropriative imagery. Instead, as one can observe when examining the 'parisdrag' hashtag on Instagram, a plethora of French performers deploy English on their social media profiles.[13] Although this strengthens my argument that this usage has diverse motivations – including the creation of cross-cultural communities, a perception of English as suited to conveying LGBTQ+ performance, and a desire to increase traffic to one's profile – these impetuses can coincide with an insistence on deploying transphobic language or culturally appropriative imagery, as we see from the profiles of Holly White and Rebecca Show Transformiste.

Moving beyond the perception of drag as subversive

As my critiques of language use in French subcultures and on *Drag Race* have demonstrated, classifying drag as necessarily reactionary can overlook the diversity present in given subcultures. In the following analysis, I will begin to trouble the classification of drag as subversive – a description which first appeared in Judith Butler's discussion of drag queen performance in *Gender Trouble* (1999: 186–9). Three key problems arising from this positioning merit attention here. First, as Julia Serano demonstrates in 'Reclaiming Femininity', positioning certain forms of gender expression and performance as subversive can create a hierarchy in which forms of gender expression and performance which do not meet the same criteria are classified as inferior or even as upholding patriarchal standards (2012: 182). As Serano argues, this attitude is particularly problematic when it is directed towards feminine forms of gender expression (ibid.), as it feeds into the societal dismissal of femininity. Second, this positioning can mean that problematic behaviours are dismissed when committed by artists whose work is classified as subversive; as the work is seen as breaking boundaries, the problematic behaviour is excused as constituting part of the transgression. Finally, as Sam Bourcier argues in his nuanced analysis of Judith Butler's work, this positioning can place an unfeasible 'burden of subversion' (2012: 154) on performers, and particularly on trans and gender non-conforming people, whose work has been positioned as subversive due to their gendered identities and practices. I suggest that as this approach can have a particularly negative impact on trans people, a transfeminist approach to drag should avoid it, concentrating instead on examining the techniques and attitudes at work in given subcultures and performances.

Significantly, however, my rejection of the positioning of drag as subversive does not preclude a recognition of the important work which certain performers are undertaking to make their subcultures more inclusive. I want to focus first on the French 'drag queer' collective Les Paillettes. Les Paillettes utilize commonplace drag accoutrements – such as wigs, make-up and glitter – while tackling political issues, such as homophobia, Islamophobia and racism, and their capacity to create intersecting forms of oppression.[14] At one event, Les Paillettes member Malik read the piece 'Je suis', a nuanced yet irreverent analysis of what it means to live in France as a cis, gay, Muslim man.[15] This piece typifies Les Paillettes' technique of incorporating texts into their shows alongside live vocals and lip-synch performances (Héraud, 2015: n.p.), and facilitates their aim of creating queer, political drag while having fun. Malik's choice to tackle Islamophobia and intersecting forms of oppression, while using humour, renders his piece similar to the disidentificatory work of Vaginal Davis, which José Estaban Muñoz analyses in 'The White to Be Angry' (1998: 93–115).

Drag queens versus the world

I turn now to the work of two UK-based drag queens, whose work critiques oppressive structures and behaviours. Both performers have appeared at Bar Wotever's Non Binary Cabaret, an event which aims to elucidate gender and sexuality through performance art.[16] Marilyn Misandry is a trans femme, whose powerful drag mobilizes existing drag tactics, such as lip-synching and comic asides, and combines these with a personal reclamation of femininity and a biting critique of transmisogyny. In one provocative performance, Marilyn deploys music and sound bites from *The Silence of the Lambs* (1991) in order to highlight transmisogynistic tropes in film and television.[17] Equally, Victoria Sin, a non-binary performer, highlights the idealization of white femininity by deploying heavy white facial make-up and by combining the aesthetics of Jessica Rabbit and Marilyn Monroe. Sin's performances underscore the labour involved in performing femininity in a misogynistic society. One performance, in which Sin makes a sandwich, clearly satirizes the misogynistic attitude typified by the one-liner 'now make me a sandwich'.[18] Despite their talent, both performers have experienced discrimination from those who believe that drag queen performance should be performed exclusively by cis gay men.[19] This attitude, which makes it harder for performers like Sin and Misandry to get work, foregrounds the need for a transfeminist approach to drag. Formulations which define drag as 'performing as the opposite sex' rely on the supposition that there are two discrete sexes which naturally oppose one another, and are unable to encapsulate non-binary performers like Sin and Misandry. Such definitions also erase women who perform as drag queens and men who perform as drag kings. Instead, a transfeminist approach to drag, which positions drag as a performance of masculinity, of femininity, or of aspects of masculinity and femininity, can account for performers of all genders. Moreover, in moving its focus away from binary performer/performed oppositions, a transfeminist approach facilitates closer attention to what is happening onstage.

Drag kings versus the world

I now turn to the valuable work of the Kings of Colour Initiative and of drag king cabaret event Boi Box. Although many performers and event organizers in London work hard to make the drag king scene inclusive, there are currently more white drag kings than black and minority ethnic drag kings performing in London. The current number of black and minority ethnic kings may have been shaped by the rise in hate crime since the vote for the United Kingdom to leave the European Union in June 2016.[20] Many drag events take place in the evening, and performers may be understandably unwilling to travel late at night. In order to combat the lack of representation, drag king Zayn Phallic launched the Kings of Colour Initiative, which organizes events dedicated to black and minority ethnic drag kings, and which offers mentoring to new kings of colour.[21] The first two Kings of Colour events were held at The Glory, a pub and performance venue, in August 2017 and January 2018, and took over the space from Drag King Cabaret night Boi Box. The third event organized by Zayn Phallic and the KOC Initiative took place at Bar Wotever at the Royal Vauxhall Tavern in February 2018. In August, the lineup of talented performers included Romeo de la Cruz, whose powerful performance protested against Donald Trump's attempted policy which would have banned transgender people from serving in the United States Armed Forces.[22] Alongside their work in the Kings of Colour Initiative, Romeo de la Cruz is one of two Boi Box ambassadors, who aid the Boi Box organizers drag king Adam All and alpha femme Apple Derrières in creating a supportive event for all attendees.[23] In their six years of running Boi Box, which is now the longest-running drag king night in London, Adam and Apple have worked hard to ensure that their event is a welcoming space for all performers and attendees (Stokoe, 2016: 104–6). Equally, by presenting an onstage couple that includes a bashful, sensitive man, who is attracted to conventionally feminine activities, and a forceful, loving woman, who insists on being taken seriously, Adam and Apple make it clear that all forms of gender expression are worthy of respect. While drag subcultures need to continue to progress, the hard work of performers such as Adam All and Apple Derrières, Marilyn Misandry, Zayn Phallic, Les Paillettes,

Romeo de la Cruz and Victoria Sin contributes to creating inclusive scenes, which challenge oppressive structures and behaviours, as well as examining gender norms.

In concentrating on a range of performers, performance styles and subcultures in the UK and France, this chapter has indicated the diversity of current drag cultures. As I have argued here, this diversity is one key reason why classifying drag as subversive or reactionary is not productive: this classification cannot account for the range of performance styles, performer intentions and performance contexts present in current drag subcultures. Using a transfeminist approach, this discussion has equally demonstrated that these classifications can create a hierarchy, which dismisses performances which do not meet particular conditions, as well as placing unfair expectations on performers. Scrutinizing the language employed by performers in French subcultures and on *Drag Race* has enabled me to elucidate a range of complex power dynamics, including the positioning of English as *the* language for conveying matters of LGBTQIA+ performance and embodiment. Perhaps most significantly, this chapter has begun to demonstrate the value of a transfeminist approach to drag performance. As shown in relation to the work of Marilyn Misandry and Victoria Sin, approaches which rely on the formulation of drag as 'performing as the opposite sex' are unable to account for the work of non-binary performers, or for those whose gender aligns with the gender that they perform onstage. Equally, such approaches stand in stark opposition to drag's rich history of gender-diverse embodiment. By avoiding such reductive formulations, a transfeminist approach to drag can provide insights into a wider range of art forms, as well as facilitating a closer analysis of what is happening onstage.

Notes

1   At the time of writing, this volume is due to be published with Routledge in November 2019.
2   To access this interview, please visit: https://www.theguardian.com/tv-and-radio/2018/mar/03/rupaul-drag-race-big-f-you-to-male-dominated-culture (accessed 2 June 2018).
3   One example of this mutual use of language can be observed in the attribution of the name 'Visage' to Michelle Visage due to her performance style in the club context in which she first met RuPaul. For more information, see Jones, 2015.
4   This article can be accessed via the following link: http://www.vulture.com/2016/03/rupaul-drag-race-interview.html (accessed 15 January 2018).

5 In an interview with Rico Gagliano and Brendan Francis Newnam (2017), RuPaul comments: 'That's what drag is about. We're mocking the ego. We are mocking identity. The *concept* of an identity'. In an interview with Seth Abramovitch (2017), RuPaul states: 'Drag is about irony and making fun of identity ... It's really about reminding culture not to take itself so seriously'.

6 In an abridged interview with Daniel D'Addario, RuPaul comments: 'To be that particular about words, you have to be in a place where you're not under attack. I believe that those same people, right now, are so under attack that ain't nobody got time to be dealing with "Did you call me a he or a she?"'.

7 In his documentary *Pier Kids: The Life* (2019), Elegance Bratton elucidates the epidemic of homelessness and poverty among the Black and Latinx LGBTQ+ youth who participate in New York's contemporary ball culture. See also Jones (2013) for Jones's article on the prospective release of the film.

8 Rebecca Show Transformiste's Instagram page provides clear examples of the use of English hashtags, such as 'dragqueen', and references to *Drag Race,* alongside transphobic terms such as 'shemale'. This page can be accessed at the following link: https://www.instagram.com/p/BVbbAQjlzIB/?taken-by=rebecca.show (accessed 20 January 2018).

9 Holly White's Instagram page features hashtags such as 'realness' and 'drag queen' and includes culturally appropriative imagery, such as his 'Geisha' look. This page can be accessed at https://www.instagram.com/p/BSETkpSAOzG/?hl=en&taken-by=mikahollywhite (accessed 20 January 2018). In *Travelling Goods, Travelling Moods: Varieties of Cultural Appropriation* (2012), Christian Huck and Stefan Bauernschmidt define cultural appropriation broadly as the 'use of something valued by members of one culture by members of another culture' (232), while highlighting the centrality of power and profit to other definitions of the term.

10 These guidelines are available at http://www.haut-conseil-egalite.gouv.fr/IMG/pdf/hcefh__guide_pratique_com_sans_stereo-_vf-_2015_11_05.pdf (accessed 30 January 2018).

11 Field's paper 'Hermeneutical Injustice and the French Genderqueer Experience' was delivered at 'Spotlight on Genderqueer' at the University of Warwick in 2013, and can be accessed via YouTube: https://www.youtube.com/watch?v=2fOz9s_oSqQ (accessed 20 January 2018).

12 I translate Greco's title as 'A Plural Self: the presentation of the self in drag king workshops. Interactional issues, categorial issues, and political issues'. This article is not yet available in English.

13 This hashtag can be accessed via https://www.instagram.com/explore/tags/parisdrag/?hl=en (accessed 20 January 2018).

14 For an introduction to Les Paillettes, see Héraud (2015). Les Paillettes, who were performing together at the time of writing, no longer work together (Héraud, 2019).

15 For a transcript of 'Je suis', please visit http://yagg.com/2016/04/01/je-suis-par-malik/(accessed 23 January 2018).

16 For more about Non Binary Cabaret, curated by Ingo Cando, please visit their Facebook page: https://www.facebook.com/nonbinarycabaret/ (accessed 23 January 2018).
17 To discover more about Marilyn Misandry, please visit her website: http://marilyn-misandry.com/ (accessed 23 January 2018).
18 To find out more about Victoria Sin, please visit her website: http://victoriasin.co.uk/ (accessed 23 January 2018).
19 Sin talks eloquently about their experiences of discrimination in the following article: https://www.theguardian.com/lifeandstyle/2017/jul/10/workin-it-how-female-drag-queens-are-causing-a-scene (accessed 23 January 2018).
20 The statistics detailing hate crime and racist incidents recorded by the police in England and Wales from 2016 to 2017 can be accessed at the following link: https://www.gov.uk/government/statistics/hate-crime-england-and-wales-2016-to-2017 (accessed 23 January 2018). An article by Lizzie Dearden (2017) in *The Independent* discusses the increase in hate crime following the vote on 'Brexit' and the terrorist attacks in March, May and June.
21 More information about the Kings of Colour Initiative can be found on their Facebook page: https://www.facebook.com/kocinitative/ (accessed 23 January 2018).
22 For more information about Romeo de la Cruz and their forthcoming performances, please visit their Facebook page: https://www.facebook.com/MxRomeoDeLaCruz/ (accessed 12 August 2019). For more information about Trump's announcement of his attempted policy, please visit https://www.theguardian.com/us-news/2017/jul/26/trump-says-us-military-will-not-accept-or-allow-transgender-people-to-serve (accessed 24 January 2018).
23 For more about Adam All, please visit their website: http://www.adamall.co.uk/ (accessed 24 January 2018). For more about Apple Derrières, please visit her Facebook page: https://www.facebook.com/apple.derrieres (accessed 24 January 2018).

References

Abramovitch, Seth. (2017). 'RuPaul on Trump, Transgender Issues and How Drag Race Became a "Touchstone for Young People"'. *The Hollywood Reporter*, 9 August. Available online: https://www.hollywoodreporter.com/news/rupaul-trump-transgender-issues-how-drag-race-became-a-touchstone-young-people-1027510 (accessed 16 Jan. 2018).

Anthony, Libby. (2014). 'Dragging with an Accent, Linguistic Stereotypes, Language Barriers and Translingualism'. In J. Daems (ed.), *The Makeup of RuPaul's Drag Race: Essays on the Queen of Reality Shows*, pp. 56–73. MacFarland.

Bourcier, Marie-Hélène [Sam]. (2012). '"F***" the Politics of Disempowerment in the Second Butler'. *Paragraph*, vol. 35, no. 2, pp. 233–53.

Butler, Judith. ([1990] 1999). *Gender Trouble. Feminism and the Subversion of Identity*. New York and London: Routledge Classics.

Crenshaw, Kimberlé. (1991). 'Mapping the Margins: Intersectionality, Identity Politics, and Violence against Women of Color'. *Stanford Law Review*, vol. 43, no. 6, pp. 12421–99.

D'Addario, Daniel. (2017). 'RuPaul on Identity in the Trump Era: "Don't Pick Battles with Your Allies"'. *Time Magazine*, 12 June. Available online: http://time.com/4813260/rupaul-drag-race-interview/ (accessed 18 Jan. 2018).

Dearden, Lizzie. (2017). 'Hate-crime reports rise by almost a third in year as Home Office figures illustrate EU-referendum spike'. *The Independent*, 17 October. Available online: http://www.independent.co.uk/news/uk/crime/hate-crimes-eu-referendum-spike-brexit-terror-attacks-police-home-office-europeans-xenophobia-a8004716.html (accessed 23 Jan. 2018).

Enke, A. Finn. (2012). 'Introduction: Transfeminist Perspectives'. In Anne Enke (ed.), *Transfeminist Perspectives in and beyond Transgender and Gender Studies*, pp. 1–15. Philadelphia: Temple University Press.

Gagliano, Rico and Brendan Francis Newnam. (2017). 'RuPaul: 'We're God Playing Dress Up. That's What Drag Is About''. *The Dinner Party Download*, 24 March. Available online: https://www.dinnerpartydownload.org/rupaul/ (accessed 16 Jan. 2018).

Greco, Luca. (2012). 'Un Soi Pluriel: la présentation de soi dans les ateliers Drag King. Enjeux interactionnels, catégoriels et politiques'. In N. Checuti and L. Greco (eds), *La Face cachée du genre: Langage et pouvoir des normes*, pp. 63–83. Paris: Presse Sorbonne Nouvelles.

Héraud, Xavier. (2015). 'Paillettes: À la rencontre des "drag queers"'. *Yagg*, 22 November. Available online: http://yagg.com/2015/11/22/paillettes-a-la-rencontre-des-drag-queers/ (accessed 23 Jan. 2018).

Héraud, Xavier. (2019). 'Clap de fin pour les Paillettes, le groupe de "drag queers" parisiennes'. *Komitid*, 23 January. Available online: https://www.komitid.fr/2019/01/23/clap-de-fin-pour-les-paillettes-le-groupe-de-drag-queers-parisiennes/ (accessed 30 Aug. 2019).

Huck, Christian and Bauernschmidt, Stefan. (2012). 'Trans-Cultural Appropriation'. In Christian Huck and Stefan Bauernschmidt (eds), *Travelling Goods, Travelling Moods. Varieties of Cultural Appropriation (1850–1950)*, pp. 229–51. Frankfurt and New York: Campus Verlag.

Jones, Daisy. (2015). 'Michelle Visage: "I could out-vogue any female"'. *Dazed Digital*, 20 November. Available online: http://www.dazeddigital.com/artsandculture/article/28502/1/catching-up-with-the-world-s-straight-talking-drag-mother (accessed 15 Jan. 2018).

Jones, Saeed. (2013). 'Could "Pier Kids: The Life" Be The Next "Paris Is Burning"?' *Buzzfeed*, 27 November. Available online: https://www.buzzfeed.com/saeedjones/could-pier-kids-the-life-be-the-next-paris-is-burning?utm_term=.utGak9y36#.wwbJ3lENG (accessed 20 Jan. 2018).

Jung, E. Alex. (2016). 'Real Talk With RuPaul: The drag supermodel of the world on how straight people steal from gay culture, meeting David Bowie, and why educating the youth is a waste of time'. *Vulture, Devouring Culture*. Available online: http://www.vulture.com/2016/03/rupaul-drag-race-interview.html (accessed 15 Jan. 2018).

Kohlsdorf, Kai. (2014). 'Policing the Proper Queer Subject, RuPaul's Drag Race in the Neoliberal "Post" Moment'. In J. Daems (ed.), *The Makeup of RuPaul's Drag Race: Essays on the Queen of Reality Shows*, pp. 74–94. MacFarland.

Levitt, Lauren. (2013). 'Reality Realness: Paris Is Burning and RuPaul's Drag Race'. Texts 3.1 Mediascapes and Connectivity. Available online: https://www.academia.edu/34978776/Reality_Realness_PARIS_IS_BURNING_and_RUPAULS_DRAG_RACE (accessed 20 Apr. 2016).

Marcel, Mary. (2014). 'Representing Gender, Race and Realness, The Television World of America's Next Drag Superstars'. In J. Daems (ed), *The Makeup of RuPaul's Drag Race, Essays on the Queen of Reality Shows*, pp. 19–37. MacFarland.

Muñoz, José Esteban. (1998). 'The White to Be Angry: Vaginal Davis' Terrorist Drag' in *Disidentifications, Queers of Color and the Performance of Politics*. Minneapolis and London: University of Minnesota Press, pp. 93–115.

Paris is Burning (1990), [Film]. Dir. Jenny Livingston. United States: Miramax Films.

RuPaul's Drag Race, Season 9 (2017) [TV series]. VH1, 23 June.

Serano, Julia. (2012). 'Reclaiming Femininity'. In A. F. Enke (ed.), *Transfeminist Perspectives in and beyond Transgender and Gender Studies*, pp. 170–183. Philadelphia: Temple University Press.

Stokoe, Kayte. (2016). 'Are Drag Kings Still Too Queer for London? From the Nineteenth-Century Impersonator to the Drag King of Today'. In S. Avery and K. M. Graham (eds), *Sex, Time and Place, Queer Histories of London c.1850 to the Present*, pp. 97–114. London: Bloomsbury Academic.

Stokoe, Kayte. (2020) *Reframing Drag: Beyond Subversion and the Status Quo*. London: Routledge.

Swamy, Vinay and Mackenzie, Louisa (eds). (2019). 'Legitimizing "iel"?' *H-France Salon*, vol. 11, no. 14. Available online: https://h-france.net/h-france-salon-volume-11-2019/ (accessed 12 Aug. 2019).

Taylor, Verta, and Rupp, Leila J. (2004). 'Chicks with Dicks, Men in Dresses: What It Means to be a Drag Queen'. In S. P. Schacht and Lisa Underwood (eds), *The Drag Queen Anthology: The Absolutely Fabulous but Flawlessly Customary World of Female Impersonators*, pp. 113–34. New York and London: Routledge.

The Silence of the Lambs (1991) [Film]. Dir. Jonathan Demme. United States: Orion Pictures.

Wittig, Monique. (1992). 'The Mark of Gender'. In *The Straight Mind and Other Essays*, pp. 76–89. Boston: Beacon Press.

8

Not a Cock in a Frock, but a Hole Story

Drag and the Mark of the 'Bioqueens'

Stephen Farrier

When it comes to talking about the kind of work I want to deal with here, the normative languages of gender in relation to drag begin to fail – almost all terms misfire or fall short in one way or another and when a term appears to fit, it only does so for a short while. It is not only an academic matter to get the terms of a discussion like this right; it is fundamental for reflecting the politics, community and spirit in which this kind of performance takes place. The work that I deal with in this chapter is female drag, the performers of which are known popularly at the time of writing as bioqueens or faux queens. Before I make my way to talk about a specific performer, rather than unquestioningly use those currently popular terms as identifiers here – 'bio' in bioqueen is short for biological woman, and 'faux' in faux queen emphasizes fakeness, more of which below – I start with a rather more specific and loquacious construction: at the base of this kind of work are, generally, people assigned female at birth (AFAB) performing in drag, using forms and costume looks similar to those associated with people assigned male at birth (AMAB) performing in drag as it is commonly perceived. For the purposes of this chapter, because the definition above is rather too wordy and bioqueen as a term persists in circulating in the community, I follow a number of performers and academics and refer to them as bioqueens with an understanding that this is an inadequate and potentially contentious nomenclature (bioqueens as a term appears in popular media – for instance, see Gander (2016), Alexander (2019) and Leighton-Dore (2019) – and in academic writing, see Berbary and Johnson (2017), French (2017), Khubchandani (2015) and Rupp, Taylor and Shapiro (2010) and countless theses and dissertations in the area).[1] I am also using it as a term to help surface the way that misogyny circulates in the contexts in which these performers work.

This chapter is concerned not only with the idea that gender is germane to drag (I would venture that it is difficult to think of any performance form in which gender does not play a fundamental role) but also that it is a performance form that often signal-jams normative uses of gender in performance. For the discussion here, it is important to investigate the relationship and function between gender and form onstage for bioqueens. This chapter looks to the way in which bioqueens challenge a number of norms developed in drag culture and performance. In the process of looking at the challenges bioqueens' work presents, the chapter will also mark the ways in which some responses to such challenges can be seen as doing the work of patriarchy. However, not wanting to replicate the idea that drag is more importantly about the offstage gender of the performer, I am keen to point out that this chapter is not wholly focused on the politics of bioqueens' work being in the drag space per se. Rather, later in the chapter, I focus on a specific bioqueen, Holestar, and the modes of performance she employs in her work that relate to other histories and historical forms of performance. While this chapter's impulse is to place practice as its prime motivator and not focus too much on community politics (because this takes us away from the performance), before reading Holestar's work, there are some important detours to the politics around bioqueens that it would be remiss not to touch on. I turn first, though, to a structuring image for the chapter, that of the 'mark', or being 'marked'. This image serves a dual sense, in part as a way to navigate through some of the political issues the chapter develops, and also as an approach to describing bioqueen performance that pays mind to the way in which it relates to other kinds of drag performance.

The mark is a means to identify different kinds of drag work. Drag is often marked by a particular performance tradition; as an example in the US context, a performance might be marked by pageant traditions or habits; in the UK context likewise, a performance might be marked by pantomime forms, traditions and conventions. Similarly, drag as a form borrows from itself – queens and kings often appropriate what they see, replicating images and blending new ideas from them – a process whereby a performance is marked by that from which it borrows or references. Thus, the idea of a mark or several marks being present in the performance means that the focus of the analysis of the work of bioqueens here is not so much an attempt to account for the sex and/or gender of the performer under the wig or make-up, as this is too limiting an approach, but on how the performance itself contains traces of other works. The idea of the mark also extends to the materiality of the performer, who often is physically marked by the costume they wear, often corseted, or pressed tightly. Thus, costume can leave a physical mark, and this chapter emphasizes performance as a material practice.

When looking at this kind of performance, mark describes the trace of performance form on drag; it may also be useful for examining the way that bioqueens are marked by an audience (that is, ranked or valued), sometimes literally in drag competitions and other times more subtly in relation to common expectations of what makes a queen, a process experienced sometimes as misogyny by bioqueens, as discussed below. Of course, being marked can also mean being struck by an experience in a positive and/or negative fashion, so as a thematic touchstone it could also be used to talk about audience experience; though that is not a focus for the discussion at hand, it might be useful for future study. In performance, identity labour and gender onstage, work is marked in some way with that which is not present – it contains embodied historical material manifest in form. Often, for a community it also contains and enacts a resonant politics.

It is important not to sidestep the impact on the performance and community of the AFAB person dragging up in this context. Often, in the chatter about bioqueens (and Holestar notes this below), the question 'Is this drag?' is often a conduit to materializing misogyny, social indignation and sometimes accusations of cultural appropriation (Bird, 2018; Hall, 2017; Nicholson, 2017). These responses have material consequences; misogyny in particular obviously impacts women's lives and should not be let off the hook when reading about this kind of performance work. Thus, for this chapter, when a bioqueen is performing, drag is drag because of its relation to performance. The point of the discussion here, importantly, is not to measure if it counts as drag – I will leave that to others – but to examine what proceeds from analysis when a drag-is-drag position is taken.

Importantly then, without attempting to account for the motivation of female drag queens or make an analysis of their journey with drag – because this is looked at by others (Shapiro, 2007; Rupp, Taylor and Shapiro, 2010) – this chapter speaks from the positive position that bioqueens are drag performers. I take the position that a bioqueen doing drag performance is drag performance. This tautology is purposeful: because, for this chapter, the focus is on performance form, the kind of performance outweighs the kind of person performing it, though of course these things are deeply connected. While it is important to note the connections between the performer and gendered and sexed material realities offstage, the imperative of the discussion here is the performance, which should not be primarily determined by the presumed/assumed biological make-up of the person doing it. Although recourse to the idea of the 'real biological' sex of the performer is difficult to resist in these discussions, I stand with Rachel Devitt, who says,

> Pinning the definition of drag so fixedly on a binary, sex-based concept of crossing not only belies the rich wealth of gender identities that inform contemporary gender performance and drag but also reifies the

naturalness of that binary ... If drag must entail a cross to the 'opposite' of one's 'true' identity, then that original, that biological sex-based identity becomes normalized and immobile, thus denying both the validity of the performer's self-identified gender and the power a drag performance has in questioning gender 'realness'. (Devitt, 2006: 30)

My position for this chapter – drag is drag because of its links to other forms of performance – does not follow the flow or focus of much of the work about queens and kings. For instance, Rupp et al.'s essay in 2010 sets out to be 'the first systematic comparison of drag queens and drag kings', such that their discussion 'enhances our understanding of the gendered dynamics of drag' (277). In their important work, they look for the differences between drag kings and queens and come to note how drag kinging and queening tend to function differently in the lives of the people that practise it. At the end of their study, which is specifically focused on kings and queens in Key West and Santa Barbara in the USA, they note:

What is striking is that participation in DBT [Disposable Boy Toys, a kinging troupe] facilitated self-reflexivity about gender identity at a very high level, which led to significant changes in the identities members claim. The drag queens did not experience the same kind of questioning about gender as a result of their performances; rather, gender transgression played an important part of bringing them to drag but they did not develop the same kind of complicated gender identities and analysis. This is no doubt in part, at least, because of the different histories of drag queens and drag kings in the gay and lesbian community. (284)

Although Rupp et al. mention bioqueens in their work, their study examines the relationship between the offstage and onstage gender of the people in the groups they investigate. Given the audience contexts in which this kind of work happens, it is important to pay attention to this relationship; yet, such a focus tends to be drawn to offstage gender and not place much emphasis on the labour most stages require, and performance often appears in these kinds of critical discussions unproblematically (that is, without recourse to its history, tenor or tropes). To be clear here, this is not a unique feature to Rupp et al.'s work but reflects the shape of many of the discussions in this area. Yet, as noted above, this chapter will engage to a small extent with the materiality of offstage gender identity, so I will touch on what bioqueen drag brings up in this sense, that more prevalent drag forms might not.

Even with a drag-is-drag aphorism established and a desire not to give air to a position that questions the legitimacy of bioqueens as drag performers (see Cracker, 2017), the discussion here should look to the common monikers bio- or faux queen in terms of their relation to sexism, as these expressions are also used as a catalyst for the production of misogyny because they can mark the bioqueen as either wholly related to biology in a way that generally AMAB cisgendered queens are not, or somehow fake or faux in their work, in a way that often such drag queens patently are, but are not negatively marked as such (their kind of fakery in some way does not stimulate the same kind of interrogative position). This inequity in title itself can be read as enmeshed by, and produced in, sexism. What each term does is to, in some way, mark (as in rank) the bioqueen differently than if they were male-identifying, which for some may be fair enough, as bioqueens are unlike cisgender-dominant drag queens in obvious ways. However, such a difference often only looks to offstage life and an identity position lived there, and in the final analysis it only really matters if there is an adherence to what Devitt above notes about the reification of gender categories (its only 'real drag' if it is a biological male doing it). Such discussions of the acceptability of bioqueens have the effect of focusing on the body doing the performance to the exclusion of what the body is doing in/with the performance (and the performance form). Because AMAB cisgender drag performers are not held to the same kind of scrutiny, discussions that look mostly to supposed or assumed biology (as if this were an easy category in this context), and that do not take account of the form of the work, mark women and trans performers in a lesser position simply by dint of particular configuration of biology or identification. This lesser positioning is not only about the delicate nature of the definition of performance form; it has material impacts.[2] In the nomenclature, both terms focus on the female body (bio emphasizing biology and faux as in a fake male) in a way that drag as a title for an AMAB cisgender performer does not. Additionally, given that it emphasizes binary sex, the bioqueen tag might not neatly fit trans-identified drag performers, and the 'faux' part of the phrase 'faux queen' can be read as an extension of the idea of trans women as somehow fake, which has unacceptable implications. In the community languages of the work I am concerned with here, there is an implicit bias at play that supports a kind of men-only club, a club that only seems to level claims of legitimacy at women and trans performers (while simultaneously and ironically fundamentally understanding 'realness' as construction) – a club that I do not want to support with this chapter. Consequently, I turn now to what the performance and performer does, through the experiences of a bioqueen.

Holestar

Holestar is an award-winning bioqueen who has been working since the late 1990s in the UK and Europe. Her performance work is at times seriously political, playful, comedic and controversial and feels very much based in camp drag and art practice. She works in a gig economy, appearing in bars and at parties while also making her own one-woman shows and pop records – as well as working as a dominatrix and running fetish nights in other venues. Her onstage look mirrors drag queen fare, larger-than-life energy, quick wittedness and drag make-up (enormous eyes); most often she would fit into what Steven Schacht (2002) sees as the glamour queen area of drag, and her comic verve deserves recognition too, which aligns with Schacht's delineation of camp queens. My reading of her work is that despite her international profile, her work is shot through with British drag form commingled with cabaret (see Figure 8.1).

Figure 8.1 Holestar. Image by Alisa Connan.

When she performs, whether at a bar or club, hosting an evening's entertainment or in her one-woman shows, she sings live to backing tracks. Although she may lip-synch in some of the work she does on film, most of her performance work involves her live singing. She sings covers, re-worked popular and club songs, and her own material. Her performance work also involves patter – off-the-cuff comebacks – in and around the songs she delivers live. Her performance, comprising her look, singing live and verbal wit, is marked by its relation to historical forms of drag. It is clear that Holestar understands the complexity of what she does, but she expresses it simply on her blog:

> drag is in the art, not your gender. There are women doing it, bearded queens, there are trans people doing drag. Now that's progress! Anyone can do drag, just research and respect its heritage and make it your own. (Holestar 2015)

Her connection to heritage is interesting here because the work she does pays mind not only to historical forms of community (particularly her understanding and knowledge of trans identities and queer culture) but also to the performance form. Although there is an open acknowledgement of history in lots of contemporary drag – particularly histories related to US forms (Poletti and Rak, 2018) – much of this does not make it into performance work, whereas Holestar's work is marked by this history. Not only does she embody historically rooted forms, she has a desire to record the importance of the scene in which she works, thereby preserving current work. For instance, she was a key personality of the film *Dressed As A Girl* (2015), which charts the drag scene of the East End of London and pays as much attention to the performers and their stories as it does to the kinds of performance that are done. What is clear in the film is that Holestar is treated as a drag performer, just like everyone else (though it does trace issues of misogyny in the context in which she works). The film shows Holestar's work playing excitingly along the border of arthouse trash and popular working-class forms of drag, and in a subtle way, music hall variety performance. Her work evades easy classification in that it plays along perceptions and genre edges yet is very present and boldly about fun.

In her one-woman show *Sorry I'm A Lady*, this connection to telling the past through the present is also manifest.[3] In the show, Holestar recounts her journey to and with drag as she moves across Europe via her honourable discharge from the armed forces, her training as a commercial photographer, her work as a dominatrix and the development of her drag persona. The performance is part biography, part variety show (with original and covered songs) and part engagement with LGBTQ+ politics. She has performed versions and fragments of the show in arthouse nightclubs, university campuses, shop windows and cabaret venues. In the work, she comes back to the idea that she is a female-identifying person negotiating a patriarchal world. Consistently she returns to talking about self-making through the roles she played and plays (soldier, sex worker, drag queen), and she marks the material reality of her world, her life and her health (mental and physical) while performing numbers themselves marked by other performance forms (variety, queer solo works, pop culture). *Sorry I'm A Lady* is profoundly queer as a work; it is too slippery to solidly define, and, likewise, her own sense of self is queer too in that she defiantly shifts across identity positions (pop performer, dominatrix) and occupies apparently non-compatible roles in her life. So, with an ironic nod to the title of her show, she is not any ordinary lady by normative standards, and she is not sorry about it.

If drag is mainly seen as playing the disjunction between the in/apparent biology of the performer and the presented gender of the character (which is usually an assumption by an audience), then this dislocation is not at stake in Holestar's work. If the audience do not already know from the beginning of the work that she is not an ordinary drag queen (that she is a bioqueen and not an AMAB cisgender queen), she makes it clear within the first moments of the show. *Sorry I'm A Lady*, then, is not about how well Holestar makes an illusion of her drag, apparently being a man-in-a-dress, or a cock-in-a-frock as older local queens might say, only to reveal that she has been a 'real woman' all along. Instead, Holestar's drag in this work is the enactment of queerness. Holestar's persona onstage is the real deal; the audience see Holestar the persona emerging (indeed, in other works Holestar does her make-up onstage) rather than the body of the performer being hidden behind or underneath the surface of the performance. What strikes me in the work is that it is ultimately about survival: she starts the show with the question 'who am I?' and ends it with 'despite it all, I am still here'. As the work traces fragments of her life – poignant, funny, upsetting and disgusting moments – it does so in a way that shows a lack of consistency has marked Holestar's existence, and in the piece the logic emerges that because of the bioqueen's playful undecidability, the space offered by drag seems a logical place to live in for a while (though she has been doing it for about nineteen years at the time of writing, which shows a fluid permanence). Drag for Holestar reads not so much as a character put on and taken off in the dressing room (or the back of a taxi); it is deeply part of how she negotiates the world. I do not think this is unique to Holestar; it describes many drag performers and is a force present in much of the drag I have seen and discussions I have with performers, but what is clear is that Holestar's performance work might be useful for talking about gender or identity fluidity, but this does not constitute it; rather, the work enacts Holestar's queerness marked by a number of performance forms. Elements of the energy present in *Sorry I'm A Lady* are rooted in popular performance and encourage audiences to vocalize their engagement. For instance, even when not playing in a nightclub setting, Holestar uses a microphone. Of course, for the sung segments of the show it is used to amplify her voice over the backing tracks and it gives a particular nightclub quality to the performance. When she sings without accompaniment and speaks through the microphone, this club characteristic remains. This is a mark of cabaret on the work. In particular when I saw her performance in a university, the use of the microphone was marked by relations to popular performance and brought to the setting a sense of the nightclub. This aesthetic mark has an impact on the audience and its responses in that, through the form of the work and its mark of the pub/club/bar, spectators felt free to respond as if they were in a bar or a club. Holestar's strategy in *Sorry I'm A Lady* is at its core one of making sure the audience have fun. Though the show is not without its political message and moments of pathos, the invitation for audience interaction (and Holestar's spontaneous comedic responses to the audience) ensures that the audience enjoy themselves, even when the message is important. Indeed, she makes the point of serious fun by making *Sorry I'm A Lady* in the way that she has, marked by forms of popular drag and cabaret – here I note cabaret's long-standing connection with political performance and agitprop, which leave their traces too on her show. This kind of performance construction implies that Holestar consciously puts together the work in a way that pulls on drag traditions – drag traditions that are very local in their flavour – although she does not express it in the academic way I have here (more of which below).

This interaction with an audience as part of the form of the work was especially present across all of Holestar's work, for instance, when at a regular London booking in 2017 (not a presentation of *Sorry I'm A Lady*) the sound system crashed, and the venue could not get it back online. Unperturbed, Holestar took to the stage and not only sang acapella (her voice being big enough to fill the venue) but also improvisationally turned the technical breakdown into a memorable moment of performance. Rather than attempt to deliver the song in a normal way, Holestar encouraged the audience to clap a beat and sing a well-known Motown song with her (Holestar sang the verses and the audience sang the chorus, over which she delivered ad-libs). This seems very similar to the way in which music hall performers would encourage their audience to sing back to the performer (Maloney, 2003). Thus, dressed in a gigantic pink glamour drag outfit, her solution to what for other queens might have been an insurmountable crisis (especially those whose work has lip-synching as a core element) was to turn the venue into an old-fashioned sing-along, marked by popular performance form. Although I would say that Holestar's work is concerned with the contemporary, it pays mind to the performance traditions from which it stems, and this unexpected rejig of the night's plans is an inadvertent demonstration of how Holestar's work is deeply connected to histories, not through telling histories directly (though *Sorry I'm A Lady* is about Holestar's past), rather through an embodied sense of how to work a stage and a room in a particular way, with a particular spirit and energy.

There are other traditions that Holestar mirrors offstage too. Like many other queens before her, she passes on her knowledge of drag to younger generations. Though she is not a drag mother, in the sense that many queens are (see Farrier, 2017), she does sit on judges' panels for drag shows and in her blog gives advice about working as a bioqueen. This is paying attention to the traditions of the form and the communities that circulate around it. In a time before the internet when information was much harder to come by, older queens were the conduit to any newly minted drag performer. Although a drag mother might give advice on make-up and dress, they also advise on performance, and it is in this last category where Holestar has appeared onstage on a panel helping younger performers hone their acts.

What marks Holestar's work as contemporary is this mark of the past – there is a clear attitude in her performance work and in interviews of recourse to the past, of her current practice connecting to a lineage of drag performers. Her rootedness through the form signals to an audience a longevity and an important insistence on understanding where the form came from. Her work then speaks about current issues as linked to a past in a way that is not existent in many other performers I have seen. There is an energy in her work that notes that a knowledge of history of the form is important, particularly in the current rapidly shifting scenes of drag – positioning the idea that knowing your roots is a survival skill.

These survival skills are a mark too, one that is a trace of the challenge of working as a bioqueen in a patriarchy. What has been consistent for Holestar and other female drag queens is the presence of misogyny in audiences, venues and bookers (see Holestar in Ashenden and Green, 2018). Thus, the work she has done has been policed by patriarchy and homonormativity as it manifests in some places in gay culture, and Holestar has challenged this where she is able. However, Holestar likewise has been challenged, but not by those who work to maintain dominant norms. Holestar has been challenged by some audience members around language use with regard to trans identity. In turn, Holestar has engaged with the challenge by questioning the points made about her commitment to trans people and politics. In relation to these kinds of identity politics, Holestar, speaking in *The Guardian*, says:

I don't want to offend other people and it won't be cool for everybody, but I've been doing this for longer than anyone else as a female drag queen and in some ways I've got the right to do it, because of that longevity. (Nicholson, 2017)

At some level the work that Holestar makes is marked with the understanding of (and maybe frustration about) the complexities and fluidity of gender, identity and sexuality, not least of all because, during her performance career, she has seen the rise of queer ideas and her sex work brings her into contact with an assemblage of sexualities, identities, genders and bodies. If there is one thing that consistently marks Holestar's performances, however, it is her negative attitude to privilege and entitlement. In a punk-like way, her work tests through drag performance what is possible and acceptable, and she challenges entitlement. For some, her performance manifests a challenge simply by dint of her being a bioqueen; for others it is hearing her talk about her sex work in her one-woman show. While being interviewed for *The Guardian*, Holestar notes that her challenge also extends to those who have studied drag academically, in whom she sees a privilege that manifests as 'snooty' (in Nicholson, 2017) and exclusive. In some way, this last challenge is about a knowledge of theory pitted against the embodied knowledge of performance (she has come across people who imply she does not know what she is doing because she apparently has not read enough Judith Butler, for instance). This kind of academic elitism mirrors the sexism aimed at bioqueens and sits well with Holestar's general resistance to entitlement and her distaste for the non-inclusive way she has experienced some aspects of her working life. Indeed, there is a sense that this position in relation to drag and academia highlights the often-exclusive nature of higher education and how so often the understanding of drag performance does not deal with the material realities of the body and life of the performer; rather, drag serves to reify theories of gender or fluid identity as if the performer has no sense of those ideas.

But for my consideration here, things function the other way around. That is, Holestar's work has left its mark on my thinking of what drag is and can be. Where I would not question a performer's veracity because they have not read gender theory, I would with a knowledge of Holestar's work question the veracity of gender theory. The mark the work has left then asks that I pay mind to the lineages of the form, and as such I respond to the theory not as generative in this situation (though, of course, sometimes it is in other contexts) but as a set of ideas and languages with which to describe the work I might watch. And, in the final analysis, drag and drag performers do not like being told what to be, and with that they continue to press their resistive mark.

Notes

1   There are other terms as well that I have come across to describe female drag queens – femme queens and hyper queens, for instance.
2   It was reported in *The Telegraph* that a bioqueen was dropped from a commercial campaign because it was discovered she was a cisgender woman; see Bird (2018).
3   'Sorry, I'm a Lady' is also a pop single by Baccara, released in 1977.

References

Alexander, Rae. (2019). 'Meet the Trans, Non-Binary and Bio Queens Who Deserve a Spot on "RuPaul's Drag Race UK"'. *KQED*, 9 January. Available online: https://www.kqed.org/pop/108023/meet-the-trans-non-binary-and-bio-queens-who-deserve-a-spot-on-rupauls-drag-race-u-k (accessed 24 Feb. 2019).

Ashenden, Amy and Green, Robert (2018). 'I'm a woman, dominatrix and a drag queen: Meet Holestar, the queen tearing up the rulebook'. *Pink News*, 1 October. Available online: https://www.pinknews.co.uk/2018/10/01/im-a-woman-dominatrix-and-a-drag-queen-meet-holestar-the-queen-tearing-up-the-rulebook/ (accessed 24 Feb. 2019).

Bird, Steve. (2018). 'Virgin drops drag queen "for being a woman"'. *The Telegraph*, 29 September.

Berbary, Lisbeth A. and Johnson, Corey W. (2017). 'En/Activist Drag: Kings Reflect on Queerness, Queens, and Questionable Masculinities'. *Leisure Sciences*, vol. 39 no. 4, pp. 305–18, DOI:10.1080/01490400.2016.1194791.

Cracker, Miz. (2017). 'As Drag Become More Inclusive, What Makes a Queen a Queen?' *Slate*, 9 May. Available online: https://slate.com/human-interest/2017/05/are-bioqueens-as-authentic-as-gay-male-drag-queens-the-art-form-is-changing.html (accessed 24 Feb. 2019).

Dressed as a Girl (2015). [film], Dir Colin Rothbart, produced by Colin Rothbart, Chris Amos.

Devitt, Rachel. (2006). 'Girl on Girl, Fat Femmes, Bio-Queens, and Redefining Drag'. In S. Whiteley and J. Rycenga (eds), *Queering the Popular Pitch*, pp. 27–41. London: Routledge, pp. 27–41.

Farrier, Stephen. (2017). 'International influences and drag: just a case of tucking or binding?'. *Theatre, Dance and Performance Training*, vol. 8, no. 2, pp. 171–87.

French, Sarah. (2017). 'Queer Femme Drag and Female Narcissism in Yana Alana's Between the Cracks'. In *Staging Queer Feminisms: Sexuality and Gender in Australian Performance, 2005–2015*. London: Palgrave Macmillan.

Gander, Kashmira. (2016). 'Can a woman be a drag queen? I spent a day with a Rupaul's Drag Race contestant to find out'. *The Independent*, 24 May.

Hall, Jake. (2017). 'Why do some people want to stop women performing drag?'. *Dazed*, 6 November. Available online: http://www.dazeddigital.com/life-culture/article/37963/1/why-do-some-people-want-to-stop-women-doing-drag (accessed 24 Feb. 2019).

Holestar. (2015). 'How to be a Female Drag Queen'. Available online: http://holestar.blogspot.com/2015/02/how-to-be-female-drag-queen.html (accessed 31 May 2018).

Khubchandani, Kareem. (2015). 'Lessons in Drag: An Interview with LaWhore Vagistan'. *Theatre Topics*, vol. 25, no. 3, pp. 285–94. Available online: https://muse.jhu.edu/ (accessed 24 Feb. 2019).

Leighton-Dore, Samuel. (2019). '"Drag Race Thailand" features first ever cisgender female contestant'. *SBS*, 15 January. Available online: https://www.sbs.com.au/topics/sexuality/fast-lane/article/2019/01/15/drag-race-thailand-features-first-ever-cisgender-female-contestant (accessed 24 Feb. 2019).

Maloney, Paul. (2003). *Scotland and the Music Hall 1850–1914*. Manchester: Manchester University Press.

Nicholson, Rebecca. (2017). 'Workin' it! How female drag queens are causing a scene'. *The Guardian*, 10 July. Available online: https://www.theguardian.com/lifeandstyle/2017/jul/10/workin-it-how-female-drag-queens-are-causing-a-scene (accessed 24 Feb. 2019).

Poletti, Anna and Rak, Julie. (2018). '"We're All Born Naked and the Rest Is" Mediation: Drag as Automediality'. *M/C Journal of Media and Culture*, vol. 21, no. 2. Available online: http://www.journal.media-culture.org.au/index.php/mcjournal/article/view/1387 (accessed 24 Feb. 2019).

Rupp, Leila J., Taylor, V. and Shapiro, Eve I. (2010). 'Drag Queens and Drag Kings: The Difference Gender Makes'. *Sexualities*, vol. 13, no. 3, pp. 275–94. https://doi.org/10.1177/1363460709352725.

Schacht, Steven. (2002). 'Four Renditions of Doing Female Drag: Feminine Appearing Conceptual Variations of a Masculine Theme'. *Gendered Sexualities*, vol. 6, pp. 157–80.

Shapiro, Eve. (2007). 'Drag Kinging and the Transformation of Gender Identities'. *Gender & Society*, vol. 21, no. 2, pp. 250–71. https://doi.org/10.1177/0891243206294509.

9

Destabilization through Celebration

Drag, Homage and Challenges to Black Stereotypes in the Practice of Harold Offeh

Kieran Sellars

Harold Offeh steps onto the stage at the Chelsea Theatre, London, as part of the two-day performance programme *Just Like A Woman: London Edition* (November, 2015). Wearing a black leotard and heels, Offeh takes the pose of Marlena Shaw on the album cover of *Take a Bite* (1979). The song 'Shaw Biz/Suddenly It's How I Like to Feel/Shaw Biz' begins to play, and Offeh remains perfectly still. Offeh maintains this pose for the song's duration with his left hand placed upon his left collarbone and his right hip popped to the side, mirroring Shaw with acute accuracy (see Figure 9.1). This pose is followed by the wide squat of Melba Moore from her 1979 album cover *Burn*, which is then succeeded by the replication of Barbara Cheeseborough's famous wide-mouthed scream on the cover of Funkadelic's album *Maggot Brain* (1971). The culmination of this performance, entitled *Covers*, comes when Offeh removes the leotard to expose his naked body, which he then covers in oil, as he attempts to replicate Grace Jones' impossible arabesque from the cover of her album *Island Life* (1985). As the song 'Slave to the Rhythm' plays, the audience are witness to Offeh's attempts to hold a pose that was created and heavily manipulated through visual trickery by Jones' then partner Jean-Paul Goude. Thus, with each of the poses becoming physically more demanding, Offeh sets himself an impossible task in his attempts to emulate Jones (see Figure 9.2).

This chapter seeks to unpick the reasoning behind these flirtations with failure and to consider these recreations as moments of homage that seek to destabilize, in Clémentine Mercier's terms, 'the cliché of the black sculptural woman with the oiled body' (2017). I will argue that Offeh's carefully choreographed moments of stillness in these poses offer a destabilization of these images by using drag as a means of critical celebration. Offeh's homage to these female black singers and models acts as a recognition of their often-

Figure 9.1 Harold Offeh in *Covers*. MAC – Birmingham 22 May 2015. Photo by Timothy James Photography.

unnoticed labour, while also challenging the fetishized, mediated depictions of these women. Offeh offers a strategy through drag in performance that attempts to deconstruct stereotypes by framing these women through his queer body. Considering the ideologically charged nature of these poses when they are realized through a male body dressed in heels and a black leotard, this chapter will argue that Offeh's embodiment of these women moves beyond a co-opting impersonation by a male body and instead acts as a challenge to normative gender ideologies.

This investigation of *Covers* is further supported by the consideration of other performances by Offeh, including *Keep It Up! Keep It Up!* (2017), which represents Offeh's, and Grace Jones', own experiences of immigration and migration through the act of hula hooping and highlights the unrecognized skill and labour that Jones put into her performances; and *Snap Like a Diva* workshops (2012–17), which explore the origins of 'snapping' from 1980s black gay culture, analysed in this chapter to highlight, through a queer black sensibility, the connection between posing and gesture in Offeh's practice. This chapter concludes by arguing that an overt exposure of the male body does not diminish the performance of drag but rather serves to complicate the performances and engagements with gender that Offeh offers his audiences.

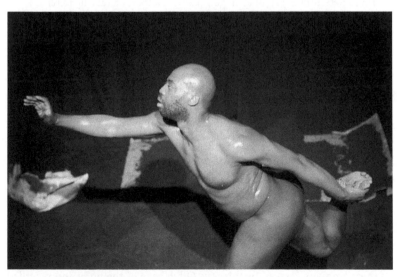

Figure 9.2 Harold Offeh in *Covers*. MAC – Birmingham 22 May 2015. Photo by Timothy James Photography.

Evoking presence and absence through drag

In his essay 'The Performance of Unmarked Masculinity', Ramsay Burt makes reference to the experimental choreography of the twentieth century and the ways in which it 'sometimes found chinks in the armor [*sic*] of normative gender ideologies that could be opened up and exploited to stage alternative masculinities' (Burt, 2009: 150). I would argue that *Covers* can be considered as a dance performance which finds and exploits the vulnerabilities in normative gender ideologies through its carefully stylized choreography. Posing and holding these poses is of particular importance to my argument that Offeh is able to deconstruct racial stereotypes while simultaneously articulating an alternative engagement with gender through his use of drag in this performance.[1] By performing as, or rather echoing poses of, these women, Offeh produces a performance that in one instance recreates these famous music album covers and also draws these women onto the stage with him.

Indeed, Burt goes on to state that

> the kinds of presences that dancers project and the absences they call to mind determine the points of view that spectators can take up in relation to the performance. Point of view both enables and restricts the ways in which embodied memories and histories, that are shared by performer and spectator, are evoked during the performance. (ibid., 154)

This is evident in *Covers*, with these women's images, and sometimes voices, present on the stage evoking a shared and embodied memory between Offeh and his audience. Such embodied presence is complicated, however, by absence, as Offeh's male body can never fully realize and replicate the poses exactly. One could argue that with the music from these albums playing throughout the performance, these female artists are made to appear absent, their disembodied voices failing to belong to the live, male body presented to the audience. This draws a connection to drag techniques, such as the lip-synch – Stephen Farrier suggests that 'those who lip-synch make a more direct relation to a body in the past and, as such, relate to temporalities as porous' (2016: 205). Offeh is arguably highlighting this porousness in *Covers* by evoking shared memories that the spectator and Offeh may have of these women's careers. In this way, Offeh's use of the body and recorded sound highlights, to return to Farrier, how drag can operate 'in part, as a manifestation of a voice and channel into the past' (ibid., 192). With Offeh's body being materially present in the performance, and the women's bodies not, there is an embodied trace of them on his body through his enactment of their poses. By his failing to recreate these poses perfectly, the porousness of temporalities, as Farrier suggested above, is made even clearer, with these women impacting Offeh's body. In this moment, I argue that this 'channel into the past' is manifest in these instances where the women on the album covers are brought into the present, while Offeh simultaneously vanishes imperfectly into the female artists through the poses.

The poses that Offeh adopts in *Covers* are themselves ideologically charged when one considers how they change when they circulate through a male body dressed in heels and a black leotard rather than an apparently lithe, Amazonian body. In conjunction with these costume elements of drag, the queer potential of these poses comes from the challenges to gender norms that Offeh enables with the stances. This notion of queer potentiality in relation to posing is also evident in Joe Goode's performance of *29 Effeminate Gestures*, originally performed in 1987, drawn upon here to further consider the queer, male body in relation to stylized, effeminate movement. Goode's performance takes the audience through twenty-nine gestures that are deemed effeminate, insofar as these gestures are deemed to feminize men when articulated through their bodies. David Gere, in his writing on Goode's performance, argues that 'to perform against the grain is to exist in a state of radical self-consciousness. And to exist in a state of radical self-consciousness is to resist the determinism of gender naturalism' (2001: 371). By 'perform against the grain', Gere is referring to Goode's engagement with effeminacy, arguably in performance and non-performance contexts, and its potential to challenge normative gender ideologies through one's own radical, gendered self-consciousness. Indeed, this can be perceived to be operating within Offeh's performance in *Covers*, with his replication of these women's poses embodying the gestures that were previously circulated through female bodies. I am cautious in my wording here, using the phrasing 'gestures that were previously circulated through female bodies' rather than 'feminine gestures', as I do not seek to limit the challenges that these women, particularly Jones, are making to normative gender ideologies in their own work. What is of interest here is the shift that takes place when these poses are performed through Offeh's body.

The significance of these poses is again foregrounded when one considers, as Jacki Willson argues, that 'any practice that uses the female body is working within a cultural system that is not value-free. Attempting to reconfigure or reconstitute the meanings produced by the already tainted female body by using that very same body is obviously problematic' (2008: 56). Referring here to the dominant, white heterocentric system of representation, one can frame Offeh's performance of these poses as queering the potentially fetishized and racialized representations of these women. Indeed, this can also relate to Offeh's own body, with his queering of these poses also calling on the audience to consider how he is asking his male body to be framed. Cultural critic bell hooks suggests that 'for black bodies, the fear has not been losing touch with our carnality and physicality, but how to be in touch with our bodies in a way that is liberating, that does not confine us to racist/sexist paradigms of subjugated embodiment' (1994: 130). Thus, Offeh in his material embodiment of these women uses his exposed black, male body as a means of reframing these women; and with the images of these women projected alongside Offeh's live body, they also reframe him.

Indeed, it is worth noting that this engagement with presence and absence is heavily dependent on mediated versions of these women, with (sometimes significantly) edited images of their bodies and recordings of their voices being the way in which these moments of embodied memory are created. This is particularly pertinent to the model Barbara Cheeseborough, as she does not sing or feature on the album that uses her image. Thus, Offeh is not only embodying women who are musicians and universally well known, such as Jones, but also women who are located more specifically within certain industries, such as Cheeseborough. In this way, some of the women are not necessarily known by name, rather by their body. It is ironic, therefore, that on this particular cover, only Cheeseborough's head is visible, appearing in the image to be buried up to her neck in soil. By replicating the poses of women like Cheeseborough, Offeh is arguably inhabiting these women and reclaiming space for them within public discourse. With these images being the primary mode through which the audience are able to encounter and engage with these women, however, this form of mediation in performance requires further consideration.

I suggest that the replication of the poses from these album covers can be framed within the style of tableaux vivant. Guilia Vittori, in her discussion of Ann Carlson's performance *Picture Jasper Ridge* (2012), which included tableaux vivant that were based on archival photographs, is useful here in her consideration of drawing on mediatized images in performance. Vittori suggests that

> The tableau vivant format provided the performance with a different effect of presence than a staging of the subject would have allowed. Still reenactments make the photograph a performance; yet they maintain the image within the limits of the object, avoiding the development of narratives. Each tableau vivant created an ambiguous play of impersonation and alienation among subjects photographed, performers, and spectators, raising ontological questions. (2016: 86)

Indeed, Vittori's assertion here echoes those made by Burt regarding how presence and absence can be shared by performer and spectator. Vittori's positioning of the relationship between the photograph and the tableaux, creating 'an ambiguous play of impersonation and alienation', is particularly relevant to Offeh's engagement with drag in this performance, with his attempts at impersonating these stars, both succeeding in its parody and failing in any attempt at fully articulating these images. Through the use of the tableaux vivant, our engagement with Jones and the other women in this performance is able to transcend the mediated spectacle. Through replication as an act of homage, Offeh is able to evoke the presence of these women via a reconsideration and challenge to the male, mediatized and fetishistic reading by which these images are often framed. It is important to note, however, that this challenge to fetish is further complicated by Offeh covering himself in oil and posing naked, and this opening up of the body to readings of fetish and the exotic are examined later in the chapter.

This use of drag to destabilize fetish bears particular consideration, as the audience are only able to engage with these women through mediated frames, such as Jones in the highly manipulated image created by Goude and through her track 'Slave to the Rhythm'. I would suggest that Offeh's queer tableaux enables a drag performance that does not conflate these women with just another mediatized spectacle, but rather presents them as figures of power and agency. This queering comes, in part, from the poses that Offeh chooses to hold in his tableaux, with the effortlessness of the mediatized album covers broken down by revealing the labour that has previously been hidden.

The acknowledgement of unrecognized labour and skill is also highlighted in Offeh's 2017 performance, *Keep It Up! Keep It Up!* For the performance, Offeh taught himself to hula hoop, as he states, 'part in recognition of Grace Jones' performative act of hula hooping for 10–15 mins [sic] at her concerts, while singing' (2017). By learning to hula hoop and positioning himself in locations in Syracuse, New York State, that are associated with Jones, Offeh creates performative moments which seek to highlight Jones' skill and talent while his own selection of hula-hooping attempts, lasting only a minute or so, highlight his lack of skill in comparison to Jones. In this performance, as in *Covers*, Offeh attempts to emulate Jones but inevitably finds himself coming up short. Royster states that '[Mariam] Kershaw notes the importance of [Jones'] experiences as a runway model, as training ground to think critically about body, look, and movement, as well as "rapid, multiple reinvention"' (2009: 85). Here, Royster highlights Jones' modelling career as a form of performer training, which not only transformed Jones physically but also provided the basis of her frequent reinventions of image, many of which played with the boundaries of normative gender representation and embodiment. Offeh's attempt at matching Jones' training and attention to detail in *Keep It Up! Keep It Up!* highlights the unrecognized work and labour of Jones' performances.

Grace-ful: Posing and snapping

Although Offeh strips naked later in *Covers,* he arguably maintains drag in his performance particularly by engaging with gesture. Through the act of posing, Offeh is able to offer his audience a reframing of his gendered body through choreography without any physical transformation taking place. Offeh is not attempting to look exactly like, or pass as, the women depicted in these covers and is instead using his body, rather than the transformational effects of costume and make-up, to engage with gender in this performance. As Gere argues of Goode's performance of *29 Effeminate Gestures,* 'beauty lies in going against the grain, a concept that can easily be translated in choreographic terms when so-called feminine gestures are performed on a male body' (2001: 360). Though I agree with Gere's assertion that these evocative challenges to gender in performance create moments of beauty, they are also symbolic of the anxiety such challenges instil in what remains a pervasively heteronormative society. Burt argues that 'men within the Western dance profession have, for the last century, been a source of social anxieties because dance performance can sometimes make visible a correlation between the way men relate to their bodies and the way male power is preserved' (2009: 151). By positioning his nude body onstage while drawing on the drag aesthetics of costume and feminizing gesture and choreography, Offeh is arguably sublimating the power that the clothed male body holds within the heteronormative, phallocentric economy.

With this queer engagement and display of his body, Offeh not only cultivates the anxieties that Burt suggests the dancing male body can evoke, but also uses his body to challenge the commonly upheld relationship between the male body and power. This social anxiety clearly resonates in the challenges Goode's performance makes, with Gere arguing that it is

in *29 Effeminate Gestures,* in which Goode's excessive effeminacy could easily be interpreted as the symbolic realization of an extroverted strategy of resistance. The message: Take your gestural socialization off my body. I will 'choreograph' myself as I please. Excess is enabled when the chains constraining one's corporeality break and shatter to the floor. Exaggeration, then, is Goode's dramatic demand for gestural freedom. (2001: 357)

Operating through his own form of excess, Offeh uses the iconic poses of these women as a form of gendered subterfuge to not only liberate these women from the confines of fetishized consumerism, but also to rid his male body of the 'gestural socialization' that Judith Butler would argue is culturally engrained in us all (2007: xv).

This liberation from 'gestural socialization' is also evident in Offeh's two-hour *Snap Like a Diva* workshop (2012–17), which features a shift in the ways in which posing and gesturing enter into his practice. Whereas *Covers* sought to evoke challenges to normative gendered paradigms by evoking poses and gestures that came from black women, the *Snap Like a Diva* workshop draws on the movements of snapping, which Offeh states is 'derived from the Black American gay sub-cultures of the 80s and 90s and consists of series of grand movements that allows participants to communicate and attain diva status' (2017). Thus, whereas the poses of women were the focus of *Covers*, the *Snap Like a Diva* workshop situates its engagement with movement within a black, queer sensibility. The workshop, led by Steve Nice and Offeh, as his drag alter-ego Divana (see Figure 9.3), seeks to 'offer participants of all abilities an opportunity to learn about the history of snapping. Then through a practical

Figure 9.3 Harold Offeh as his drag alter-ego, Divana. Photo courtesy of the artist.

session participants will acquire the basic skills to communicate and perform fabulous and expressive moves. The session will end with a grand snap diva contest where participants will battle for the honour of being Grand Snap Diva' (2017).

Divana is one of Offeh's most overt engagements with drag in performance, but one which, as in his performance of *Covers*, does not seek to make a realistic impersonation. Rather, as Divana, Offeh creates a drag persona on which the male and female bodies are able to interweave. Offeh's facial hair remains and his chest is exposed to reveal that no padding or make-up has been used to create the impression of breasts, and though neither of these are particularly new to drag performance, they both highlight the ways in which Offeh does not seek to erase or hide his male body. By pairing and making his male body visible alongside the aspects of drag, Offeh creates performances where his male body is able to operate in dialogue with his use of drag. This notion of dialogue and communication can be further considered in relation to Marlon T. Riggs' writings on drag queens and race. Riggs questions 'can we talk? But of course we can, queer diva darling, if you abide by the rules of the dominant discourse, which means, in short, you must sing someone else's tune to be heard' (1992: 101). Indeed, by making his male body visible alongside the drag in his performance, Offeh challenges the dominant discourses to which Riggs makes reference. Through drag and the evocative snap, Offeh is able to articulate a challenge to dominant, white discourses by positioning his engagement with these concepts in direct relation to his black, male body.

The stylized movement of snapping, and the battle to be crowned Grand Snap Diva, echoes the heavily coded practice of voguing and the competitions which took place in the Harlem ballrooms from the 1960s onwards (Johnson, 2001: 13). By teaching others to snap like a diva, Offeh offers a 'fabulous' and 'expressive' (to use his words) performative strategy in alternative ways of moving through public space. I position Offeh's engagement with the poses of the women in *Covers* as an act of celebration and homage that presents a reconsideration of the way their bodies are framed. Offeh once again uses movement as a means of challenging its normative gendering through an engagement with the queer art of snapping. In this way, the use of drag and a focus on movement offer Offeh's audiences ways of considering how the male body can confront, make vulnerable, and challenge normative gender. Though Offeh makes use of drag costume elements in his workshop – wigs, make-up, clothing associated with women etc. – his use of his body can clearly be framed likewise as an act of drag, with choreographed movements performing and reinscribing gender onto his body.

The nude drag act

Offeh's black leotard in *Covers* takes on new resonance when he removes it for the final pose of the performance, Jones' 'impossible' arabesque. In this moment, the functionality of the leotard is echoed in the functional manner in which Offeh removes it.[2] There is no attempt at a fetishized, slow reveal of the body as Offeh removes his clothing; instead this moment of undressing and the subsequent application of oil on his body could be viewed as quotidian and task-like. Though this particular way of undressing is a clear choice and I read it as a challenge to the fetishized depictions of the nude black male body, it would be naïve to suggest that Offeh is able to perform outside of an eroticized gaze completely. Willson argues that 'the tease acknowledges both the powerlessness and control that earmarks veiling and nakedness and by wavering in that hazy halfway house intervenes knowingly in this process of revelation, the process of using and losing power' (2008: 184). Though I do not frame Offeh's removal of his clothes as a striptease, Willson's idea of performatively undressing as both a moment of empowerment and disenfranchisement is pertinent in considering Offeh's exposed body in performance.

Roland Barthes and his oft-referenced writings on the striptease are also useful in considering the theorizing of movement and its links to the erotic potential of the naked body. Barthes, in his discussion of the dance which accompanies the striptease, suggests that

> the dance, consisting of ritual gestures which have been seen a thousand times, acts on movements as a cosmetic, it hides nudity, and smothers the spectacle under a glaze of superfluous yet essential gestures, for the act of becoming bare is relegated to the rank of parasitical operations carried out in an improbable background. (2000: 85–6)

Barthes is useful in considering what happens when the nude body is exposed but no movement takes place as in the case of *Covers*. I have already argued that the mundane way in which Offeh removes his outfit challenges, but is arguably unable to resist, an eroticized gaze, but with Barthes' positioning the movement of the dancer as a process which 'hides nudity, and smothers the spectacle under a glaze of superfluous yet essential gestures', the stillness of Offeh's body and its connections to the erotic require unpicking. Indeed, Willson argues that 'the tenuous balance between power and desire is never going to be resolved. The objecthood of the body gives us the potential to be both empowered and co-opted back into the system' (2008: 77). Thus, if immobility is linked to the fear of revealing the nakedness of the performer,

Covers appears to operate on the cusp of a seemingly erotically charged display, with Offeh's exposed body in one instance acting as a moment of empowerment over normative gender ideologies while also at risk of being drafted back into an arrangement of eroticized display.

This engagement with stillness resonates with André Lepecki's theorizing on the dancer's body and stillness as a means of challenging the commonly held assumption that the dancer's body must be constantly in the midst of motion to be considered dancing (2006). André Lepecki makes use of Nadia Seremetakis' notion of the 'still act' as a strategy of resisting 'historical dust' by examining how the 'dust' settles onto the body (1994: 12). Lepecki defines historical dust as

> not a simple metaphor. When taken literally, it reveals how historical forces penetrate deep into the inner layers of the body: dust sedimenting the body, operating to rigidify the smooth rotation of joints and articulations, fixing the subject within overly prescribed pathways and steps, fixating movement within a certain politics of time and place. (2006: 15)

This engagement with stillness as a means of examining the historical forces which have shaped and influenced the body can be used as way of analysing Offeh's choreography in *Covers*. Offeh's stillness offers a means of making his nakedness overt, but through Lepecki these moments of stillness can also be considered as points in which the 'historical dust' of the black male body can be examined. As Lepecki states, 'against the brutality of the historical dust literally falling onto bodies, the still-act reshapes the subject's stance regarding movement and the passing of time' (ibid.). Here, one can read Offeh's moments of stillness as acts which challenge readings of the black male body. As hooks suggests, 'to break with the ruling hegemony that has a hold on images of the black male body, a revolutionary visual aesthetic must emerge that reappropriates, revises, and invents, that gives everyone something new to look at' (1994: 138). In this way, Offeh's attempts at holding his poses arguably shake off the weight of fetishized and stereotyped readings of his body and move away from 'fixing the subject within overly prescribed pathways and steps' (Lepecki, 2006: 15). By deploying stillness as choreographed movement, Offeh highlights how his body and those of the women he imitates have been literally and figuratively shaped by dominant structures of power.

Though I have argued that Offeh's nudity in his work is not inherently sexual, I also contend that the act of removing his clothes is an acknowledgement of the ways in which black bodies are consumed in popular culture. By placing his body in this vulnerable position, Offeh mirrors the ways in which the women in the album covers have also had their bodies framed and eroticized. Judith Butler's germinal text *Gender Trouble* is useful for the further consideration of Offeh's use of nudity in relation to dominant structures of power because he maintains elements of drag even though he is naked. Butler questions,

> Is drag the imitation of gender, or does it dramatize the signifying gestures through which gender itself is established? Does being female constitute a 'natural fact' or a cultural performance, or is 'naturalness' constituted through discursively constrained performative acts that produce the body through and within the categories of sex? ... gender practices within gay and lesbian cultures often thematize 'the natural' in parodic contexts that bring into relief the performative construction of an original and true sex.[3] (2007: xxxi)

Considering this notion of 'thematiz[ing] "the natural" in parodic contexts', I suggest that Offeh's naked male body is itself a type of drag performance, as the audience see the semi-nude Grace Jones reimagined through the total nudity of Offeh. Returning to Burt and Vittori's writings regarding the cultivation of presence and absence through an engagement with archival images and embodied memory, it would appear that Offeh's exposed, male body continues in this vein of carefully cultivating the presence of Jones within his own body. However, this is not only a performance of parody or imitation made to highlight the performativity and constructed nature of gender that Butler references. But with the complete exposure of Offeh's body, while Jones remains partially clothed, the audience see a complication in the recreation of this image with the male and female body converging in these moments of posing.

Conclusion

In his performance of *Covers*, Offeh deploys gesture, movement and nudity to speak to the ways in which the black body, both male and female, is fetishized in art and popular culture. In his practice Offeh engages with costume elements of drag, such as the black leotard, to speak to notions of training and rehearsal that the album covers presented to the audience are unable to express. Throughout *Covers*, Offeh reframes his male body through carefully choreographed moments that are able to exceed the limits of normative gender associated with male bodies and bring the women that he is emulating onto the stage with him. Certainly, rather than diminish his performances of drag, Offeh's nude, male body acts as another tool with which normative gender can be challenged, disavowed and thrown aside, offering instead a reframing of his body, and those of the women that he performs, in order to challenge the fetishized black body in performance. With a focus on movement and the body, this chapter has sought to highlight how an engagement and overt exposure of the male body do not diminish the performance of drag but rather serve to complicate the performances and engagements with gender that Offeh offers his audiences. Through carefully choreographed moments of stillness, Offeh is able to draw attention to centuries of historical dust that lies on his body. By aligning his male body alongside elements of drag, Offeh creates performances which do not seek to impersonate the women, but rather to emulate their presence and celebrate their work.

As the song 'Slave to the Rhythm' draws to a close, Offeh, who has held and fallen out of Jones' arabesque numerous times, now covered in sweat as well as oil, steps out of the pose and picks up the leotard and heels that he had previously removed. He offers his audience a small bow and a 'thank you' before exiting the stage, gone before he has a chance to take in his audience's applause. I have framed my analysis of this performance as an homage to these women and their work, and it appears as though Offeh has left the applause for the women he has carefully drawn out of our embodied cultural memory.

Notes

1   A new photographic series, entitled *Lounging* (2017), has been developed by Offeh as an extension of his performance of *Covers*, which explores the depictions of black men on album covers lounging and reclining. This has been highlighted here to draw attention to the connections Offeh is making between black bodies and normative gender ideologies, engaging with not just female but also male bodies to explore representations of the black body in performance.

2   The black leotard also has clear connections to work and labour processes through one's rehearsing and training in the dance studio.

3   It is worth noting that Butler went on to clarify after *Gender Trouble* in *Bodies That Matter* (1993) that she was thinking of ballroom culture when she was considering the power of parody to both challenge and reconsolidate dominant gender norms (ibid.: 85). Thus, there are further connections to be drawn between Offeh's engagement with drag to challenge the 'naturalization' of gender through his naked body in this instance and his *Snap Like a Diva* workshops, which draw on the codified, gendered movement of the ballroom scene.

References

Barthes, Roland. (2000). *Mythologies*, trans. Annette Lavers. London: Vintage Random House.

Burt, Ramsay. (2009). 'The Performance of Unmarked Masculinity'. In Jennifer Fisher and Anthony Shay (eds), *When Men Dance: Choreographing Masculinities Across Borders*, Oxford: Oxford University Press, pp. 150–67.

Butler, Judith. (2007). *Gender Trouble: Feminism and the Subversion of Identity*. Oxon: Routledge.

Butler, Judith. (2011). *Bodies That Matter: On the Discursive Limits of 'Sex'*. Abingdon: Routledge.

Farrier, Stephen. (2016). 'That Lip-Synching Feeling: Drag Performance as Digging the Part'. In Alyson Campbell and Stephen Farrier (eds), *Queer Dramaturgies: International Perspectives on Where Performance Leads Queer*. Basingstoke: Palgrave MacMillan, pp. 192–209.

Gere, David. (2001). '29 *Effeminate Gestures*: Choreographer Joe Goode and the Heroism of Effeminacy'. In Jane C. Desmond (ed.), *Dancing Desires: Choreographing Sexualities On and Off Stage*. Wisconsin; London: The University of Wisconsin Press, pp. 349–81.

hooks, bell. (1994). 'Feminism Inside: Toward a Black Body Politic'. In Thelma Golden (ed.), *Black Male: Representations of Masculinity in Contemporary American Art*. New York: Whitney Museum of American Art, pp. 127–40.

Johnson, E. Patrick. (2001). '"Quare" studies, or (almost) everything I know about queer studies I learned from my grandmother'. *Text and Performance Quarterly*, vol. 21, no. 1, pp. 1–25.

Lepecki, André. (2006). *Exhausting Dance: Performance and the Politics of Movement*. London: Routledge.

Mercier, Clémentine. (2017). 'Brassages en Revue au Mac/Val'. *Libération*, 18 June. Available online: http://next.liberation. fr/arts/2017/06/18/brassages-en-revue-au-macval_1577674 (accessed 11 Jan. 2018).

Offeh, Harold. (2017). *Harold Offeh's Website*. Available online: http:// haroldoffeh.com/ (accessed 4 Jan. 2018).

Riggs, Marlon T. (1992). 'Unleash the Queen'. In Gina Dent (ed.), a project by Michele Wallace, *Black Popular Culture*. Seattle: Bay Press, pp. 99–105.

Royster, Francesca T. (2009). '"Feeling like a woman, looking like a man, sounding like a no-no:" Grace Jones and the performance of Strangé in the Post-Soul Moment'. *Women and Performance: A Journal of Feminist Theory*, vol. 19, no. 1, pp. 77–94.

Vittori, Giulia. (2016). 'A Mediation on Stillness: Ann Carlson's *Picture Jasper Ridge*'. *TDR/The Drama Review*, vol. 60, no. 2, pp. 83–102.

Willson, Jacki. (2008). *The Happy Stripper: Pleasures and Politics of the New Burlesque*. London: I.B.Tauris.

10

Gender Euphoria

Trans and Non-Binary Identities in Drag

Olympia Bukkakis

Oly Stash   When I no longer think about my gender being misperceived, where my desires and manifestation of my identity are viewed in the way that I intend them to. Like a running feedback loop of projected and received energy that match each other.

Cheryl   A state in which I have become my idealized gendered self entirely; any dissatisfaction with my gender identity has ceased.

Britney Smearz   Whoah. Let me ponder.

Collapsella   The moment you feel comfortable and 'whole' about yourself in your current body, even if it breaks binary definitions.

Oozing Gloop   I.COINED.IT.

Dollar Baby   The feeling of joy when one's gender is recognized correctly. It's a feeling that can be caused by being able to play with gender however one wants, a feeling of taking it lightly because it's lost its threat.

Bree Zilla   It is like existing in a space that is powerful and joyful, where all the complexities of my gender just float without me having to explain them or think about them.

Psoriasis   A celebration of individuality. It shouldn't be forced, it comes from within. It shouldn't be expected, it's part of a process that an oppressed individual might go through.

Victoria Sin   A utopian ideal, a point we can work towards and try to model with drag.

Rhyannon Styles   A unique feeling of immense pleasure.

Umlilo the Kwaai Diva   Being completely happy with the gender you are comfortable with on the spectrum. It's taken me a long time to really accept myself, my body, my flaws and everything in between, and now I've reached a '0 fucks given' approach to the way I see myself in relation to the world and that gives me a bit of gender euphoria from time to time. I don't know if gender euphoria can really exist for us in South Africa or other parts of the world where queer bodies are still a site of violence inflicted by society so it always creates a dysphoria because of the risk involved in loving yourself.

Kaye P. Rinha   The strong feeling that gender is something fluid and cheerful. It invites us to be free and creative with it instead of limiting us to borders.

ShayShay   It can be achieved in spaces where my gender doesn't matter at all. Where my clothes are not seen as representations of my gender. And the amount of make-up (or lack thereof) I have on is not perceived as a costume. My fluidity means that I am constantly mixing masculine and feminine traits. If I am in a state where I feel free from thinking about how others are interpreting my gender, that is my 'Gender Euphoria'.

(Definitions of 'gender euphoria', field research, 2017–18)

Since beginning to do drag in 2009 while studying for a bachelor's in gender studies and social theory, I have seen my work and the work of those around me through two very distinct lenses. There is the more practical side, which involves all the tattered wigs and dresses found on the street, all the toilet-cubicle change rooms and late nights with eyelashes torn off in inebriated, pop-fuelled ecstasy, all the trash reassembled into glamour. Then there is the theoretical side. Influenced by Judith Butler, Michel Foucault and a bunch of other queer thinkers, I have often considered my work and my identity as a drag queen as a way to navigate the world as a non-binary transfeminine person. I have developed this text over the course of two years in which I have taken steps to assert my gendered identity and these efforts have had a profound impact on my work. The ideas that I outline here have been developed as a drag lecture performance and then later as a (drag) contemporary dance piece. So, while this is a theoretical discussion of drag, those who do it, and the spaces in which it takes place, this text is also a product of my drag practice. It is both *about* and *of* drag.

First, a bit of background. The last few years have borne witness to an increasing visibility for trans people. Caitlyn Jenner's curated and sensationalized coming out, Chelsea Manning's struggle against governmental oppression and Laverne Cox's fame are just three examples of what has become a cultural moment in the West. This has been a catalyst for a public discussion around the limits and boundaries of trans and queer identities. Because of the very low public literacy when it comes to gender, many transfeminine commentators have had to publicly explain that they are not, in fact, drag queens.[1] This has led to a broader discussion online and in other media about gender, sexuality and the artistic and social meanings of drag practice. This discussion is long overdue and is still only in its early stages. At the same time, the meteoric rise of drag culture into the mainstream through popular television show *RuPaul's Drag Race* has led to a greater understanding of the existence of drag, but it has also caused a calcifying of what drag spaces and practices are and what they mean. This in turn has fostered a common assumption that there is a solid and stable boundary between drag and trans identities. That is to say, people now often understand a drag queen (or king) as a cisgender person who dresses as the 'opposite' sex for entertainment, art or fun, whereas a transgender person is someone whose gender does not align with the biological sex they were assigned at birth. This understanding has settled into a kind of binary opposition.

Given the scope and scale of these public discourses, a certain amount of simplification is understandable. But while it is true that collapsing this binary is both incorrect and potentially hurtful (many trans people have never had anything to do with drag), trans and drag identities (all identities really) are nowhere near as stable as all that. Non-binary and trans people have always been an integral part of drag communities, spaces and events, even if we have not been their most visible face. As one such person, I am interested in our experiences of, and contributions to, drag culture.

To get into this issue, it is important to use a variety of approaches. I am going to refer to Judith Butler. Her work, and that of many other queer theorists, has been invaluable in articulating queer experience and informing political action. But most queer lives happen outside academic spaces, so it is vital that these theories are grounded and relatable to trans and queer-lived experiences and material realities. Also, there are already enough people talking about us. I am interested in what we have to say. So, I have interviewed a number of trans and non-binary drag performers and event organizers from a variety of national, artistic, gender and sexual backgrounds. They are:

Britney Smearz   A Californian queen who along with Silk Worm makes up a 'duo of drag wives politically committed to the lolz'.

Psoriasis   A Berlin-based performer who has a politically charged drag practice that deals with 'harassment and abuse inside of the queer community and the very personal horror of living in between multiple cultures and identities' as well as videos of cats in space.

Oozing Gloop   A green monster and oracle from the UK who deals in 'pontificating, Lisa Simpson as the Lizard Queen and transgressive tattooing and tarot reading'.

Victoria Sin   A non-binary performer in London who is concerned with 'femininity as it exists and is idealised in the western world' in the context of its colonial histories.

Fox Pflueger   A quing living in Melbourne who uses 'camp lip-syncs of party bangers' to represent archetypes of femininity and masculinity.

Oly Stash   An assigned-female-at-birth (AFAB) non-binary performer from California living in Berlin whose practice 'exists in the context of drag, but is not always perceived as drag'. They make performances using characters such as The Androgynous Monarch 'to show that we don't need the binary and we never did'.

Bree Zilla   A performer in Melbourne with a genderqueer persona called Glitterfist, 'a filthy pleasure prophet using spoken word and striptease to lure audiences into a world where ambiguity is worshipped and pleasure is powerful'.

Dollar Baby   A 'post-drag slutty satanic witch embracing darker subjects like healing from trauma through BDSM, radical vulnerability, and loss of hope in the current political situation'. They were also a member of the Faux Real collective, which put on performance events centring trans, non-binary and women drag performers.

Kaye P. Rinha   A Berlin-based performer and organizer creating spaces where 'gender is not binary and where you are invited to love your body no matter how it looks'.

Collapsella   A model and gutter sensation from San Marino living in Berlin. Her work varies from 'acoustic-ish reinterpretations of mainstream hits with new lyrics focused on hedonism to spoken word pieces layered over hard techno music that aim to challenge Berlin's hyper-masculine culture'.

Cheryl   A middle-aged divorcée from Brooklyn with a heart of gold and a libido to match. She rewrites lyrics to songs and makes performances that deal with 'the refugee crisis, right-wing populism, 18th century opera, body positivity, existential crisis, musical theatre, *The Exorcist*, aquatic bestiality, food as a medium of performance art, DIY cinema, and all manner of figures of pop culture'.

Rhyannon Styles A trans woman from London who used drag as 'a tool to find an identity within the queer community'. Despite not having performed in drag since 2015, she now considers elements of drag practice one of the ways she cements and performs her female identity to the world.

Umlilo the Kwaai Diva A South African performer and musician who began performing in the drag circles of Cape Town. She has since moved into underground music circles that she feels have 'a better understanding of breaking the mould whereas traditionally queer drag spaces felt a little too boxed'. Her whole ethos has been 'to break through space as an interdimensional being that cannot be confined by genre, by space, by time, by gender, and by race'.

ShayShay A performer and organizer of The ShayShay Show living in London. They run events with a political focus and believe that 'there is something very powerful about the type of collective healing that can occur from performance'.

Nearly thirty years after Butler alluded to its subversive potential in *Gender Trouble* (1990), the ramifications of drag for gender in general are still hotly contested. In using drag performance as an example in this book, Butler pointed to the performative nature of gender and argued against the authenticity of sex as a biological truth and of gender as a cultural given. There was a backlash against this argument from many sides, in particular some radical feminists even argued that Butler's work helped give rise to a queer movement that was seeking to infiltrate and debilitate a lesbian feminist movement and politics. They argued that by muddying the waters of sex and gender Butler was doing the work of the patriarchy and distracting and confusing people from the real work waiting to be done.[2] Butler was holding up what they considered 'men parodying women' as feminist icons, sidelining 'real' women in their own fight.

So, the big debate in the 1990s was between a bunch of queers (inspired by Butler) arguing for a drag that destabilized gender and a bunch of radical feminists arguing that drag is an act of patriarchal mimicry. Butler addressed this controversy in her follow-up book, *Bodies That Matter* (1993), explaining that the simple act of putting on the clothes of a certain gender (e.g. through drag) does not constitute her idea of gender performativity. She writes, 'Drag is subversive to the extent that it reflects on the imitative structure by which hegemonic gender is itself produced and disputes heterosexuality's claim on naturalness and originality' (1993: 125). Oly Stash says, 'often the culture of drag (especially more conventional/mainstream drag) has a lot of internalized misogyny that makes it impossible to abolish some hierarchies between performers, especially those based on my perceived gender as one of the only AFAB performers in the community'. Psoriasis adds, 'I don't think [drag] directly affects my "gender experience" because there are too many gay dudes who do female impersonation drag that are still considered to be "the correct way to do drag" so when I show up in my black and white painted face and only little clothes, people will assume my gender to be male.' These are sentiments echoed by both Victoria Sin and Dollar Baby. Therefore, a distinction needs to be made here. Drag culture and spaces are not subversive just because they are places where one puts on the clothes and mannerisms of the 'opposite' sex. They need to play host to a drag that is critical in some way. In order to be political, drag needs politics. Or to put it another way, drag as a performance form in itself is neither feminist nor sexist. Rather, sexist drag performers are sexist and feminist drag performers are feminists. It is up to everyone else in the community to work out which is which and why. So in fact drag is neither the bogeyman of Butler's critics, nor is it necessarily always the radically subversive tool many queers claimed it to be on the basis of her writings.

In addressing the various readings and misreadings of *Gender Trouble*, Butler says,

> The bad reading goes something like this: I can get up in the morning, look in my closet, and decide which gender I want to be today. I can take out a piece of clothing and change my gender, stylize it, and then that evening I can change it again and be something radically other, so that what you get is something like the commodification of gender, and the understanding of taking on a gender as a kind of consumerism … when my whole point was that the very formation of subjects, the very formation of persons, *presupposes* gender in a certain way—that gender is not to be chosen and that 'performativity' is not radical choice and it's not voluntarism … Performativity has to do with repetition, very often the repetition of oppressive and painful gender norms to force them to resignify. This is not freedom, but a question of how to work the trap that one is inevitably in. (Kotz and Butler, 1992: 83–4)

The last sentence here is vital. If we cannot break free of the gender binary and go running in the fields streaming glitter and poppers fumes in our wake, what are we doing here? I asked my interviewees what drag makes possible for them because I was curious about how they were 'working the trap'.

Britney Smearz   It makes me feel comfortable looking hot. This sounds flippant, but it's not. Drag enables me to be open to a necessary and actually very affirming and loving form of objectification, without feeling like I'm voiceless or worthless.

Psoriasis   I don't know if I could say that I benefit from drag a lot regarding my everyday gender experience since it is dominated by white gays who pass as men out of drag, so I only have a few people I can talk or relate to.

Oozing Gloop   A way to express myself independent of medical narratives.

Victoria Sin   Drag allows me to explore parts of my gender which are not possible because of the body I exist within.

Fox Pflueger   Drag has helped me find my identity as a faggy trans boy who loves getting dressed up femme. I've always been a 'tomboy' or 'butch' but something about spending time backstage and on stage with queens has really helped me identify with my gender more than I could have imagined. Although I am often gendered in the feminine, e.g. 'Hey Girrrllll', I still feel my gender is more seen, heard and respected than in most other social situations.

Oly Stash   On a daily basis I would love to be perceived as an individual outside of the binary; however, I will probably always be read in relationship to the binary. In the context of drag, I get to be whatever gender I want.

Bree Zilla   Drag makes it possible for me to express more of my gender, makes my gender more visible, allows me to share it in ways I can't always do in everyday life. Drag makes possible the embodiment of how my gender feels, in a flesh meets fantasy kind of space.

Dollar Baby   Drag enables me to be the fierce woman I could be in a parallel universe. It makes me feel sexy and empowered and good about my femininity. It's partly a 'what would be if ...' kind of game that enables me to play with gender-based expectations that usually tend to give me gender dysphoria.

Collapsella   So far I think it has allowed me to blur my own gender lines further than I imagined.

Cheryl   It allows me to express my idealized gendered self in a public forum that not only accepts this presentation but encourages and funds it.

Rhyannon Styles   Drag allows me to navigate the world in a female identity. Drag was first and foremost my way of expressing to the world my desired gender. Before the use of pharmaceutical medication, female dressing was (and still is) a primary tool, allowing the realization of my female self.

Umlilo the Kwaai Diva   I think drag makes it easier to dress how I feel inside and to articulate what I'm inspired by at that moment in time. It helps me to also transcend traditional gender roles. I use my drag to blur the lines across the gender spectrum but not so much to emulate a certain gender.

What is notable about these responses is that they express a common understanding of the outside world as a place dominated by an oppressive gender binary, and also that the drag space (sometimes) offers a reprieve from that world. The ways in which this relief manifests are varied (and beautiful) but there is a common sense of the generative potential in the play that drag allows. A while ago I was having a discussion with Oozing Gloop about how drag affects and interacts with my gender and experience of gender dysphoria. We were talking about the medicalization of trans existence and how this offers an intelligible identity but also grounds the trans existence as one defined by suffering. While we were comparing this medicalized gender discourse to how gender operates in some drag spaces, Gloop suddenly rejected the idea that she suffered from dysphoria, spontaneously claiming 'I experience *gender euphoria*'. We were very excited by this. We wondered, if gender dysphoria is a medical term that can be deployed to achieve access to medical treatment and social recognition, what options would gender euphoria make available? Perhaps if gender dysphoria was what we experienced in our everyday lives being gendered as men, gender euphoria is what we make possible through drag.

Inspired by this idea and curious as to whether it held water with other drag performers, I asked my interviewees to define this term. Their responses make up the beginning of this essay. Cheryl's response strikes me as particularly succinct: 'A state in which I have become my idealized gendered self entirely.' Many of them related this concept to their experience of drag. This led me to believe that gender euphoria is the moment where the performer is not compelled to justify their various bodily contours and fixtures, the positioning of fat deposits and musculature. The drag artist in the drag space is (consciously) performing gender, and for a moment no one expects any of it to make sense. Bree Zilla puts it beautifully: 'hanging out with fellow performers or audience regulars I'm at ease even if I'm standing around wearing a gold dildo, hairy blue tits and a glowing mirrorball clit. No one questions or gives a shit.' Existing and working in drag spaces can offer a moment free from the compulsion to create a stable, solid and coherent gendered identity. Signifiers momentarily detach from the signified and there is no doctor, administrator, relative or thug demanding to know who you 'really' are.

I thought further about what this term could mean. Euphoria is a necessarily temporary state of heightened well-being. No one can stay euphoric forever and just like with drugs, coming down from gender euphoria can cause anxiety and depression; the walk home, the U-Bahn, the taxi are dangerous places and the high can vanish quickly. So, it is not a question of total liberation. But neither is it totally divorced from the outside world. Britney Smearz talks about drag as a kind of 'queer world making'. She says, 'the queer bar is a fantasy world with real implications'. In a similar vein Oozing Gloop explains, 'my drag basically is me dragging myself through life. There actually is no difference between it and my day-to-day, only one's on volume 2 and the other's 11. "Drag" is 11 [...] More and more I am abstracting it from bar culture and inserting it into spaces it has never been used, i.e. the countryside of East Anglia.' However, it is not an easy relationship; Cheryl notes, '[drag] never allows me to cross the line into reality; in the sense that though I find acceptance from the public around me, everyone knows it is merely an illusion. They all expect to me return to the gendered state that they are more accustomed to as soon as they have finished enjoying the performance.' I encountered a number of different relationships between these spaces and their outsides; Umlillo responded: 'I think [my drag] is actually me in an exaggerated form and it changes from space to space or whatever I'm feeling at that point. I live in a city where queers can't really walk around in the most fashion-forward fashion or you might get into trouble, so I do find myself editing myself depending on the space I'm going to just for safety purposes. If I had it my way I'd be in drag all day everyday.' So, in different contexts for different people, drag stretches out beyond its traditional spaces (or it does not) and this euphoria has a strong spatial component. This means that it is vital to understand not just the performances and identities that exist in drag but also the economies and the architecture of these spaces in which it takes place.

Practically, drag is a performance form that has a particularly strong relationship with its social context. It has grown out of a community that has often been marginalized and shunned, and while its current emergence into the mainstream has brought it a broader audience, it maintains a specific relevance to queer communities and spaces. Drag, even when done in a heteronormative zone, almost always refers back to a queer space. The broader relationship between queer politics and the materialist left is beyond the scope of this essay, but Nancy Fraser offers an important insight when she insists on the necessity of 'situating [post-structuralist and queer theory] in relation to macro-sociological structural theorizing, including political economy and institutional analysis' (1998). This is obviously a tall order for a small-scale drag organizer, but in this context it is worthwhile to look at what it means in material terms to create a space where gender euphoria can take place.

To better understand my own experience organizing the queer performance platform *Get Fucked* (which the reader can catch a glimpse of in the accompanying photo, Figure 10.1), I asked some trans and non-binary drag event organizers some questions specifically related to how they create these spaces and I noticed three main factors: accessibility, discourse and consciously providing space. Dollar Baby, ShayShay, Kaye P. Rinha and Cheryl all acknowledged that there is a tension between making these events sustainable by taking enough money at the door and ensuring

Figure 10.1 Olympia Bukkakis at *Get Fucked* in 2016. Photo: Brigid Cara.

that the space remains accessible to queer and trans communities that are often economically disadvantaged. Cheryl and ShayShay both mentioned advertising a certain door fee but having a policy of not turning anyone away for lack of funds as a way of resolving this. In terms of accessibility for people with disabilities (for example, through wheelchair-accessible venues and interpreters for the hearing impaired), Kay P. Rinha and Dollar Baby both spoke about the difficulties in accommodating this while at the same time maintaining financial accessibility. The fact remains that even with a large amount of unpaid labour on the part of the organizers these spaces need to be financially viable in order to be sustainable, and very often this places restraints on how inclusive they can be. Therefore, a considered attempt to juggle constraints in terms of funding and accessibility is a key factor in terms of maintaining these spaces and events.

Another important factor that arose from the interviews is the discourse that takes place. ShayShay writes, 'I want my show to be a safe haven from the crazy world … but I am sure to engage in discussions about the very real troubles of our world and the threats to our communities.' Cheryl makes a similar point, explaining that her events 'are very much separate from the outside world; aware of its existence and continually engaging with it from a critical standpoint'. So, a key element of their events is that they are places where (leftist) discourse is encouraged and facilitated. This can include discussions or performances that problematize the conventions of drag.

Dollar Baby also stresses the need to provide space for people who are usually not centred in many drag spaces, such as women, trans people and people of colour. By explicitly stating that Faux Real was a space for women, trans and non-binary performers, they wanted to 'create a space for people that are not only "accepted" in a framework that is not made for them [such as traditional gay male-dominated drag spaces], but one where they can co-create their own space – literally TAKE up space'. Cheryl and ShayShay also indicated that the audience at their events are encouraged to take part in the event through dressing up and participating in performances, and in this way the community is also provided with a space to explore their gender presentation.

These strategies all contribute to a specific mode of drag that is common to many of the performers I interviewed. The kinds of spaces outlined here play host to a drag that does not seek to imitate binary gender (as contestants of *RuPaul's Drag Race* are encouraged to), but explode it. As Dollar Baby puts it, 'Drag done by trans and non-binary people seems to automatically challenge everything that drag stands for. "Passing" as the other gender isn't a goal because the relationship between one's own body and "the other gender" is already way too complex for it to work out.' This contradiction of being unable to dress as the 'opposite gender' generates conditions which can give rise to a multiplicity of gendered expression, and this is where the radical potential of drag lies – not in attacking the gender binary out of a commitment to a political principle, but rather in constructing situations and paradigms that make our lives and our selves possible. In creating and proliferating drag spaces where 'natural' sex or gender is not assumed but problematized, we make room for a kind of democratic playfulness that can be used to create new ways of gendered being: we take the first steps in becoming ourselves. We begin to build a home in which we might comfortably be able to live. Still it is important not to valorize or overemphasize the political importance of this play. Structural heterosexism and transphobia will not be toppled by drag alone, and many drag spaces remain inaccessible or hostile to trans and non-binary people. In outlining the utility of drag as a tool and space for liberation, I am not trying to suggest that this is a complete political programme or even a movement. Very often this is an isolated and rare phenomenon. However, if we work hard at these spaces, if we ensure that these spaces are as accessible and safe as possible, if those who spend time in them and watch the shows we create become our allies, perhaps this can become an important step in building a movement towards the mass proliferation of these homes: a kind of movement for social housing, so that every person could have a comfortable place to exist.

Notes

1   Some examples of this discussion may be accessed at https://thinkprogress. org/the-quiet-clash-between-transgender-women-and-drag-queens-297a9da4c5f6/ and https://everydayfeminism.com/2014/04/trans-women-not-drag-queens/.
2   An example of this view can be found in Jeffreys (2006).

References

Butler, Judith. ([1991] 1999). *Gender Trouble: Feminism and the Subversion of Identity*. New York: Routledge.
Butler, Judith. (1993). *Bodies that Matter: On the Discursive Limits of 'Sex'*. New York: Routledge.
Jeffreys, Sheila. (2006). *Unpacking Queer Politics: A Lesbian Feminist Perspective*. Cambridge: Polity Press.
Kotz, Liz and Butler, Judith. (1992). 'The Body You Want: Liz Kotz interviews Judith Butler'. *Artforum*, vol. 31, no. 3, pp. 82–9.
Fraser, Nancy. (1998). 'A Future for Marxism'. *New Politics*, vol. 6, no. 24. Available online: http://nova.wpunj.edu/newpolitics/issue24/fraser24.htm

11

The Tranimal

Throwing Gender out of Drag?

Nick Cherryman

Drag is, for many, a way to highlight the flaws inherent in the social construction of sex and gender – the gender fluidity inherent in drag performance emphasizes the behaviour disconnect between social expectations and regulations, and the reality of the performance of gender itself. However, while this suggests that gender and sex are absolutely integral to the drag performer, and to mainstream drag artists, the tranimal style of drag performance is one which, while aware of the gendered nature of typical drag, makes an explicit effort to ignore it.[1] While seemingly contradictory – this attempt at explicit ignorance – this attitude reflects how the tranimal style and aesthetic embrace gender through the very refusal to engage with it in socially accepted ways. Judith Butler, in *Bodies that Matter*, describes drag as 'subversive to the extent that it reflects on the imitative structure by which hegemonic gender is itself produced and disputes heterosexuality's claim on naturalness and originality' (1993: 125). Butler is referring to how the drag performer is able to highlight the lack of innate essence that is often socially assumed to be part of someone's biological sex as it is performed and perpetuated in heteronormative culture. That is, being biologically male, for example, does not necessarily mean that the subject behaves in a masculine or 'male' way as dictated by social norms. It is the social constructions of masculinity or femininity that are assigned to the biological body and thus repeated in a *'stylized repetition of acts'* that dictate the regulatory behaviours that control subjects' bodies (1988: 519, italics in original). In their performances, the tranimals attempt to work outside the social structures that regulate gender in an attempt to undermine the absurdity of these very constructs. Despite this, there is an awareness of their inability to fully act outside the structural nature of gender, and the movement negotiates these structures of gender through 'chaotic freedom of expression' (Lecaro, 2018), and despite working with the aim to break free from these rigid structures of presentations of gender, it is unable to fully ever escape hegemonic gender readings.

The tranimal movement was founded in 2008 by Austin Young, Squeaky Blonde and Fade-Dra Phey and conceived as a participatory performance artwork, first shown at Machine Project Gallery in Los Angeles, in which 'visitors enter a Tranimal-assembly-line where they undergo a transformation with after-portraits by Austin Young' (*Confuse-a-Tron*, 2011). Museum visitors enter into the exhibition and invited artists, alongside Young, Blonde and Fade-Dra, add another aspect to the visitors' look, so the final look is a mélange of artistic views with no singularly created aesthetic vision. Young, meanwhile, states that 'new looks [were created] using soft sculpture and found objects with an intentional aesthetic to subvert ideas of beauty and gender' (email conversation with author, 2019).

Mathu Anderson, the make-up artist famous for creating the iconic look and style that helped make RuPaul famous and for being an early member of the Club Kids, was an invited collaborator in 2010 at the Hammer Museum event and describes the archetypal tranimal as 'a dirty, vicious, available drag queen. They work with whatever's at hand. They have no scruples, no morals, and no guiding aesthetic voice other than "it works"' (*Damiana*, 2010).[2] Others, such as drag queen Willam Belli, describe the aesthetic, in what are notably gender-neutral terms, as 'punk + clown + avant-garde = tranimal' (2016: 19). *Queerty*, a gay lifestyle and news website describes it this way:

> Tranimal: A.K.A. 'terrorist-drag'. Tranimal drag deconstructs fashion and makeup, often using found objects, elements of surrealism and mixes of performance art, punk rock, racial and social issues. These drag queens often purposely use unkempt wigs and clothing. Most still hide male attributes, but don't necessarily shave or tuck [hide the male genitals], creating a constant push and pull between the genders. (Turner, 2014)

Austin Young cites the look as being based on the 'drag style of Squeaky Blonde and Fade-Dra... and has roots in [Young's] experiences with photographing Leigh Bowery and the San Francisco and New York Drag Scene in the 80s and 90s' (email conversation with the author, 2019).[3] Jer Ber Jones, another invited tranimal artist at the Berkeley Art Museum and Hammer Museum, focuses on deliberately distancing the movement from mainstream drag. In an interview for *Vice* magazine, he describes the origins and the name of the movement:

> The animal part of the name is purely from seeing someone working one of those more theatrical looks and thinking that they look like a wild animal among all the pedestrian trannies who just look like *RuPaul's Drag Race*

contestants. I'm very into letting yourself become as ugly as fuck, and appreciating the ugliness of mainstream culture, like bigoted Christianity, Shrek, Ugg boots, and the Martha Stewart lifestyle. All that is ugly and mundane, but also kind of beautiful and mesmerizing. (Clifton, 2012)[4]

For Jer Ber Jones, the definition of tranimal drag involves removing oneself from the existing structures of mainstream drag, which are, themselves, already distanced from the socially accepted rules that regulate gender. Instead, Jer Ber Jones uses bestial language not only to distance his performance from human readings of gender but to remove an anthropocentric view on what can be accepted as drag in the first place. The removal or displacement of human gendered signifiers on the bodies of the tranimal performers has the potential to disrupt the gendered reading of the subject entirely for the viewer. The human viewer's expected reading of a human body is fractured into several parts that no longer make a 'whole'; that is, although individual elements of the performer have recognizable elements of a human body, they do not work as an entire body itself. Recognizable body parts play a role in the look, although the overall 'body' of the performer is rendered unreadable (see Figure 11.1).

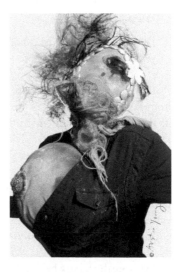

Figure 11.1 Left: Austin Young, untitled tranimal portrait, 2011, Tranimal Workshop at *Confuse-a-Tron*, Berkeley Art Museum, curated by Mark Allen. Right: Austin Young, untitled tranimal portrait, 2011, Tranimal Workshop at *TRANSylvania Mania*, curated by Darin Klein, Hammer Museum, Los Angeles. Tranimal Workshop is a participatory artwork by Squeaky Blonde, Fade Dra Phey and Austin Young and guest artists.

For Jer Ber Jones, drag is not necessarily restricted to the realm of the human, and he reduces his reading of drag down to the most minimal of aspects. For example, in an interview on the *Transformations* series with James St James he says:[5]

James St James (JSJ)   You disappeared off the face of the Earth.

Jer Ber Jones (JBJ)   I went to the desert to reclaim my spirit.

JSJ   …and this was about two years ago?

JBJ   Yeah.

JSJ   And you are in a house, by yourself…

JBJ   By myself. Where I can sing and dance and record at 3 o'clock in the morning if I want to.

[…]

JBJ   During Christmas I wrote Lady Bunny an email and said that I can get away with doing drag with just one simple nail now […] Drag became minimal and…

JSJ   And you pulled everything back […] and you are now down to just one nail…

JBJ   One red nail; instead of corsets and make-up. […] For a couple of years now it's come down to just one drag nail. (*Transformations*, 2015)[6]

In reducing his drag down to its most basic elements and isolating himself from society, Jer Ber Jones removed the performative element of drag (in its theatrical sense) on which the queens in, say, *Paris is Burning*, *RuPaul's Drag Race* or *Dragula* thrive. The audience that the queens rely on is removed entirely and drag develops into a singular and insular experience. In this instance, drag becomes about how the performers read themselves, no longer reliant on the contextual support that surrounds the audience-reliant queens. In doing so, the gendered elements of the performance are removed entirely. Jer Ber Jones and James St James discuss the theoretical background of this in the same *Transformations* interview:

JSJ   So, the theory behind it is…?

JBJ   Availabilism…

JSJ   It's a constructivist [*sic*], where you take bits and pieces – a stream of consciousness – and it becomes part of who you are. (*Transformations*, 2015)

In the same interview, it is revealed that the materials that Jer Ber Jones is going to use to 'transform' James St James come from two 'garbage bags full of trash' that he brought to the filming studio. Jer Ber Jones creates his outfits from 'trash', which look chaotically constructed but have been meticulously built, and he refers to shows where he created headpieces out of old parking tickets he found. Through these types of construction, the tranimal performer has the potential to shock anyone witnessing the creations, be it an audience member, a casual observer or even the performer doing drag. Because audiences are not entirely sure what they are seeing at first glance, this drag created from 'trash' and other found items – i.e. availabilism – can shock. With the tranimal performer, instead of reading the drag performance as an explicit presentation playing with gendered stereotypes, the audience are enjoined to re-evaluate how the performance of gender and its stereotypes are constructed in the first place.

Given the fluidity of the terminology used in both scholarship and drag performance and the instability of the definitions themselves, such as the shifting roles of drag house mothers and fathers and the pronouns drag queens often use to define themselves and others, these performers occupy a 'non-place' – or perhaps a non-specific but fluid space – on the field of gender. Therefore, I am reluctant to place or even accurately define a specific location on a spectrum or terrain of gender, as the instability of these roles means that any placement on these measures of gender risks redefining and re-taxonimizing these subjects – placing them on another locus of gender definition, and into an altogether different category as restrictive as the very social boundaries of gender these drag artists flaunt in the first place. It is the very state of being, created by the liminality of the performances themselves, that creates the space I term the queer-'other'. This space exists in the gap between performance spaces, be it ballroom, nightclub, online and/or broader society, and is a space that is often in flux and paradox. If the tranimals exist in this space – in a state of liminality – there can be no innateness of being, much as Butler posits, and the state of being is instead constructed by the very state of flux that exists. That is, by being in a place of instability the performers then adopt the new identity of instability, which paradoxically becomes their most stable identity. Such a reification of instability exists in the interpersonal relations between the queens and contextual scenarios that surround them. The performance of the queens on and offstage and their interactions with each other (such as the role of house mothers and fathers) shape this state of flux. The tranimal movement of drag works both within and without this queer-'other' in that they deconstruct and reshape the way the subject is able to visualize gender in the first place – an ossification of gendered constructs alongside socially constructed stereotypes of gender.

This subversion of stereotypes resists typical readings of gender in the performance of the tranimal, which stands in contrast to mainstream drag. Owing to the proliferation of discourses of drag in recent years, in no small part because of the success of Emmy award–winning *RuPaul's Drag Race*, a particular expectation of who and what a drag queen is has arisen. Much as mainstream drag comes to represent *another* gender altogether removed from, yet integrally linked to, the social idea of the gender binary and of the codification of gendered acts, the 'drag queen gender' that exists in the queer-'other' has congealed and reified its position in society's expectations when presented in the media. RuPaul, for example, in response to accusations that drag is an impersonation of women, wrote on Twitter, 'I do not impersonate females! How many women do you know who wear seven inch heels, four foot wigs, and skin tight dresses?' (RuPaul 2013). While not as solid as the regulatory structures surrounding 'male' and 'female', I argue that there is a social expectation that the drag queen must fall into one of two very broad categories of performance. The first is the queen who attempts to look aesthetically pleasing in a realistically feminine way (according to social expectations of femininity). They have a focus on fashionable costumes and looking convincingly socially feminine through clever make-up (sometimes problematically referred to as 'fishy').[7] The second category often aims for less 'realistic' or naturalistic depictions of femininity, and it embraces the duplicitous nature of performing genders different from one's own for the purposes of comedy, often acknowledging the fact they are a biologically assigned male dressed as a drag queen.[8] However, for both of these categories of queens, performances of gender remain, for those observing, as just performances – albeit influenced by the performer's out-of-drag personage. The viewer acknowledges the skill or the quality of the performance, but the performance always remains tempered by the fact that it is 'fake', that is, it is still a performance where the main focus is on the blurring of the social readings of gender binaries in the first place, regardless of the intent of the performer. Therefore, the tranimal's disengagement with gender is as a result of a heightened social awareness of what drag may constitute, and the fact that social expectations of drag rely on the performance blurring or reinscribing perceptions of gender for the audience. It ties tranimals into a paradoxical loop from which they cannot escape: by attempting to disengage from gender as a part of their performance, more attention is drawn to gender than had they embraced it in their creations and performance in the first place; it becomes noticeable through their lack of engagement with gender.

Because of the social expectations carried with 'drag' as a concept or social idea, one of the most immediate questions an audience asks, when observing the tranimal performer, is what gender am I supposed to be looking at, and what gender is the performer underneath? This is further complicated by the involvement of the audience as models in the participatory performance 'factory-line', as the performer may conceptualize themselves in one way, and the viewer of the performer in another way altogether different. In so doing, the performer pushes (consciously or unconsciously) for a reconceptualization of the drag performance space for the audience as a place to 'genderfuck' or a place where the viewer would expect to look at gender being played with, to one where it ceases to be, or at least attempts to cease to be, concerned with gender at all.[9] This disruption, or perhaps undermining, of the structures that govern gender and the drag performative arena changes the way one must read tranimal performers in the first place. With this in mind, how can one read a tranimal drag performance as gendered if there is no clear evidence of a 'stable' gender originally? Does this mean it is possible to do genderless drag if the very social structures of gender are removed from the drag performance in the first place?

The removal of the gendered structures of tranimal drag comes about owing to the apparent genderless/gender-obscured nature of the performer on stage; that is, the drag performance is attempting to function outside socially regulated readings of gender. By this, it is often hard to tell if the tranimal is biologically assigned male or female as their bodies are so distorted by the effect of the drag itself, and thus it becomes meaningless to even attempt to investigate gender or sex (as it is socially constructed) in the first place.[10] This stands in contrast to the drag queen who may strive for realism in their performance, as it is consciously dependent on gender stereotypes being distorted – that is, the performance is appreciated (at least partly) because of the skill employed in deceiving the eye. Alternatively, for example, a trans-based performer may rely on the audience being very aware that it is a trans-influenced performance to make the very point the performer attempts to elucidate.[11] In contrast, the only reference to gender in some cases of the tranimal movement is the occasional use of the term 'drag queen' and what that connotes. This term is muddled, however, among different collaborators, with some embracing and others dismissing the term. This leads one to analyse the effect that the tranimal performer has on ways to theorize gender – often through extreme exaggeration of gendered body parts to the point where they are laughably absurd or weirdly misplaced (see Figure 11.2).

The displacement or complete removal of gendered signposts on the drag performers' bodies draws focus to, and critiques, the very social characteristics that the audience use socially to define and read gender, readdressing both social conceptions of gender and what it means to be a drag performer or performance artist. While mainstream drag is still often (inaccurately) solely

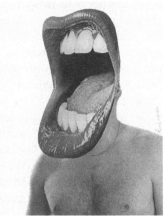

Figure 11.2 Left: Austin Young, *Portrait of Squeaky Blonde*, 2013. Right: Austin Young, untitled tranimal portrait, 2018. Tranimal Workshop at 'Sleepless: Free Radicals' at Dorothy Chandler Pavilion, Los Angeles, curated by Fulcrum Arts. Tranimal Workshop is a participatory artwork by Squeaky Blonde, Fade Dra Phey and Austin Young and guest artists.

perceived as the male subject dressed in a feminine way, the tranimals render the very reading of gender as not only impossible but futile. There is a double irony included in the performance of the tranimal for the social reading of 'drag': the first is the expectation of performing the socially 'incorrect' gender ('mainstream drag'); the second is being unrecognizable as performing this wrong gender in the first place. That is, the single irony of 'typical' drag performance is undermined by the very difficulty of reading tranimal drag in a gendered way; one is unsure of the gender and sex of the performer, and thus the gender confusion is doubly ironic as the performance becomes unrecognizable in the role of fulfilling the gender-blurring society expects in drag. This attempted reading of the tranimal body disrupts the normative reading of the gendered subject, and the viewers' expectations are jarred by what they observe.

The question remains, however, whether or not the tranimal movement is able to function within the framework Butler posited before, that 'drag is subversive to the extent that it reflects on the imitative structure by which hegemonic gender is itself produced and disputes heterosexuality's claim on naturalness and originality' (1993: 125). Tranimalism does fall under this theoretical reading of drag by Butler, but in a different way than she originally meant, given that tranimal drag arose post publication of *Bodies that Matter* (1993). The idea of availabilism and the creation from apparent detritus, the concept where the work or performance is constructed using the materials that are immediately available to the performer when creating the performance, allows a reconceptualization of drag performance as a piece of gender subversion. By only taking what is available right at that moment, the movement indicates the way that society frames subjects in social situations as not only about gender, in contrast to the focus of 'typical' drag. By attempting to step outside the structures that govern and regulate the binaries of gender that inform mainstream drag, and within which the queer-'other' oscillates and is fluid, the tranimal tries to redefine the rules that structure the arena of performance in the first place. The tranimal is, through this aesthetic reclaiming of society around them, able to comment on the social readings of gender itself – they are able to draw attention to all they like or dislike and comment on it through the drag itself (or what Jer Ber Jones called the 'ugly as fuck' or 'Martha Stewart' lifestyle) and embrace it to make it mesmerizing.

To argue that social commentary and performance of tranimal drag are completely removed from gender would be a mistake, however. In much the same way that the very nature of drag implies a gender-based performance, gender performativity is so enmeshed in the social structures that surround the subject that gender is inevitably involved in the performance, even if there is an attempt to deliberately distance oneself from it. Even if the subject were able to divorce themselves entirely from the gendered structures that surround them from their creation, the projection of that performance to others (be it via an email discussing a single nail as a form of drag or a series of photographs in a workshop) means that the tranimal is once again inserted into the heteronormative matrix of socialized gender. The very act of viewing the tranimal reinserts them into the gendered structures of society – the performance for a viewer inevitably means that the viewer reads them from these structures themselves. For example, the act of a single fingernail being painted red may not be innately gendered in the eyes of the performer, but the viewing of it by others draws on the social structures of which the viewer is part: social readings of nail polish and the colour red immediately link the nail polish to gendered readings and queries whether or not it asserts or subverts the gendered structures ('Is that a man?' 'Is that a feminine activity?' 'What does it mean that they've only painted one fingernail?'). The inability to disconnect social readings of gender by the audience or reader is apparent in all the tranimal performances. The viewer searches for glimpses of recognizable or definitive displays of gender, such as chest hair and beards – masculine traits – or exaggerated lips and breasts – feminine traits – and attempts to reconceptualize these, sometimes blurring the two in the same images. One feature that carries through the tranimal images, however, is the blurring or distortion of the face. Jer Ber Jones describes it thus:

> Yeah, the stretched and torn pantyhose over the face is probably the key tranimal look. I never liked it, but considering a lot of us queens are actually pretty butch dudes, and we like our facial hair, it's a good way to cover that up without having to shave your face clean. They work particularly well for the guys who would otherwise be scrubbing 26 layers of paint and lipgloss off their faces to become a dude again so they can go out and turn tricks [participate in sex work]. (Clifton, 2012)

The action of distorting the face warps or belies the features of the tranimal performance without distorting the performer's actual features underneath. It grants a temporality to the degendering of the performer, but in so doing acknowledges that the performer themself must return to a world where society reads subjects as gendered – that is, they wish to keep their facial hair because they are 'butch dudes' and hope to prostitute themselves to others as socially read men later in the evening, in this example. Even if the tranimal is able to subvert the typical gendered readings of mainstream drag, they are tied outside their tranimal performance by the performativity of gender in mainstream society and are unable to avoid the full degendering nature hoped for by the tranimals. Instead, as one can become a tranimal and then 'become a dude again', the embodiment remains as ephemeral as the performance itself.

The destabilization of gender and performative norms is taken to an extreme through the tranimal movement. Through deliberate attempts to deconstruct and question what drag is, they are able to redefine how the gendered subject is viewed. Their attempt at removing gender from the performance of drag altogether leaves the viewer unsure of the performance they view. However, the viewers themselves remain as gendered subjects and society remains structured around gendered norms. In much the same way that the queens in *Paris is Burning* rely on the audience to read and judge their success of performing gender accurately, the tranimal is reliant on the viewer struggling to read their gender accurately; that is, tranimalism relies on resisting the viewers' attempts to solidify their reading in one particular gendered position. This complicates the performance, as the viewer of the tranimal is pushed to re-evaluate what they are looking at and search for gender in the performance. The lack of immediate gender signifiers and the subsequent search for sexual characteristics forces the tranimal back into the gendered structures they are pushing against. With this said, while the tranimal is unsuccessful at removing gender from their performance as they require a viewer, they are successful in forcing a refocusing of what gender constructions the audience read onto the subject. So, while drag that exists outside gendered readings and subjectivity is a theoretical ideal and one that can never (at least for the contemporary viewer) be fully realized in practice, the theory and analysis behind the tranimal performance can still act as a useful tool for querying performances of gender.

Tranimal drag is, then, able to force reconsiderations of gender, in both the theatrical sense and the Butlerian reading of gender as a performative sequence of acts (conscious and unconscious). Gender is broken down and then reconstructed simultaneously through the tranimal performer. While the nature of the theatrical drag performance is one that is ultimately ephemeral and destined to end, the theory that this work has aimed to elucidate points out the very ephemeral nature of gender in the first place. To pass as convincingly gendered in society and then remove the very structures that force the gendering in the first place is not to remove gender altogether, but it is able to point out the liminality of the gender performance itself. Thus the subject can perform 'man' and 'woman', or even another gender altogether – one built on resisting social binaries within the queer-'other'. However, society has yet to reach a point where the subject is able to convincingly perform as genderless. The subject is permanently forced into gendered structures by those around them, and the viewers of the performer define the gendered nature of the performance, regardless of the performer themselves. Although the tranimal pushes the boundaries of gender for theoretical enquiry, and attempts to step out of these constructs of gender, they are not entirely successful. They do, however, pave the way for more experimental types of drag and open the dialogue between viewer and performer in conceptualising upcoming constructions and conceptions of drag.

Notes

1   Mainstream drag, that is, the style of drag performance that rests, most commonly, in the social consciousness of what 'drag' means – often comedy and with a strong focus on drag as a man in women's clothes. Although drag obviously encompasses much broader categories than this limited

definition, socially it remains the most common interpretation of what 'drag' is.

2   The Club Kids were a group of club personalities in New York in the late 1980s to early 1990s and included, most notably, Michael Alig, RuPaul, James St James, Amanda Lepore and others. They became famous for being able to throw good parties, and clubs would often hire them to appear in the evenings for promotional purposes.

3   Leigh Bowery was a performance artist known for his outlandish costumes and as a club-night promoter. Famous in his own right as an icon of the club scene of the mid to late 1980s, his shows pushed the boundaries of taste at the time, and he often garnered attention owing to his controversial performances. Fade-Dra Phey and Squeaky Blonde clearly draw on the aesthetics of Leigh Bowery in their own performances.

4   The use of the term 'tranimal' has been interpreted by some as damaging given the combination of the words and the complicated and often injurious history behind the word 'tranny'. This term is, in some respects, historical, and the original founders of the movement – Young, Blonde and Fade-Dra – have not specified exactly the origins of the term publicly. The word itself remains controversial in drag communities and, while acknowledging the toxic and hurtful history of the word, I mean to engage with it academically in the context quoted. I am aware that while parts of the trans+ community have reclaimed the word in an attempt to detoxify it (as other LGBTQ+ communities have with other slurs), not all members of the community are comfortable with it and it remains a deeply problematic word for some, rooted in a difficult history.

5   *Transformations* is a series where James St James invites make-up artists and drag performers to 'transform' him into a signature look while he interviews them.

6   Jer Ber Jones also has an entire YouTube channel based on the concept of a single red nail encapsulating drag called 'NailTapper' – where the camera focuses almost exclusively on the single red nail he has painted pointing at relatively innocuous things such as pictures of meat in fast food restaurants ('Lucky Meat') or on Christmas ornaments ('Caressing Christmas') with orgasmic moans in the background.

7   Examples of this include Courtney Act, April Carrion, Miss Fame and RuPaul.

8   Examples of this include Lily Savage, Bob the Drag Queen, Bianca Del Rio, Lady Bunny and Ginger Minj.

9   Genderfuck: the term used for styles of drag that, arguably, do the opposite of tranimalism – i.e. draw the attention even more explicitly to the gendered nature of the performance rather than ignore it completely. Examples of genderfucking include performers such as Conchita Wurst (also known as 'The Bearded Drag Queen'), who won the 2015 Eurovision Song Contest, the British drag queen Le Gateau Chocolat, and political drag movements such as the Sisters of Perpetual Indulgence, who dress up in nuns' habits and often work on promoting safe sex and AIDS awareness.

10   Despite drag movements that also push, pull and play with the expectations
     of 'mainstream' drag (see bioqueens or Club Kid–inspired drag as
     examples), the deliberate attempt to nullify the structures of gender in the
     tranimal is notable. These styles of drag are becoming more well known
     and there is an undeniable shift in focus in conceptions of 'mainstream'
     drag from more 'traditional' drag to that which twists gender away from
     expected drag conventions.

11   Examples of trans-specific performances and performers include UK
     performer Kate O'Donnell, founder of *Transcreative* performance company,
     and Brooklyn-based transmasculine drag king K. James.

References

Belli, Willam. (2016). *Suck Less: Where There's a Willam, There's a Way*. New
     York: Hachette Book Group.

Butler, Judith. (1988). 'Performative Acts and Gender Constitution: An Essay
     in Phenomenology and Feminist Theory'. *Theatre Journal*, vol. 40, no. 4,
     pp. 519–31.

Butler, Judith. (1993). *Bodies that Matter*. New York: Routledge.

Clifton, Jamie. (2012). 'Why Be a Tranny When You Can Be a Tranimal?', *Vice
     Fashion*, 26 June. Available online: https://www.vice.com/en_uk/article/
     ex7wkw/tranimals-jer-ber-jones (accessed 30 March 2017).

Confuse-a-Tron. (2011). Part of Machine Project. Words taken from
     advertisement of event. Available online: http://machineproject.
     com/192011/workshops/at-the-berkeley-art-museum-mp-confuse-a-
     tron/(accessed 12 Feb. 2018).

'Damiana at the Tranimal Workshop at the Hammer Museum' (2010).
     dailyfreakshow YouTube channel. Available online: https://www.youtube.
     com/watch?v=WpjsTzUS7Vg (accessed 12 Jan. 2018).

James St. James and Jer Ber Jones. (2015). *Transformations* YouTube
     series for WOWPresents. Available online: https://www.youtube.com/
     watch?v=3qYsCHTMF8w&t=76s (accessed 4 Jan. 2018).

Lecaro, Lina. (2018), 'Austin Young's Tranimals Come Out after Dark', *LA
     Weekly*, 31 July. Available online: http://www.laweekly.com/arts/austin-
     youngs-tranimals-come-out-after-dark-9708410 (accessed 3 Aug. 2018).

RuPaul. (2013), *RuPaul's Drag Race* [Twitter feed], 3 June. Available online at:
     https://twitter.com/RuPaulsDragRace/status/341638123953995776

RuPaul's Drag Race (2009–Present), [TV programme], USA: Logo TV.

Turner, Paige. (2014). 'The 11 Most Common Drag Queen Styles',
     Queerty, 3 June. Available online at: https://www.queerty.com/11-common-
     drag-queen-styles-20140603 (accessed 6 Jan. 2018).

12

Drag Kings and Queens of Higher Education

Mark Edward

From drudgery to dragulous

Throughout my teenage years in the 1980s I was a school refuser. My only qualifications on 'officially' leaving school included a vocabulary of acidic wit to help survive daily homophobic assaults (more of which below, but see Edward, 2014a, 2015), a leather bomber jacket, bleached blond and blue hair, and an ability to recite every word of the 'in your face' 'Tales of Taboo' sung by the American performance artist Karen Finley. I delighted in playing this, rather loudly, on my stereo. I am from a small semi-rural village outside Wigan in the UK. One of the major local public houses of the day, Henry Africa's, was located just a mile up the road from my family home and primarily focused on working-class entertainment and a good night out.[1] At the age of 16 I began to sneak in through the back door. I discovered an underworld of cheap glamour, cabaret dancers and drag queens. This northern fun pub celebrated my emerging gay identity and delighted my senses with all things queerly spectacular and kitsch.[2] Here, I met the established drag queen Chris D' Bray, who became my mentor and drag mother and gave me the drag name Tallulah Tongue.[3] The art of drag was handed down from Chris, a more experienced drag queen; I became a drag 'daughter' (see Farrier, 2017). Learning the ropes of drag was a lengthy progression of becoming and could not be easily fast-tracked, nor easily accessed in that geographical or historical context. During this era there were no overnight YouTube sensations or drag Instagram stars. There was no click of a button to an online tutorial. The skills had to be learned through mentorship – make-up, tucking, wig styling, sourcing affordable jewellery, lip-syncing and padding – learned by eventually moving up or down in the working-class northern pubs and clubs circuit. There existed a ranking of drag, a sort of drag 'hairarchy'.[4]

> Hairarchy is a play on the word hierarchy where drag has a culture of hand me downs or 'drag me downs'. Aside from passing on routines, make-up tips and discarded garments there is an unnoticed mentorship that occurs in each drag performer. True professional drag queens, like academics, always reference their source material within performance. If they do not (unlike academics) they are often bitched and bad word is spread around the sub-culture. (Edward, 2014b: 159)

During my early days of drag I gave some performances for free under the watchful eyes of various matriarchal drag personas, who were critical yet offered much guidance after my performance had been surveyed by public spectatorship. Drag, in some ways, had begun to save me as a young gay teenager. During my school days and early teens, I was plagued by homophobic abuse and subsequent depression and anxiety, resulting in medication – I survived eventually by becoming more resilient, as opposed to experiencing less homophobia. Drag gave me a sense of social and cultural identity and honed my ability to deal with daily homophobic verbal and, sometimes, physical abuse (see Figure 12.1). Moving on from my teenage coming of age,

Figure 12.1 Mark Edward performing at Henry Africa's in 1989. Photo: Chris D' Bray.

I returned to education a little more confident, first training in vocational studies and then taking courses in performing arts, namely dance and drama. This allowed me access to higher education; I studied for a BA (Hons) in live art, contemporary dance and drama at university. This education gave me the skills and confidence to become a dance theatre-maker, live art practitioner and contemporary dancer. Later in my life I studied for a master's degree in dance studies, followed by a PhD in performance research in autoethnography and mesearch (2018). These qualifications complemented my career in lecturing in further and then higher education.[5]

LGBTQIAA[6] but where is the D?

In 2012 I co-created an immersive art installation titled *Council House Movie Star*.[7] Within this work, I lived in a life-size house inside a gallery for several weeks as an aged and lonely drag queen. Students were involved in both performing and spectatorship. Mobilizing research into my teaching, in 2015 I opened the closets on my drag experience and authored the first UK drag module in higher education, as far as I am aware, which was validated by Edge Hill University – Edge Hill had the valour and insight to authorize a drag andragogy.[8] The module was not a whim. It was informed by the interests of the performing arts students who were incorporating drag into their own performance making. It was carefully planned through rigorous benchmarking against governmental standards for higher education within the UK. Moreover, it was subjected to an internal and external validation to confirm its quality and rigour. The rigour required at this level of study allowed me to embed research-informed teaching within the curriculum design.[9] The module garnered a vast amount of media attention, with one news story reaching 2.4 million 'likes' online. The news of the module spread across Russia, the USA, Canada, Mexico, Australia, New Zealand, Japan, Brazil, Ireland, Spain, France and other places.

Educationalist Douglas Gosse explores a queer curriculum model and highlights the need for interconnecting the personal with the performative:

A queer curriculum model incorporates anti-oppressive pedagogies. Considering the multiplicity of human beings and incorporating spiritual, physical, moral, intellectual, and emotional factors should persist. Rigorous questioning and dialoguing can help students to relate to course material and their own lives, thereby helping them to interrogate their own values and responsibilities. (Gosse, 2004: 34)

There is clear consensus among academics that the curriculum diet we have been offering needs diversifying (Hawley, 2015). Sumara and Davis argue that queer theory exposes the sexual and, in fact, 'explicitly heterosexualized' (1999: 191) nature of pedagogy and the curriculum. They point out that heteronormative structures are limiting to students and their learning experience: 'interrupting heteronormativity, then, becomes an important way to broaden perception, to complexify cognition, and to amplify the imagination of learners' (ibid.). Studies of sexuality and gender existed within the academy, popularized by feminism, women's studies, studies of sexuality and the emergence of queer theory. The 2010 Equalities Act in the UK legally compels organizations, including higher education institutions, to protect individuals in terms of equality, diversity and inclusivity. In relation to minority sexualities, this module reflects this legislation in curriculum content and module design. In such terms, drag can be considered an appropriate term for queer visibility, rupturing repetitions in performance and parody.

In addition to looking at 'high art' sources, including Shakespearean drag, the module offered a critical reading of gender and sexuality in performance alongside the use of 'low art' aspects of performance, which emerge from popular or alternative culture. Jack Halberstam observes how low theory pushes 'through the divisions between life and art, practice and theory, thinking and doing, and into a more chaotic realm of knowing and unknowing' (2011: 2). The module sought to use both low and high art as points of departure. I also saw the module as a rediscovery of all I felt had been lacking in my own (in)formal drag education. It was a rejuvenation of a performance form that had been edited out of my professional performance career. Drag appeared to be lacking visibility in the alphabetical soup of acronyms and somehow needed to be brought into the academy.[10] This autobiographical drag process became part of my queering and querying the academic curriculum for performing arts students and foregrounding drag in higher education. Collaboratively, the education process allows an exploration which furthers queerness, engages debate on the rupturing of binary structures, resists categories and explores a sense of authenticity within students' research work in drag performance.

Similarly, drag, like queer, should be disruptive to 'traditional and dominant ideas about research' (Adams and Holman Jones, 2011: 110) and to (re)presentations and notions we may have of drag. It is important to note that many higher education institutions have diplomatically controlled queers/queerness (Miller and Rodriguez, 2016; Oldfield and Johnson, 2008; Pinar, 2008; Tierney, 1997), since queers are not new to the academy yet have lacked a 'visible' presence, as Miller and Rodriguez state: 'Queers have been part of the academy since its creation. Fear and institutional policies, however, have created constraints that have kept those academics from being their authentic selves' (2016: xvi). Therefore, this optional Level 6 module gave another platform for academic staff to share their skills and experiences of drag, discuss personal historical involvements with LGBTQIAAD crusading, and analyse relationships between self, scholarship and performance making.[11] Students needed to engage with theories around marginalization, gender as a product of social processes (Butler, 1990, 1993, 2004), sexualities and identity, and the ways in which performance might be deployed in the service of specific political and cultural agendas. Through a consideration of the performativity of drag performance, my intention with the module was for it to be wholly interdisciplinary. Therefore, tracing the trajectory of drag in performance including the presentation of drag in historical contexts, the writing of the module was to combine postmodern theories of gender, including feminism, and queer theory alongside complex performance skills. The rigour of the module was to challenge and empower the students academically, physically and holistically, giving them the opportunity and encouragement to ask mature questions on patriarchal structures that can render divergent forms of performance while also introducing them to key concepts around heteronormativity, homonormativity and their social obligations as enlightened emerging queer/drag artists.[12]

I saw that drag's popularity could engage my undergraduate students, who were a mix of gay, bisexual and heterosexual young cis men and cis women. The module asks the students to study a brief history of drag to uncover its political activism as a key player in LGBTQ+ history and rights. My previous live art and dance theatre teaching had always been a type of magpie for drag, borrowing elements of drag performance embodied from my earlier days: lip-synching, performing old school 'routines' and using camp and parody to queer gender.[13] I had previously performed in my own person-as-research/practice-research work in 2012, which focused on my life through my drag persona, Gale Force, and I had performed in 2004 in drag as the character Penny Change in Penny Arcade's autobiographical work *Bad Reputation* (see Mercier in Volume 2).[14] Aside from my drag days in the studio and theatre, drag had sparked media interest, a 'drag trending' (mainly) in youth culture, through RuPaul's drag competition, which is broadcast internationally.

However, my writing of this drag module was not intended to institutionalize drag but to ensure that students recognize its diversity and understand that the recent surge of drag should not be put into a scholarly and performative vanity case, as drag is not easily boxed into neat readable frameworks, nor should it be reduced or measured, for example, without due attention to the critical and performance differences of localized drag traditions – differences that need unpacking (or untucking) while also resisting the mainstreaming of drag forms present in the international circulation of *RuPaul's Drag Race*. It could be argued that there is drag amnesia when it comes to current drag performance. It would appear that *RuPaul's Drag Race* has a monopoly on representations of drag within the media; this has arguably dwarfed (or dragged) other forms out of the spotlight, giving way to a specific line of drag aesthetics and language that are increasingly placing drag into a specific (make-up) box. I felt this amnesia or turning away from local forms needed to be covered in the sessions to address a reductionist attitude about how drag is read, through which some local forms are relegated.

Brennan and Gudelunas's edited collection *RuPaul's Drag Race and the Shifting Visibility of Drag Culture* (2017) explores these issues of American centrism, marginalization, exclusions and inclusions, such as the 'occasional, thorny inclusion of Puerto Rican contestants' (2017: 3) and other considerations worthy of exploring. My intentions in developing the module were to educate and steer students away from only engaging with the superficiality of drag. I wanted to show that although drag TV shows are a good and valid touchstone for reference (and for easy access to a drag world), they are also a springboard for further discussion of what is and what is not present. For instance, there is an absence of honest talks on issues surrounding HIV/AIDS and violence (Brennan and Gudelunas, 2017).[15] Likewise, the use of the term 'fishy', which could be seen as insulting towards women, needs to be brought into discussion.[16]

Recent media attention surrounding bioqueens (biologically female drag queens) also opens interesting and relevant debate on challenging stereotypes of what constitutes a drag queen, as well as drag appropriation/drag borrowing from an established form that has predominantly been male to female and not female to female. It reveals how women are now playing with performative femininity, through hyper-feminized personas with strong performance identities emerging. Holestar, the UK-based bioqueen, is a prime example of this. Although I do not feel suitably qualified to critique bioqueens (see Farrier, this volume), the changing landscape of drag means that this is a hot scholarly topic which I wanted to bring into the drag module. Similarly, questions need to be raised surrounding kinging, and debates need to be had on how various drag king representations of men and masculinity represent certain types of toxic masculinity, which have ultimately and historically oppressed women.

My drag mother, mentioned earlier, Chris D' Bray, was invited to teach on the module.[17] He sought to challenge the students by engaging with theory to understand complex language and drag lineages, in a move away from the bandying of 'catch-all' phrases with little historical understanding of those drag ancestries, and where certain language has been constructed through hardship and secrecy (Polari) and in many ways as a form of survival.[18]

Creativity, critical thinking and chaos

Critiquing drag or critically thinking around drag performance is to pierce and enter into dialogue. Such dialogic analysis opens up drag spaces for students to explore the more complex layering of drag and its 'perpetual becoming' (Browne and Nash, 2010: 1). Thus, the perpetual becoming and *the evolution of drag* were inherent to the curriculum design, as the interdisciplinary focus created a rich discourse around the art form. Drag critique involves engaging the 'Cs': content, critique, critical thinking, creativity, chaos, curriculum design. My bringing the form into the academy is not about sanitizing the method or trying to shoehorn drag into a neat linear pathway for an equally neat linear academic framework or drag dissection. I wanted to dodge a 'drag matrix' like that of Judith Butler's 'heterosexual matrix' (1990: 45) and put forward questions about drag fluidity and a need for the avoidance of a hexis or in this case a 'drag hexis', a stable structure. Rather, the module focused on unravelling and revealing, and at the same time not being able to arrive at a final unchanging drag destination as 'there are fewer answers than questions' (Gosse, 2004: 33). I was also conscious of not wanting to run the risk of producing work that did not allow for Halberstam's low art. I embraced learning processes which were messy, playful and risk taking, which resisted docile forms of regurgitated drag set against a specific measurable criteria.

My authoring of the module was to ensure the content focused on the disordered processes of drag, moving away from the commercialization of the form where people are presented with a glossy marketable product rather than a development. The critiquing and exploration of drag involved viewing historical footage of international drag performers and their works and the discussion of how these foundations are critical to understanding how drag forms have mobilized or influenced contemporary works. My aim was to explore a historic overview of drag performance within various geographical contexts. Fuelling the practice-based work was a focus on various aesthetics of drag, including the American character actor Divine and the merging of performance art with a trashier drag aesthetic, seen in much footage of Leigh Bowery's performance and nightclub happenings/ works and, likewise, David Hoyle's politically charged stand-up projects. It is debatable whether Bowery and Hoyle can be classed as drag, as they appear to defy categorization, yet they do come under the umbrella term of queer and use drag elements in their performances.

The mocking, queer/drag bashing, family acceptance and societal hardship that I watched, as a 16-year-old, in Harvey Fierstein's 1988 film *Torch Song Trilogy* influenced some of my thinking and theorizing around intended workshop content and helped to draw comparisons for the students to understand how these issues are still partly mirrored in contemporary TV documentaries. Also, *RuPaul's Drag Race* has had an impact on the embryonic development of gaming with drag characters on social media for an online community that can secretly engage in 'drag wars'. The drag merchandising of clothing, board games, and so on has also allowed people to become drag fashionistas and participate in drag role play. This too was to be explored as the module developed.

Yet, the module also considers hidden or uncovered footage of local and national drag forms, to be explored in a university setting, which had its roots and routes in the development of the drag explosion that seems to be sweeping across the UK. The module also includes ethnographic studies of drag settings through a visit to the renowned Funny Girls drag show bar based in northwest UK (Blackpool). By enlightening students about drag lineages and the historical context of male and female impersonation (drag kings and queens), they could evaluate and re-evaluate geographies of drag. Thus, the offshoot of their practices were both departure points and launchpads of new emerging methods. Students undertaking this module could also consider the ways in which performance intersected with other identities and aesthetics, forming discourses such as theories of gender performativity and performance. Students also consider themes of ethnicity; drag and race(ism); class and drag; subculture and drag performance; applying gender to the stage; drag and issues of identity; mothers and daughters – mentorship and collaboration in drag performance; artistry of drag – make-up, wigs and costume, moustaches and frocks; humour and lip-syncing.[19] More importantly, students engage in reflective critiques of their own position in the performance, a method I call elsewhere 'mesearch' (Edward, 2018).

Conclusion

For many years I have had 'dragulous' fantasies/visions of making differences in lives and expanding people's learning experiences through drag pathways for students. Personally, and in performance terms, there is a transformation as students don their critical thinking caps, wigs, false tits, rubber cocks, binding gear, leathers, sequins and moustaches (this list is not exhaustive), giving people the transferable and employable skills to either sashay away into other avenues of work or shantay and stay on the academic runway of drag theorizing and performance making.

While the relatively safe spaces of academia have often been at the forefront of theorizing about gender and sexuality in terms of the development of queer studies, drag is only now joining this body of work. This institutional validation of my drag module is testament that drag as an area of study within performance is academically credible, intellectually stimulating and creatively unbound, and it offers opportunities for self-realization. This highlights the importance of drag studies in permeating the academy and hopefully, eventually, filter into the everyday, offering radical potential to question and challenge normative structures of gender, class, race and social privilege on the ground. I have witnessed, and experienced, the hardship and struggles many queens and kings have gone through, and go through, because of financial difficulties, family rejection, homophobia and/or insecurities of work. But at the same time I have seen the younger 'draglets' welcomed into experienced and matured drag communities that have given young LGBTQIAA, and D, a sense of belonging, a family life and much-needed support through acts of kindness, mentoring and positive role modelling. It is also important to note that while theorizing and discussing my drag module in a liberal university in the UK, there are many people in the world who are denied access to study or work because of their non-normative sexuality or gender.[20] The power of heteronormativity and veiled or explicit homophobia still has a strong foot in numerous institutional doors throughout the world. There are many people who are privileged and take their choices of studies and freedom of expression for granted, yet there are those who cannot. Only by fighting, dislodging and moving knowledge forward can we lessen the struggle (which is real) and hope to transform and deconstruct globally oppressive ideals.

We are in exciting times through the renaissance of drag. Drag must not lose sight of its queer roots; it must remain in flux. The point of this flux is that it is wholly queer, ephemeral, multiple, creative and unbound. As I have written elsewhere on issues of binaries, categorization and queer, 'the essence of queer is to remain unrecognisable and to remain resistant to classification and methods' (Edward, 2018: 77). Current trends, shifts and new practices are ensuring the form defies pigeonholing. Drag does not find its roots within the higher education academy; rather, its roots are found in resistance, rupture and re/presentations. It is right that the academy explores these roots, connecting non-normative presentations of gender and sexuality, performance and subcultural art forms. To truly research, teach and learn about drag, academics should not view drag from ivory towers, but engage with the communities in which it is formed.

Notes

1   Henry Africa's was based in Standish (near Wigan) and in Scunthorpe and Oldham (all in the north of the UK). See D' Bray (2021).

2   It was during this period of my life that I was also part of the inception of the 1988 UK countercultural movement of acid house and illegal raving. My early teenage years were a complex mix of learning high-camp drag performance and participating in a drug culture that allowed me to revolt against mainstream heterosexual discotheques, authoritarianism and have freedom of expression while being part of exciting subcultural groups. For further reading see Edward (2015).

3   Other drag performers working in Henry Africa's at the time were Davinia, Roxy Duvall, Roxy Hart, Miss Martell and Crystal Starr. Alison (Ali the Dancer) and Panda Jazz also danced throughout the week.

4   Tucking is the act of ensuring the penis is 'tucked' away to give the appearance of a vagina. It is similar to drag kings and the 'binding' of their breasts to ensure a flat-looking chest.

5   Further education in the UK is for school leavers (usually 16 to 18 years of age) to study for further qualifications to gain entry into university or to gain employment skills through vocational training. Higher education in the UK is for those who are 18 years of age or older and wanting to study for a university degree.

6   You may be forgiven for thinking that a cat has just crawled across my keyboard. However, this is one of the current acronyms to denote lesbian, gay, bi, trans, queer/questioning, intersex, ally and asexual.

7   This immersive live art installation was in collaboration with Rosa Fong, Mark Fremaux, Karen Lauke and Olivia du Monceau. A range of established artists and students were invited to perform in this epic interdisciplinary project. The work attracted viewership from the everyday passer-by and established writers, performers and activists such as Bette Bourne and his partner Paul Shaw, David Hoyle, Gerry Potter/Chloe Poems, Paris Lees and Mickey Poppins.

8   Edge Hill University is based in the UK. Its mission is to harness the creativity, knowledge and commitment of its staff to promote its values and enhance its activities, while providing outstanding student experience. In 2017 it was awarded 'Gold' for the Teaching Excellence Framework (TEF) and in 2014 was named 'University of the Year' by *The Times Higher*.

9   Furthermore, in terms of the intended learning outcomes on successful completion of the module, students would be able to [1] explain and evaluate critical theories relating to drag in its historical and contemporary contexts; [2] embody the focused and sophisticated artistry, craft and technique of the drag performer in the independent and autonomous creation and presentation of drag; [3] present with insight the outcome of research and

intellectual engagement in drag performance studies, adhering consistently and accurately to the required standards of academic scholarship.

10 See endnote 6 in case you have missed a gem.

11 Level 6 is the final year of undergraduate study for students in UK universities.

12 Homonormativity was coined by Lisa Duggan (2002). In brief, the term refers to the depoliticization of lesbian and gay culture, and how heterosexual institutions are upheld within the culture. Michael Warner popularized the term 'heteronormativity' in the introduction to *Fear of a Queer Planet* (1993). The term refers to the normalization of heterosexuality within society and culture.

13 For further reading on drag and magpie/scavenger performance making see Edward and Newall (2021).

14 Arcade never gave me the name Penny Change in *Bad Reputation*; it was I who asked other performers to call me this during the rehearsal process.

15 The UK TV series *London Drag Queens* is not a drag competition. However, it does give a backstage look at various drag/queer/trans lives and the daily struggles of working in drag, dealing with HIV and medication, mental health challenges, family narratives, relationships and overcoming adversity.

16 The word 'fishy' is used to denote a drag queen who excels at presenting as female.

17 Julia Griffin, senior lecturer in dance at Edge Hill University, was the module leader.

18 Polari is a form of complex slang historically used within UK gay subcultures.

19 Formative assessment was employed throughout the module in the form of entries in a weekly journal or online blog, of approximately 300 words per entry, with a minimum of six entries. The rationale for this assessment was to provide the students with an ability to document their positionality in relation to the module content. As part of the module, students could reflect on the practice and theory of the module and on personal research findings about the culture and politics of drag performance. They then used this reflection as a tool for discussion within their tutorials, at which point the tutor offered oral feedback. Within practical workshop sessions, students were required to explain and evaluate in discussion their exploratory work and the theoretical and practical development of a drag artist in performance. This underpinned the practical project work and prepared students for the summative reflective report on the practical summative assignment, where students created and performed in a drag project. This was accompanied by a final blog entry, which, with academic underpinning, constituted complementary writing, making explicit the students' practice-research/person-as-research findings and the

achieved learning embedded in the practical project. Students could work individually or in groups.

20 At the time of writing, the International Lesbian, Gay, Bisexual, Trans and Intersex Association note 134 countries in the world where laws exist to protect LGBTQ+ people in terms of discrimination in employment. Source: https://www.ilga.org/maps-sexual-orientation-laws.

References

Adams, Tony E. and Holman Jones, Stacy. (2011). 'Telling Stories: Reflexivity, Queer Theory, and Autoethnography'. *Cultural Studies ↔ Critical Methodologies*, vol. 11, no. 2, pp.108–16.

Brennan, Niall and Gudelunas, David. (2017). *RuPaul's Drag Race and the Shifting Visibility of Drag Culture*. London: Palgrave.

Butler, Judith. (1990). *Gender Trouble*. London: Routledge.

Butler, Judith. (1993). *Bodies That Matter*. London: Routledge.

Butler, Judith. (2004). *Undoing Gender*. London: Routledge.

D' Bray, C. (2021). 'Camp and Drag in the mainstream: a critical study of the Phenomenon of the British Northern Fun Pub 1973-1993'. In Edward, M. and Farrier, S. (eds), *Drag Histories, Herstories and Hairstories: Drag in a Changing Scene*. London, UK: Methuen Drama.

Duggan, Lisa. (2002). 'The New Homonormativity: The Sexual Politics of Neoliberalism' . In R. Castronovo and D.D. Nelson (eds), *Materializing Democracy: Toward a Revitalized Cultural Politics*, pp. 175–94. London: Duke University Press.

Edward, Mark. (2014a). 'Stop prancing about: boys, dance and the reflective glance'. *Equality, Diversity and Inclusion: An International Journal*, vol. 33, no. 5, pp. 470–9.

Edward, Mark. (2014b). 'Council House Movie Star: Queering the Costume'. *Scene*, vol. 2, pp. 147–53.

Edward, Mark. (2015). 'Dance: Anarchy from The Margins and Free Expression'. In Robson, C. and Gillieron, R. (eds), *Counter Culture UK: A Celebration*. Twickenham: Supernova Books, pp. 75–94.

Edward, Mark. (2018). *Mesearch and the Performing Body*. London: Palgrave.

Edward, Mark and Newall, Helen. (2021). 'The Buttcracker: Dragging Ballet into Queer Spaces'. In Edward, M. and Farrier, S. (eds), *Drag Histories, Herstories and Hairstories: Drag in a Changing Scene*. London: Methuen Drama.

Equalities Act (2010). https://www.legislation.gov.uk/ukpga/2010/15/contents.

Farrier, Stephen. (2017). 'International influences and drag: just a case of tucking or binding?' *Theatre, Dance and Performance Training*, vol. 8, no. 2, pp. 171–87.

Gosse, Douglas. (2004). 'Foundational tenets and challenges in conceptualizing a queer curriculum model'. *Intercultural Studies*, vol. 4, no. 1, pp. 32–41.

Halberstam, Jack. (2011). *The Queer Art of Failure*. North Carolina: Duke University Press.

Hawley, John S. (ed.) (2015). *Expanding the Circle: Creating an Inclusive Environment in Higher Education for LGBTIQ Students and Studies*. Albany: Suny Press.

Miller, sj. and Rodriguez, Nelson M. (2016). 'Introduction: The Critical Praxis of Queer Memoirs in Education'. In Miller, sj. and Rodriguez, N. M. (eds), *Educators Queering Academia: Critical Memoirs*. New York: Peter Lang Publishing, pp. xv–xxiii.

Oldfield, Kenneth and Johnson, Richard G. (2008). *Resilience: Queer Professors from the Working Class*. New York: State University of New York Press.

Pinar, William F. (2008). *Queer Theory in Education*. New York: Routledge.

Sumara, Dennis and Davis, Brent. (1999). 'Interrupting Heteronormativity: Towards a Queer Curriculum Theory'. *Curriculum Inquiry*, vol. 29, no. 2, pp. 191–208.

Tierney, William G. (1997). *Academic Outlaws: Queer Theory and Cultural Studies in the Academy*. London: Sage.

Torch Song Trilogy. (1988). [film] New Line Cinema. United States.

Warner, Michael. (1993). *Fear of a Queer Planet*. Minneapolis, Minnesota: University of Minnesota Press.

13

Drag Publique

The Queer Spectacle, the Emaciated Spectator and the Public Secret

Allan Taylor

Muñoz (1999: 25) recognizes that there is power in demonstrating the spectacle of queerness in that its performance makes the performer a 'disidentificatory non-citizen', and this can transform works and situations, with the performer bending cultural references for their own purposes. He describes disidentification as 'shuffling between production and reception decoding mass, high or any other cultural field from the perspective of a minority subject in such a representational hierarchy'. In his later work, Muñoz (2009: 1–10) says that performances of queerness are not a 'here and now', but embody a future that is yet to come. In this sense, performing queerness through the vehicle of drag opens up a discussion about the potential of those futures by enabling the internal identification of queerness to be read as a highly visible performance mode.

In an age where gender politics are discussed more openly than ever before in public media and terms like non-binary and gender fluidity enter common parlance, we could assume that tolerance is self-evident. However, when performances of queerness spill out of clubs, cabarets and bars and into the streets, they are still seen as spectacle: simultaneously enticing, deceptive, distracting and superficial. As Muñoz suggests, by performing queer otherness, we choose to 'disidentify' because the transformative effect of this process can illustrate a variety of discourses of power in effect and unveil unspoken normative behaviours that are not questioned. This stems from the performer's aspiration to reveal such unspoken dynamics by transforming them into a queer spectacle, initiating a visual – as opposed to verbal – dialogue about how change might happen and what that looks like.

In the following practice-based investigation, I employ the performance of drag identities and genderqueer interventions in public spaces to remove such performances from the context of a designated 'performance space' and evaluate how such identities are received when performed as an occurrence on the street and how such drag-based performances can highlight the issues surrounding the policing of the public performance of gender identity. Drawing on Read's (2013) concept of the emaciated spectator, I suggest that introducing the pathogenic quality of queerness into public streets interrogates the limits to which inner identity can be expressed and whether or not the public audiences that receive the performance can contain it. Simultaneously, drag and gender performance also has a quality of affective contagion (from Hickey-Moody, 2016) that, if not contained, has the ability to become infectious. Therefore, the pathogen starts to occupy a queer space of being public and private, spoken and unspoken simultaneously. I conclude by stating that such performances of queerness intrinsically interrogate what is said and unsaid by the spaces the queer individual can inhabit through this visual mode of performance, consequently expressing a longing from the artist for a future that is yet to pass.

Becoming spectacle[1]

In Hall's (1997: 275) idea of 'the spectacle of the Other', he describes a kind of activity he calls 'a third counter-strategy' to reverse the nature of stereotypes within representation. The strategy locates itself within the complexities and ambivalences of representation itself, attempting to contest the inherent bias of the modernist discourse of capitalism from within by challenging the stereotypes it has produced. In employing such a strategy, Hall says, the spectacle works 'with the shifting, unstable character of meaning, and enters into a struggle over representation, while acknowledging [that meaning] can never be finally fixed' (ibid.). In this strategy, stereotypes are not avoided, but used as a way to contest difference. By deploying this strategy as a practice, it can make the familiar feel strange, raising questions about underlying and unquestioned norms in the spectacle of society in general.

Because of this, I chose to illustrate 'performances' of queerness through overly exaggerated quasi-drag actions that operate outside gender norms rather than, for instance, sex performance as it speaks to Hall's idea of exposing such stereotypes of feminized behaviour for what they are.[2] At the same time, it addresses one of Butler's (2011 [1993]: 79–149) early assertions that drag 'could be' a political vehicle if it did not adhere to gender binaries. She later revisits this comment in Butler (2004), stating that

Norms can be significantly deterritorialised through the citation. They can also be exposed as non-natural and non-necessary when they take place in a context and through a form of embodying that defies normative expectation ... The point about drag is not simply to produce a pleasurable and subversive spectacle but to allegorise the spectacular and consequential ways in which reality is both reproduced and contested. (Butler, 2004: 218)

Butler illustrates that 'drag' (and the many shades of queer acts in between) can be utilized as a transgressive strategy to highlight and contest norms while creating a 'subversive spectacle'. Echoed by Kosofosky-Sedgwick (2003), she writes that the constant definition of continuity and change through the cycle of repression and liberation leads 'in many cases, to its conceptual reimposition in the even more abstractly reified form of the hegemonic and the subversive. The seeming ethical urgency of such terms masks their gradual evacuation ... It is only the middle ranges of agency that offer space for, effectual creativity and change' (2003: 12).

On commencing these investigations, I initially tried to use the rural landscapes of Cornwall, UK, as a way of playing against site. This remote and largely rural environment is a world away from the perception of queerness as a largely urban phenomenon.[3] In this sense it seemed like the rural landscape surrounding Falmouth would be a good starting point to commence the 'exaggeration' of queer identity to juxtapose what is seen as the primary perception of 'queer as urban' against 'landscape as rural'.

Dislocating the urbanized view of queer behaviour, these actions took place in relative seclusion with a very small audience: often just myself, an assistant who took photographs and whoever happened to be passing by that day. On embarking on this practice, I thought the performances would reveal something psychogeographical about the body and landscape. However, it was not until I carried out *Poor, Unsuspecting Cow* (Figure 13.1, top left) that the question of audiences and witnesses came into play. I spent the day in a field of cows that were very curious as to why I was there. After some time, they came over to me and embraced me as part of the herd, licking my clothes, my high heels and me.

The cows readily accepted me, as they had no concept of the social etiquette or appropriate social behaviours of human beings. It made me realize that by keeping the performances of queerness relatively private, I was not challenging such etiquette and power play of human publics and, in order to reach the next stage, I needed to make the spectacle more visible to human eyes, thereby engaging with the dynamics created by the implicit social relationships of simply being in a space where other people are present.

Figure 13.1 Clockwise from top left: *Poor, Unsuspecting Cow, Glamping, Angus Og* and *Wishing You Were Here.*

To counter this, I started with tiny acts of queer rebellion in populated spaces, such as in *Appliqué* (Figure 13.2), which took the form of a simple application of lipstick in public. Still practising in the various spaces of Cornwall, I would often choose to sit in the corner of a bar or café and begin to apply a light covering of face powder and lipstick while timing the camera to go off at certain intervals to capture reactions. Because the room could not see me, no one paid much attention. These 'secret acts' were hidden in plain sight and yet it would have been quite overt if anyone turned around or paid attention. The action ended once the make-up was applied.

Before commencing each action, it took me some time to gather the energy and impetus to do it. In fact, throughout all of the performances, there was always a sense of fear and apprehension. I felt I was breaking the rules, that I would get caught, ridiculed or ostracized for doing such a thing. There were two reasons I surmised why this might be happening. The first is simply that I was transgressing implicit social rules. In some circumstances this elicited anger, negative commentary and, in one instance, physical ejection from a location. The second was the force of shame. Whether this sense of shame was imposed by the public, self-inflicted or a historical combination of both, it pervaded.

Figure 13.2 *Appliqué* test shot.

For the most part, *Appliqué* remained covert and this probably added to the 'naughtiness' shown below, which was the second time I performed the action in public (see Figure 13.2). The action was 'performed' through the window to the high street. Outside, people would stop and stare, commenting and laughing. In the image, we see that there is a table of people in the background for the most part unaware of what is happening. Passers-by outside were shocked, perhaps amused, by this action. The people inside did not want to pay it attention, while the camera observed the action throughout.

The act of appliqué shown in these photographs does not have the full effect of applying a complete face of drag make-up. However, it does pierce what could be perceived to be an otherwise normative presentation of modernist masculinity (e.g. suit and shirt, shaved, sensible haircut). Through the simple act of applying one element of make-up, a flash of red ruining what might be seen as an otherwise normalized appearance, it demonstrates the fragility of normative power systems that seek to repress the underlying force of desire. But more than this, it also demonstrates the fragility of 'masculinity' itself. Moon talks about this dichotomy as a relationship between the 'white dick' (2009: 347) that has always been seen as associated with power and control that changes when it is transferred to a homosexual context. It starts to represent a masculinity under siege, and it 'makes clearly visible the inconsistencies, contradictions, and inadequacies central to all identities' (ibid.).

It is clear from the reaction to the piece when performed in public, as well as from the visual reception of the image, that this pierce through the delicate construction of gender identity is keenly felt. Though the act in itself is relatively small, it was still very much perceived as a queer thing, and for that reason the action starts to take on wider significance. With a man performing the action, it illustrates how constrained and rigid performances of masculinity are: that one step outside the performance of the masculine has the potential to slip into the space of queerness. If, however, it is seen as a gay man performing this action, then it could be seen to cite the delicacy of homonormativity: that endorsed gay behaviour imposed by normative society is easily chipped by the desire it seeks to repress, which the application of the lipstick becomes representative of.

Grindstaff (2006) talks about the blurring of boundaries between public and private gay identity when it comes to citizenship, asking whether queer citizens should work with or defy heteronormative knowledge-power by highlighting the contradictions between the 'rhetorical secret' (Grindstaff, 2006: 152) (for which he uses the example of the closet and coming out as a performative statement) and the contradictions that govern such a speech act. He argues that though society gives the illusion of acceptance, it is done through ignorance, attempting to push performances of gay sexuality into the private sphere. He writes, 'Queer resistance begins by announcing the publicness of sexuality rather than defending homosexuality in zones of privacy ... When we limit homosexuality to zones of privacy, we forgo the right to be public' (ibid.: 154).[4]

As seen in the previous images, performances that lacked the spectacle of the presence of other people or did not illustrate the potentials of social relationships reinforce the privatization and repression of queer desire. Human presence, however, starts to invoke questions around 'tolerance through ignorance' when the audience do not look. Concurrently, it invites the pleasure of gazing on such a spectacle, thereby queering the time and space in which it occurs. In the attempted ignorance, for example in *Stripper Vicar* (Figure 13.3), one cannot help but draw relationships between the figures, wondering whether this is a chance encounter or a purposeful meeting and how salacious the nature of such a meeting might be. In performing an aspect of sexuality in public, we confront the repression and desire behind such performances that we would usually not see in the public space. As such, potential spectators can draw their own conclusions about whether they engage or not with the dichotomies the performance presents.

There is at play a sense of double shame – my own shame confronted with the shamelessness of such overt performances of sexuality – leading to an effect of the live witnesses that Read (2013) refers to as 'the emaciated

Figure 13.3 Image from the performance *Stripper Vicar*.

spectator'. Playing on Rancière's (2009: 22) notion of the emancipated spectator, Read comments on one student's remark to him that they feel a sense of shame when engaging in participatory or immersive theatre and Read, having a background in community theatre, uses this idea to posit 'community' against 'immunity'. In this usage, Read posits immunity as a reaction to a sense of 'shame' from the engagement attempt. The experience stems from immunity of involvement: a way in which we might curtail our willingness to enter the contract of performance that stems from within. He says, 'Immunity does this by introducing a minute foreign element to the body, whether that be an individual, such as a patient, a community or political body, introducing a fragment of the same pathogen from which it wants to protect itself, and it is this that blocks natural development, and with it the risk of further infection' (Read, 2013: 97).

However, the audience did not have a choice in their level of involvement. The spectacle is presented to them regardless, and the doubling of shame/shamelessness can invite both indifference and excitement. As a queer presence, I was the foreign body or a pathogen with the potential to both infect and revitalize the community with this sense of queerness. As a community, it chooses to ignore or buffer itself against the act with a form of emotional and mental resistance; it will not infect them. This infection could be as simple as acknowledging that the enforced normative dress code that they employ is easily disrupted, and to raise this question and interrogate it in their own minds would be more complex and traumatizing than it is to ignore and repress it, consequently reverting to the unquestioned norms they have previously accepted. On the other hand, if they have engaged with the performance even in a passing or internal way, it can expand the horizons of what the community has the potential to move towards.

What I was mistaking for a site or place-specific investigation actually became an investigation into publics, the politics of those publics and the citizenship afforded to queer individuals in those publics. Keenan describes the idea of public as something that cannot be imagined as location: 'The "public sphere" cannot simply be a street or a square, someplace where I go to become an object or instead heroically reassert my subjectivity, some other place out into which I go to "intervene" or "act". If it is anywhere, the public is "in" me, but it is all that is not me in me, not reducible to or containable within "me"' (1993: 132–3).

In this sense, what emerges is the discourse between the questioning of the power of the individual and the relative power of the public in which they operate. What Keenan suggests is that I do not only demonstrate the difference between the public and myself, but also that the public is a part of me and it is what I as the queer spectacle cannot entirely embody at the same time. In undertaking these investigations, I express a desire to be the public, as well as to illustrate that I can *never be* wholly public, as there exist aspects of the concept that cannot be contained by that which queer performance seeks to resist. Public is not site-specific, but a mobile body that occurs both inside and outside the individual and the community at large. Only by exaggerating and performing internal and unspoken identities as a visual discourse with the ability to be witnessed by a given public can a dialogue be initiated about the contradictions of simultaneously belonging to and being outside a given community.

Shame, secrecy and strategy

Power is clearly an appropriate consideration in this work, invoking Foucault's (1990) repressive hypothesis that supposes society is governed by repression: that taboo images cannot be talked about and, moreover, that the governing of sexuality provides a key linchpin through which dominant power and law can assert itself. However, he also reveals that discourse, while producing and transmitting power, can also undermine and expose it, that 'silence and secrecy are a shelter for power, anchoring its prohibitions; but they also loosen its holds and provide for relatively obscure areas of tolerance' (Foucault, 1990: 101). This is one of his key ideas around reverse discourse that can change dominant power systems.

Secrecy lies at the very core of this power, and Taussig (1999) analyses how secrecy is at the heart of social formations as 'that which is generally known, but cannot be articulated' (Taussig, 1999: 2–5). The content is both known and disavowed, repeated and kept hidden. This simultaneous knowing and unknowing is, for Taussig, the central structuring feature of society. Secrecy is about a long-standing social structure, not a historical and contingent event.

Eaglestone (2014) picks up on this, suggesting that testimony can only be read in relation to the secrets that the public keep, and that publics are bound as much by what they do not say as what they make explicit. He says, 'Unlike shared collective memory, for example, the public secret creates not a community but an "un-community": the public knowing people binds people together who may not want to be bound together, who really have nothing in common except the secret. It creates a version of a community bound by shame and secrecy' (Eaglestone, 2014: 81).

This was evident in the next investigation, *Shopping Is a Drag* (Figure 13.4). A high street is very public, so I decided to further develop

Figure 13.4 Image from the performance *Shopping Is a Drag*.

my drag experimentation in my most gender-conforming costume in all of the experiments. However, note that I have pink hair and unnatural colours purposely selected so that it was made obvious that I was a man in a dress. I simply walked down an urbanized high street with two full bags of shopping dressed in this guise.

For the shoppers of this area, it was a supreme spectacle. People followed me down the street, but it did not feel as though they were looking for enjoyment, as instead I felt a sense of personal danger – as though this fascination was not just purely because of the vibrant colours and queerness – that could have led to something more threatening. Embodied in the photograph, the colourful contrasts with the mundane. However, even this vibrant character seems to succumb to the mundanity, making the everyday a spectacle and disrupting the normal with the unusual.

Indifference or ignorance towards the act can always be read as minding one's own business; after all, the alternative would be to have people following me around or staring endlessly. The point here is that the audience were unsure if they should or could do anything. As such the response is one of self-preservation and to adhere to the unspoken community rules, as no contract with the performer is willingly established. The community remains resolved to be unweakened and unpenetrated by the queer pathogen, upholding the discourses of power in effect.

A partial agent of this disruption is the idea of 'temporal drag', as detailed by Freeman (2010: 6).[5] Referencing the work of Cindy Sherman, Sherry Levine and Barbara Kruger, she posits the idea that temporal drag could be a way of connecting queer performativity to disavowed political histories. She writes, 'Might some bodies, by registering on their very surface the co-presence of several historically contingent events, social movements and/ or collective pleasures, complicate or displace the centrality of gender-transitive drag to queer performativity theory? Might they articulate instead a kind of temporal transitivity that does not leave feminism, femininity, or so-called anachronisms behind?' (ibid.) And though Freeman refers to the anachronisms of feminism, this could also analogize as a relationship with homonormativity, gender acceptability and the limits of gender etiquette. In this sense, by performing queer, boyish or playful gender identities, what is potentially being read across the body are the disavowed histories of queerness and the shaming of such queer behaviours as an unspoken speech act.

However, the evidence of willingness to engage was present. One teenage girl screamed at me and asked if she might take a selfie, to which I happily laughed and obliged. She acts as though it is the most surreal thing to ever happen to her in her life (see Figure 13.5).

Figure 13.5 Teenage girl takes selfie with me in drag.

Continuing on the theme of contagion, her response confirms the idea of the pathogen's potential to become affective, adopted and embraced by the body it inhabits. In this sense it becomes infectious in a way that is synonymous with the idea of infectious laughter – something we catch that is not unpleasant at all. Hickey-Moody writes that 'Art escaping the capitalist bleed is future oriented. It values difference. It makes its people, its subjects, through scrambling capitalist codes in a manifestation of untimeliness that is temporally and spatially modulated... A public is called to attention to witness the power of difference to resonate with the liveness of being different together' (2016: 538).

She writes about an idea of *affective contagion*, a reaction to which we can see from the girl with the selfie. Having never seen such a spectacle in liveness, she wanted to have a piece of this pathogen, potentially calling to her own attention her limited experience of such actions. This led to her wanting to be involved, to catch the bug, which she did in her frame of experience by taking a selfie to show that this had happened to her.

Relating back to the point about public in itself being a queer concept of a collective body composed of individuals, this girl represents what could be true for many citizens within that collective. By engaging with and identifying with the queer performer's aims and intentions, she feels enabled to express her support and identification with this individuality. By proxy, she reinforces her own uniqueness by feeling empowered enough to digest and incorporate the pathogen.

This form of engagement helps the emaciated spectator broach the secret within their own frame of their experience. Negotiations of this contract of involvement were audience-led, and this was a purposeful strategy to accentuate the idea of the artist as liberal hero exposing the shame of society's secrets. Drawing on the line of questioning of my own intentions for this vein of enquiry, it became apparent I was calling upon a purposeful and established strategy seen in, for example, Vito Acconci, VALIE EXPORT and other performance interventions prevalent in live art in the 1960s and 1970s.

Ward (2014) observes this strategy by saying:

The manipulation of the scale of the public (as though the public, or the idea of public, had become a medium) may resonate with the manipulations of the scale of objects in pop [art] and minimalism... The enclosure of the public so that it might see itself as such, as if this would necessarily produce a critique of public-formation more generally. (Ward, 2014: 19)

He articulates that this divisiveness of public/private could be seen as escape attempts on behalf of the artist, insofar as they disarticulate artistic subjectivity from the artist's own presence in the works (seen here by the use of identity play and drag rather than appearing in everyday gender-conforming wear), which is in turn disallowed from being seen as complete in itself. The overall effect, he states, is one of 'ironic self-liberation' (ibid.: 22), and this is both a positive and negative manipulation on behalf of the artist. In an optimistic way, it works towards changing perceptions by displaying this difference or raising questions about why this occurs through proactive challenges to underlying discourses in intentional acts that allow the public to recognize themselves 'as public', allowing them to question the limits of public social conduct and the extent to which their own individual identity can be expressed within it. At worst, we have to question the artist's motivation to be positioned as a conduit of enlightenment, which relies somewhat on perceiving public as bad and artist as good – and this is not always the case. What I am recognizing is that the artist intends, before executing the action, that it be seen as grating against societal norms and to some extent invoke reactions of indifference, hostility, intrigue, delight or confusion. However, only by introducing a practice of queering publics that contravenes the secrets they may keep, a dialogue is opened as to the limits of public behaviour and the influence of the individual in overcoming such limits.

By performing such acts of queerness, McCormack (2014) explains that central to subject formation is an ontological and existential vulnerability, which is not optional. She states that 'any affective relation to it is variable (it can be sensed by the subject even while it is that which founds the subject) ... The question of being can only be thought through one's ethical relation to others' (McCormack, 2014: 34).

In a sense, it is essential for me as a performer to face my own shame and experience the range of public reactions when witnessing me as emaciated spectators to illustrate that vulnerability is not an optional part of the ethics of witnessing (see Figure 13.6). It is necessary to put oneself at risk and face such uncertainty so that the leakiness of queer vulnerability, one that bleeds between existing in public and expressing its own privacy, can challenge those discourses. The insertion of a reauthored context of these spaces, which is intentionally rewritten by the performance of these drag identities, forces speculation by embodying the politics of both identity and of public space.

Moreover, it gives way to a common feeling of placelessness that is general to human experience: the feeling of being alone in a crowd, of feeling that one stands out in a bad or embarrassing way, of wearing one's shame. Taking on the role of the queer Other in such an overt and exaggerated manner illustrates that at times we can all become that person who feels as though

Figure 13.6 Image from the performance *Executive Realness*.

they do not belong. In performing drag and identity play *as spectacle* we metaphorically speak out in the most visual way in order to rally against what cannot be said verbally. Performance of drag (and associated gender) identities gives voice and breaks silence, because it is silence in itself that perpetuates and inhibits the integration and acceptance of such identity performances from being commonplace.

Notes

1 Echoing Debord (1995 [1967]: 9), who suggests that mediated activity supplants everyday life. The following account relays how employing spectacle as a queer device can, conversely, draw attention to the illusions the society of spectacle seeks to create.

2 In that sexuality can also be expressed in terms of its physical nature rather than the idea of the culture that has become associated with it. This is mentioned to highlight that there may be alternative performance strategies that highlight similar issues of queerness.

3 Bell and Binnie (2000) observe this, detailing that urban commercialization characterizes the citizenship of queerness: '[urban commercial scenes]

represent the most intelligible manifestations of gay culture to the straight onlooker ... misrecognised as representative of all lesbians and gay men as a uniformly affluent and economically privileged group ... serving to deny the material impacts of homophobia'.

4   Similarly, Kosofosky-Sedgwick (1990: 4) also identifies the silence/speech contradiction and the knowledge-bearing potential the performativity of speaking one's sexual identity holds.

5   Schneider (2011: 176) picks up on Freeman's term, suggesting that 'camp history drags the past into the present and across its differences asking for time-again witnesses to [see] moments not yet past and not present either'. To pick up on Muñoz's idea of queer futures, it could be inferred that the performance drag itself occupies a not-yet-here while simultaneously being not-quite-then.

References

Bell, David and Binnie, Jon. (2000). *The Sexual Citizen: Queer Politics and Beyond*. Cambridge: Polity Press.

Butler, Judith. (2011 [1993]). *Bodies That Matter: On the Discursive Limits of 'Sex'*. London: Routledge Classics

Butler, Judith. (2004). *Undoing Gender*. London: Routledge.

Debord, Guy. (1995 [1967]). *The Society of Spectacle*, trans. by Donald Nicholson-Smith. New York: Zone.

Eaglestone, Robert. (2014). 'The Public Secret'. In Kilby, Jane and Rowland, Antony (eds), *The Future of Testimony*. London: Routledge. pp. 69–82.

Foucault, Michel. (1990). *The History of Sexuality: Volume One*, trans. Robert Hurley. New York: Pantheon.

Freeman, Elizabeth. (2010). *Time Binds: Queer Temporalities, Queer Histories*. Durham, NC: Duke University Press.

Grindstaff, Davin Allen. (2006). *Rhetorical Secrets: Mapping Gay Identity and Queer Resistance in Contemporary America*. Tuscaloosa, AL: University of Alabama Press.

Hall, Stuart. (1997). 'The Spectacle of the "Other"'. In S. Hall (ed.), *Representation: Cultural Representations and Signifying Practices*. London: Sage and The Open University, pp. 223–79.

Hickey-Moody, Anna. (2016). 'Being Different in Public', *Continuum: Journal of Media & Cultural Studies*, vol. 30, no. 5, pp. 531–41.

Keenan, Thomas. (1993). 'Windows of Vulnerabilty'. In B. Robbins (ed.), *The Phantom Public Sphere*. Minneapolis, MN: University of Minnesota Press. pp. 121–40.

Kosofosky-Sedgwick, Eve. (1990). *Epistemology of the Closet*. Durham, NC: Duke University Press.

Kosofosky-Sedgwick, Eve. (2003). *Touching Feeling: Affect, Pedagogy, Performativity*. Durham, NC: Duke University Press.

McCormack, Donna. (2014). *Queer Postcolonial Narratives and the Ethics of Witnessing*. London: Bloomsbury.

Moon, Jennifer. (2009). 'Gay shame and the politics of identity'. In D. Halperin and V. Traub (eds), *Gay Shame*. Chicago: University of Chicago Press. pp. 357–68.

Muñoz, José Esteban. (1999). *Disidentifications: queers of color and the performance of politics*. Minneapolis, MN: University of Minnesota Press.

Muñoz, José Esteban. (2009). *Cruising Utopia: The Then and There of Queer Futurity*. New York: New York University Press.

Ranciére, Jacques. (2009). *The Emancipated Spectator*. London: Verso.

Read, Alan. (2013). 'The Emaciated Spectator and the Witness of the Powerless'. In P. Lichtenfels and J. Rouse (eds), *Performance, politics and activism*. Basingstoke, UK: Palgrave Macmillan. pp. 87–103.

Schneider, Rebecca. (2011). *Performing Remains: Art and War in Times of Theatrical Re-enactment*. London: Routledge.

Taussig, Michael. (1999). *Defacement: Public Secrecy and the Labor of the Negative*. Stanford: Stanford University Press.

Ward, Frazer. (2014). *No Innocent Bystanders: Performance Art and Audience*. Dartmouth: Dartmouth University Press.

14

'Blessed Is the Fruit'

Drag Performance, Birthing and Religious Identity

Chris Greenough and Nina Kane

Season six of *RuPaul's Drag Race* saw an increase in the religious language used within the popular series. RuPaul has characteristically adopted the language from US church groups, ending each episode with the tag line 'Can I get an "amen" in here, y'all?' The winner of season six, Bianca del Río, picked up and expanded on the religious metaphors, famously proclaiming 'Not today, Satan. Not today!', which went on to be the title of her stand-up world tour. Yet drag performance has often made references to Christian religious cultures in the form of parody, and within the West, this has been largely targeted towards Roman Catholicism due to its high level of religious aestheticism and performativity through ritual. Indeed, it could be speculated that these references serve as a form of protest or rebuke for those who have felt rejected or marginalized by traditional church teachings on homosexuality and queer lifestyles.

In this context, this co-authored chapter serves as an exploration into the relationship between drag queens and kings and their own religious beliefs. The title, 'Blessed Is the Fruit', is an annunciatory reference from the Roman Catholic prayer Hail Mary. 'Fruit' in the gay language of Polari means 'a gay man' (Denning, 2007). Chris Greenough provides the contextualization for exploring queer individual life stories as a form of theology. He sets out the parameters for discussion in the continuing and burgeoning fields of queer theologies and theologies of sexualities. What emerges as illuminating for the field of theology and religion is that individualization and the privatization of religion trump institutional forms of religion. Nina Kane offers an extended case study in relation to this. A theatre-maker and a Black Veil Sister with the Manchester Sisters of Perpetual Indulgence (SPI), Kane is also a trans* man with a theological interest in Mariology.[1] She develops gallery-based drag performances centred in feminist and queer spiritualities and community activism (Kane, 2004–18). Her recent project *Caul* focused on song and lip-synching, and proposed that drag involving these is a form of 'placental' economy (Irigaray, 1993) which enables queer people to share nurturing breath with one another and to grow into their own queer power and subjectivity (Kane, 2017a).[2] In *Caul*, Kane passed performatively between the gender binary, employing shifting tropes of conventional drag kinging and queening. The performance was framed within the biblical Song of Songs – an apocryphal text, multi-authored and polyvocal, and one which as a young queer she found essential for her own transgender 'becoming' and growth (Brenner, 1993; Lundy, 2012).[3] This discussion therefore signifies how the individualization of religion can provide a catalyst to shape and transform communities for queer-identified individuals.

Jennifer Koosed observes how 'drag culture has been the subject of documentaries, and has achieved a certain acceptance in mainstream entertainment. Yet, drag is also a site of controversy among cultural critics and theorists of gender, race and class' (2006: 344). The controversy is heightened when drag is positioned against religious identities, given the pronouncements and teachings from mainstream, and therefore dominant, Christian groups with reference to homosexuality and transgender. It is hardly surprising that a discussion of drag culture and religion exists in very few academic texts (Sullivan-Blum, 2004; McCune, 2004). Melissa M. Wilcox has conducted some pioneering research on the Sisters of Perpetual Indulgence (2012, 2018), in terms of exploring spirituality and activism among SPI groups within the USA. Dominic Janes (2015: 187) has also usefully analysed the intersection of religious drag, activism and the SPI in the UK in relation to filmmaker Derek Jarman's canonization by the group in 1991 (Fuller, 2010). However, analyses that interrogate theology, queerness and performance practice from those working 'at the dragface' are in short supply, and our collaboration here aims to fill something of that gap.

First, we look briefly at fieldwork exploring the religious identities of drag queens working at this 'dragface'; second, we explore how identities (drag, religious, performance) are interwoven, resulting in sites of complementation and conflict; and third, we aim to contextualize the religious in drag by exploring the performance project *Caul* and its placental and queer birthing foci.

Queer studies have seen a burgeoning interest within the academy, and the discipline of theology and religion has not been an exception. Within UK legislation, The Equalities Act (2010) has compelled higher education institutions to have due regard to protect characteristics relating to sexual orientation and gender. In addition to the inclusion of LGBTQ+ studies, gender studies and queer studies, this led to the first module in drag studies in higher education (see Edward, this volume). Long before this legislative milestone, early gay and lesbian theology emerged from the 1990s (see for example, Stuart, 1992, 1995, 1997). Deryn Guest, alongside others, has produced some pioneering work in the area of biblical studies for lesbian and transgender-identifying individuals (Guest, 2005; Guest et al., 2006; Hornsby and Guest, 2016). Marcella Althaus-Reid authored *Indecent Theology* (2000) and *The Queer God* (2003), and positioned God as a drag queen:

> God the Faggot; God, the Drag Queen; God the Lesbian; God the heterosexual woman that does not accept the constructions of ideal heterosexuality; God, the ambivalent, not easily classified sexuality. (2000: 95)

Drag, as a subversive form, existed long before feminism and queer theory. Its genealogy therefore extends far back beyond the framework for discussion we offer here. Yet, rather than give a historical pre-post-modernity discussion of drag, we offer a contemporary lens through which to view drag and religion. The reasons for this are twofold. First, the drag queens interviewed see their working arena as dominated by present-day youth and sex culture. Second, the queens perceive a common disaccord between their professional/performance identities and Christianity, and therefore how they reconcile this duality in everyday life is pertinent to the discussion here. Within fieldwork conducted between 2013 and 2016, Greenough engaged in a digital ethnographical study of non-normative Christians (see Greenough, 2017, 2018), and among his participants were drag queens from the UK and USA. In terms of expressing the conflict between their performative identities, as drag queens and as Christians, the following soundbites emerged from the interviews:

> After 20+ years in the business, I still get nervous before going onstage. As I'm putting on my make-up, I have this routine where I pray to God that there is no homophobic idiot in the audience and that I get through the night. I very much doubt God approves of what I'm doing on stage, especially some of the crude acts and explicit jokes. (Frau N)

> There's sometimes an emptiness when I spend time with God. And I know that's cos he disapproves of me. It's vulgar what I do. So then I just say, 'well please change it'. (Hell'en Heaven)

Studies exploring faith and non-heterosexuality (Yip, 1998, 2002, 2003a, 2003b) have demonstrated how, in the contemporary era, a negotiation of identities results in a subsequent 'turn to self' (Heelas and Woodhead, 2005: 2). None of the drag queens who participated in the study attended or claimed to be part of a church or other religious community. This privatization of identity and beliefs largely allows a reconciliation to conflicting identities. Only two queens out of the seven interviewed saw no conflict between their professional performances as drag queens and their Christian identity:

> It's simple. God made this. He made me queer. He made me creative and I make people laugh. I'm not going to beat myself up over that. (Trinny Tee)

> When I'm performing, I never seen a problem between doing that [drag] and believing in God. No. Never. She is different to me. But when I'm getting ready I do sometimes think 'should I be doing this?' (Lucy Fer)

On a theological level, the stories from the seven drag queens interviewed are important because the site of conflict is both physical, in terms of the drag work, and spiritual, in terms of the beliefs held. In Christian terms, the importance of incarnation (the divine made human) places a strong emphasis on the spiritual and physical dimensions of the human body. Drag represents the full incarnation of queer identities, within which are interwoven political and social parodies of sexual dissidence. Yet, the incarnation of drag actively performs what is impossible, as does the grand narrative of the Christian tradition. When people see a drag queen, the general response is to identify that queen as male or female, but also to identify the queen as a disruptive signifier first and foremost. That is, the disruption is read before gender. Drag does not point to an illusion of gender, rather the impossibility of gender.
    Social activist bell hooks notes that

> Cross-dressing, appearing in drag, transvestitism, and transsexualism emerge in a context where the notion of subjectivity is challenge, where identity is always perceived as capable of construction, invention, change. (1992: 145)

It is this metaphor of drag as the capacity and catalyst for change which punctuates the self-narrative from Nina Kane in the following section. Isherwood and Althaus-Reid state that 'Queer theology is an "I" theology' (2004: 6), and Kane embraces the subjectivity of offering autobiographical experiences such that the 'text poses as an interface between the author and the reader' (Koosed, 2006: 342).

Trans* identity and religious drag – self-narrative[4]

One Manchester evening, I was accosted by a large drag nun in 1950s party dress and 'shades', who invited me to 'fill her bucket' in support of a local HIV/AIDS charity. I recognized the nun as a Sister of Perpetual Indulgence, an organization I knew when working as a women's sexual health/HIV and AIDS worker in Kent in 1993. I duly filled the nun's receptacle and signed myself up to join the order. At that point in my life I was undergoing a process of collapse and transition. My 'womanhood' was crumbling under the growing recognition of myself as male – a gay man – and after suffering for years with incongruity and a feeling of living an unreal life, the world was beginning to shape a language to describe what it was I had always felt myself to be. I was still, however, struggling to articulate myself. I hung around the Manchester gay scene – alone, drunk, being read as a butch lesbian, vulnerable, lost, but determined to find a life and identity that made sense.

By 2016, I was teetotal, happier, and I had defined the gender lines for myself with more clarity. I still used 'Nina' and female pronouns with family and for professional purposes, but in other areas of life adopted a male name and pronoun use. I was manifesting with the Manchester SPI regularly and developing a new relationship to the city as Sr Polly Amarosa of the Blessed Mercy Beau Cul and Bona Aris and as my newly emerging trans* male self.[5] It was a double process of dragging, a double process of becoming. It involved many changes of clothes.

For trans* people clothing is a marker of making and remaking, of concealment and revelation. It fundamentally relates to birthing the self, of taking responsibility for one's own breath and life (Irigaray, 2002: 50). On escaping the convent she had lived in since childhood, the seventeenth-century trans* nun and soldier Catalina de Erauso first transformed her gender presentation by resewing nun garments into a suit of men's clothes. Hiding out in a liminal space just beyond the convent walls, she tells how she was

> holed up for three days, planning and re-planning and cutting myself out a suit of clothes. With the blue woollen bodice I ... made a pair of breeches, and with the green petticoat I wore underneath, a doublet and hose – my nun's habit was useless and I threw it away, I cut my hair and threw it away. (Stepto and Stepto, 1996: 4)

She successfully passes as male in her local town, but it is only when her own mother fails to recognize her that she considers her transformation complete, and she leaves to make her fortune at sea.

Becoming a Sister with the SPI offers an opportunity to birth oneself anew. While parodying conventional religious ordinations, the elevation ceremonies are also a serious and meaningful profession of faith and intention (*We Are Here*, 2019). The process is contextualized within a 'maternal-feminine' frame (Irigaray, 1993); in some UK houses, novice mistress and novice will often call each other Mother and Daughter. I suggest that the SPI profession ceremonies have kinship with other forms of gay male birthing rituals – for example, those of the eighteenth-century London Molly Houses as explored by Rictor Norton: 'The most spectacular evidence for the mollies' occasional female identification was their performance in a highly-formalised ritual during their "Festival Nights" known as "mock birth" or "lying-in"' (1992: 98). He suggests it was a form of superstition and exorcism:

> Mock birth is not so much a case of aping heterosexuals or even mimicking women, as a means of blunting the end of heterosexual prejudice. The mollies were the scapegoats, and their own sub-society needed a scapegoat whether it be a wooden doll or a Cheshire cheese. (1992: 99)

Sr Polly, for me, holds similar association, and as I came out as trans* I reflected on my practice of devising female singing street-theatre characters, and making life-model performance with the female body (Kane and Woods, 2017). While culturally affirmative of a positive and feminist femininity, these performances also worked to 'exorcize' me of an imposed girl/womanhood. Whatever role I played, whether in theatre or life, I was always a boy and man underneath (Kane, 2017b). Sr Polly marks a point of departure. In short, she is all the young girls and women I 'was', and the act of dragging as a nun has become for me a loving affirmation and exorcism of that struggle, and the girl/woman I no longer am.

A drag midwife

As Sr Polly took shape as a *momento mori* of a former female self, I battled on with growing into manhood in everyday life – a stark process involving a transgender phenomenon of double ageing.[6] In chronological years I was 43; yet in male terms, socially, I was a 'chicken' (Denning, 2007).[7] Then one Sunday, I experienced what I can only describe as a 'delivery' by a very astute and beautiful drag 'midwife'.

I was attending a regular drag show known as Sunday Service in a local gay bar. The bar has a strict men-only policy that extends to a dress code of 'masculine attire'. While drag queens thrive on the stage, punters are not usually admitted if wearing make-up or 'feminine' clothing. It is an arena that prioritizes masculinity. I had been welcomed as a trans* man by an enlightened management team, but nevertheless stood out and was read as female. I successfully headed off stares in the build-up to the show and engaged politely in conversations about trans* matters when asked the inevitable 'how did you get in here?' question; however, it was clear some punters were not happy. When the drag performer took to the stage, she noted the mood of the crowd and instantly singled me out with a light provocation. She asked me about being transgender, listened respectfully while I answered and, in a beautiful moment, turned the crowd's ambivalence and hostility round by making an affectionate and inclusive reference to me 'always being a boy at heart!' which set everyone laughing and cheering.

I was subsequently greeted warmly – even congratulated – by other punters on my 'coming out' and being accepted in the club. When singing along to an iconic rendition of Bonnie Tyler's 'Total Eclipse of the Heart', I can only describe the feeling of being in the all-male crowd as akin to a spiritual experience. I had been delivered in more ways than one by a six-foot queen in a stunning scarlet wig and shimmering dress. Watching online footage of the event later, I noted the power of her physical and vocal performance as she directed the crowd to 'SING!' or 'WAIT!' It was exactly the same energy with which a midwife shouts 'PUSH!' and it became clear that it was not only I who was being delivered by her show, but many other men in the room (Rope Wolf Photography, 2016). Embraced and nourished through song and humour, given space to breathe, grow, sing and laugh, we affirmed ourselves and one another under the strong, protective direction of an experienced and generous drag queen.

Shortly after this birthing, I was commissioned to produce a theatre project for York Art Gallery, UK, in response to the *Flesh* exhibition and devised a repertoire piece, *Caul*, inspired by *Virgin and Child* by Fiorenzo di Lorenzo (1445–1525) (York Museums Trust, see Figure 14.1). The fabric in the painting is particularly interesting. A thin, transparent drape with a gentle sheen is knotted round the Christ-child's midriff, clinging, in part, to the flesh accenting his naked toddler body. Curiously fluid, it poses a conundrum; at once visible and invisible, it both covers and reveals an emerging body. In contemplating its fluidity, I recalled the superstition of the 'caul' – the amniotic sac of fluid protecting the foetus in a womb, which some 'lucky' babies are born in, and which midwives traditionally saved to sell,

Figure 14.1 *Virgin and Child* by Fiorenzo di Lorenzo (YORAG 799). Reproduced with kind permission of York Museums Trust.

as it was said to bring luck to sailors. I became interested in the 'placental' potential of this image. It was a powerful starting point.

Contemplation of *Virgin and Child* unwittingly brought forth memories of queer-feminist spiritual interests from my early twenties (1992–7). I recalled:

Making a sculpture – *My Soul Doth Magnify* – for a women's conference based on *The Magnificat* – 'Song of Mary' (Bible), prompted by feminist theologians and thinkers, particularly Fr Tissa Balasuriya who argued – 'The significance of the "Hail Mary" would have been different if it had included an invocation for Mary's support for radical social change ... see Luke 1.52.' (Stanton, 1997[1990]: 30);

Encountering the SPI's 'Play Fair' Safer Sex campaign when working for the Health Promotion Authority;

Writing a feminist thesis on the Song of Songs, centred in philosophies of 'sexuate difference' (King James Bible, 2018; Irigaray, 1993, 2002);

Making rituals on the 'sabbats' (Starhawk: 1989 [1979]: 181–96) with an eco-feminist goddess-worshipping group, the Sisters of Gaia; receiving a card from them when pregnant featuring the *Venus of Willendorf*, with a blessing to 'enjoy always the sensuous pleasures of the flesh';

Mapping *Proverbs* (Bible) with dancers and film-makers, for choreographic research on biblical edicts and 'codes of movement';[8]

Nursing someone close to me dying of an AIDS-related illness through the last weeks of his life; wandering the hospice at night like a ghost, wearing old men's pyjamas, watched over by positive, loving, gentle Catholic nuns.

These recollections resulted in a trans*-informed spiritual dramaturgy for *Caul*, framed structurally by the Polari version of the Song of Songs or 'Chant of Chants' (Greening-Jackson, 2001–15). Rooted in ideas of 'trans-temporal drag' (Lorenz, 2012), the work prioritized drag kinging and queening as a method, and built performances from exhibited works using lip-synching, song and silence. Stephen Farrier proposes that in the moment of lip-synching,

there is a somatic link to a body in the past, to a person making the recording that serves as the base of the performance moment ... This pastness makes a connection to histories that the community see as important and that sustain the circulation of stories about itself. (2016: 196)

The connection between the past and present community engendered through this queer aesthetic was of particular interest to me, also the potential to explore breath through it. Reflecting on my experiences at Sunday Service and other drag shows, I formed the idea that song-based drag, live or lip-synched, is a form of 'placental' economy (Irigaray, 1993), which enables queer people to share nurturing breath with one another and to grow into their own queer power and subjectivity (Kane, 2017b). I aimed to extend something of this queer placenta and its 'feminist ethics of generosity' into the heteronormative and cisnormative spaces of the public gallery (Bergoffen, 2007; Kane and Woods, 2017).

Birthing 'at the dragface': *Caul* by Cast-Off Drama (2017)

I decided early on, when devising this performance, not to present a conventional canon of drag queen songs/inspirations (Farrier, 2016: 196), but rather to allow the interaction of fleshy art objects in the gallery spaces and my performer's body to select any song for exploration (York Museums and Art Gallery Trust, 2018). I spent time with artworks in the *Flesh* exhibition, 'listening' to and physicalizing their 'auras' (Benjamin, 1936) – essentially finding a song that the artworks 'wanted' to sing, with my (queer and trans*) body as mediator. The first song to emerge, however, was that drag queen classic 'MacArthur Park', resulting in weeks of studying the diction and pacing of Richard Harris, Donna Summer, the Three Degrees and Waylon Jennings in a bid to find the breath that felt most resonant to lip-synch to. I watched online videos of drag queens both lip-synching and singing it live, learning much from this. The quest for 'MacArthur Park' led to countless gender shifts as I embodied the singing patterns and sartorial choices of each singer. I was able to recall and embody/breathe Richard Harris' version without the soundtrack playing and eventually decided to lip-synch the song silently in the gallery space, allowing small phrases to be vocalized before returning to silence again. The effect of this was very powerful and allowed for the underlying 'breath score' to be expressed. Inherent 'queer temporalities' came into play when performed in the public gallery spaces, and the 'porous' nature of the drag activity revealed itself (Farrier, 2016: 198–9). It is such a well-known classic, gallery visitors opted to sing along over my lip-synch when I returned to silence or, in one case, just lip-synched it silently with me, making expansive gestures. I employed conventional drag queen tropes for the costume – sequinned dress, red stilettos, blond wig, full-face make-up and mannerisms from innumerable online drag queens.

Another resonant queer-identified song was 'Vampires' by the Pet Shop Boys. For this I built a boylesque number drawing on drag king and lesbian performance aesthetics – leather harness and strap-on dildo, leather 'boy' cap, gloves and men's knee-high boots. Choreography took inspiration from Klaus Kinski's highly camp, strangely vulnerable Dracula in Werner Herzog's *Nosferatu* (1979). I lip-synched to the whole track in performance.

'Vampires' made strategic and political uses of my exposed breasts and referenced a cunt-centred sexuality in the performance of the strap-on. The work involved a strip-tease of leather, with gloves and boots flying across the exhibition space, strategically choreographed to avoid exhibits but creating a disruptive effect nonetheless. It was transgressive and risk-taking; at one point I sank my teeth, cat-like, into a large raw fish. Most gallery visitors appeared bemused and unsettled by it, and few applauded at the end. I still consider it the best drag performance of the programme.

Some performances developed in response to my struggles as a trans* man with finding an appropriate and viable version of masculinity for myself to live by, or dealt with loss, decay, depression, disease, death and Catholicism. An investigation of saint paintings resulted in full lip-synched performances of Leonard Cohen's 'You Want it Darker' and 'Steer Your Way', and involved crucifixion imagery. I wore men's hospital pyjamas for these. Contemplation of an image of *Samson and Delilah* brought 'Troy' by Sinead O'Connor through, and led to an autobiographical, text-based, silent, semi-naked strap-on performance. 'Cut it Like a Man' explored self-harm, menstruation, gender dysphoria and haircuts; it used drag king tropes.

Masculinity, rules, obedience and ambition were themes of a long lip-synch to Pink Floyd's 'Dogs', which involved me changing from a men's business suit into pyjamas and shaving my chin in the process. It ended with a set of directions to the audience to treat me like a dog, with cards asking them to 'Take me for a walk', 'Tickle my belly', 'Tell me to "fetch"', etc. in reference to gay male 'pup play' and recent experiences of this scene.

Other performances explored femininity and breath (Irigaray, 2002). Choosing a Saturday afternoon moment when the main room of the gallery was full of visitors, I asked them to blow up balloons to help me 'build breath in the space' while I live-sang, a cappella, 'Deh vieni, non tardar' (*The Marriage of Figaro*, Mozart). The room grew in breath and colour as visitors 'huffed and puffed', balloons bouncing above and between the exhibits to opera, with a lively game of balloon football ensuing. Visitors then popped the balloons, releasing breath and laughter, dispelling the conventional silences of the gallery space.

I distributed song sheets for 'Total Eclipse of the Heart', inviting the same visitors to sing along with me to Bonnie Tyler. The performance was an homage to my drag midwife, and in preparation I had studied her physical score (choreography) and mannerisms from the online footage to bring something of her performance presence and energy into the space (Rope Wolf Photography, 2016). While performing, I became overwhelmed with a feeling of fracture – something not uncommon to those of us who live trans* lives. I became painfully aware of the contrast between the testosterone-fuelled camaraderie of the gay bar (the close proximity to other male bodies, the energy of men singing) and the open gallery with its mixed clientele – its spaces, its daylight, its lack of physical closeness/tactility. It took huge physical and vocal effort to fill the room with song and breath, and I felt the tension of battling the 'dead' flesh of exhibits with the live flesh of humans. Literally 'out of breath' afterwards, I recognized the moment as one of transition and release – a performative 'post-natal depression'.

The audience, by contrast, were euphoric and expressed enthusiasm, saying as they left that it had brought the gallery alive for them and they were seeing the spaces anew. One man said I had brought them together, if only for half an hour, 'as a community'. I had succeeded in extending the placental warmth and 'birthing' of my own drag midwife experience through song and made some crossover and connection between the different worlds. I had made others happy, but felt lonely. It brought home to me the challenges as a trans* person of working with drag outside queer-identified spaces.

A final live-singing a cappella act was 'Babe Rainbow' by Melanie. It was an expression of the 'ghost girl' in me – the girl I have let go – and related to Sr Polly. I strapped balloons to cover my whole body while dressed in full drag queen regalia, and gradually exploded each one with a pin, stripping off every item of the costume to stand naked and unadorned in a pile of rubber by the end of the song (see Figure 14.2). I then added balloons to my naked body and repeated the process. At the end of the day, there is only flesh and breath.

The performance was punctuated by an ongoing recitation of the 'Chant of Chants' (Polari Bible), performed with the aid of a small string puppet of a rooster, a deference to a higher power that maps all our fates, with love expressed nevertheless in the historic gay language of Britain's old queens and its order of queer nuns.

Conclusion

The fieldwork conducted by Greenough noted how parody about religion in drag performance tended to have negative representations on stage. On a personal level, it highlighted a conflict between dual identities of identifying as a drag performer and a Christian. Kane's experiential narrative offers a radical transformation to the reading of drag in religious terms. This meditation on drag practice opens up the possibilities of both space and performance to create anew. From a theological perspective, this new creation can signify healing and new birth. The call for being 'born again' from Jesus

Figure 14.2 Sr Polly Amarosa of the Blessed Mercy Beau Cul and Bona Aris, Manchester Sisters of Perpetual Indulgence, campaigning for LGBT* people in Chechnya, Manchester Pride, 2018. Photo: Andrew Moor.

resounds in the gospel of John, where the emphasis is on a spiritual rebirth. Kane's rebirth reflects the tropes of physical, spiritual and religious rebirth, and this is used to energize her engagement with community-focused transformations. Kane's story offers an example of practical theology for the post-modern and queer times in which we now live.

Notes

1 The Sisters of Perpetual Indulgence is a worldwide order of queer nuns, which since 1979 has promoted safer sex and challenged the stigma of HIV/ AIDS. It is dedicated to charity work, community/political activism, street theatre and challenging stigmatic guilt. Sisters 'journey' from Aspirant, to Postulant, to Novice (White Veil) to Fully Professed Sister (Black Veil). The latter two stages are attended by a ceremony – elevation then profession. (Kane, 2016; The Manchester Sisters, 2015–17). The short film *We Are Here* (2019) profiles the Manchester Sisters and features Kane discussing her 'nunself' Sr Polly Amarosa.
2 Kane's Cast-Off Drama project comprised *Queer Sundays* (community 'drop-in'), *Naked Acts: Flesh and Queer* (symposium) and *Caul* (performance); York Art Gallery, UK (2016–17).
3 The Song of Songs is a biblical text structured as a dialogue between a male and female lover accompanied by a chorus of female voices – 'the daughters of Jerusalem'. It is traditionally read as a metaphor for the relationship between Jesus Christ and the Church, or as a love poem between King Solomon and the Queen of Sheba. Feminist scholarship attributes it to female authorship, underlines its eroticism and polyvocality, and suggests it was written by a dancer-poet in Solomon's court (Brenner, 1993).
4 Nina Kane's usage of the asterisk is a personal choice related to the importance it holds for her life journey and theatre work in its inclusion of transvestism, gender and two spirit connotations.
5 Sr Polly's name combines a French joke – 'merci beau cul' ('thanks, nice arse') mispronouncing 'merci beaucoup' ('thank you very much') – with the Polari 'bona aris' ('nice arse') (Denning, 2007). Polly Amarosa is a pun on 'polyamorous'.
6 *Memento Mori* means 'remember that you will die'.
7 'Chicken' – Polari for 'young man'.
8 *Dancer's Eye* (1997), choreographer: Thea Nerissa Barnes.

References

Althaus-Reid, Marcella. (2000). *Indecent Theology*. London: Routledge.

Althaus-Reid, Marcella. (2003). *The Queer God*. London: Routledge.

Althaus-Reid, Marcella and Isherwood, Lisa (eds). (2004). *The Sexual Theologian*. London: Continuum.

Benjamin, Walter. (1936). *The Work of Art in the Age of Mechanical Reproduction*. Available online: http://web.mit.edu/allanmc/www/benjamin.pdf (accessed 5 Jan. 2018).

Bergoffen, Debra. (2007). 'Irigaray's Couples'. In Cimitile, M.C. and Miller, E.P. (eds), *Returning to Irigaray: Feminist Philosophy, Politics, and the Question of Unity*. New York: State University of New York Press, pp. 151–72.

Brenner, Athalya. (ed.) (1993). *A Feminist Companion to 'The Song of Songs'*. Sheffield: Sheffield Academic Press.

Denning, Chris. (2007). Polari. [Blog] *Polari*. Available online: http://chris-d.net/polari/.

Equalities Act. (2010). Available online: https://www.legislation.gov.uk/ukpga/2010/15.

Farrier, Stephen. (2016). 'That Lip-Synching Feeling: Dragging Performance as Digging the Past'. In Campbell, A. and Farrier, S. (eds), *Queer Dramaturgies: International Perspectives on Where Performance Leads Queer*. London: Palgrave Macmillan, pp. 192–209.

Greening-Jackson, Tim. (2001–15). 'Chant of Chants'. [Blog] *Lattie of the Polari Bible*. Available online: http://www.polaribible.org/ (accessed 5 Jan. 2018).

Greenough, Chris. (2017). 'Queering Fieldwork in Religion. Exploring Life Stories from Non-normative Christians Online', In *Fieldwork in Religion*, vol. 12, no. 1, pp. 8–26.

Greenough, Chris. (2018). *Undoing Theology. Life Stories from Non-normative Christians*. London: SCM Press.

Guest, Deryn. (2005). *When Deborah Met Jael*. London: SCM Press.

Guest, Deryn, Goss, Robert E., West, Mona and Bohache, Thomas. (eds) (2006). *The Queer Bible Commentary*. London: SCM Press.

Heelas, Paul and Woodhead, Linda with Seel, Benjamin, Szerszynski, Bronislaw and Tusting, Karin. (2005). *The Spiritual Revolution: Why Religion Is Giving Way to Spirituality*. Oxford: Blackwell.

hooks, bell. (1992). *'Is Paris Burning?' Black Looks: Race and Representation*. Boston, MA: South End Press.

Hornsby, Teresa J. and Guest, Deryn. (2016). *Transgender, Intersex, and Biblical Interpretation*. Atlanta: SBL Press.

Irigaray, Luce. (1993). 'On the Maternal Order'. In *Je, Tu, Nous: Toward a Culture of Difference*, trans. Martin, A. London and New York: Routledge, pp. 39–44.

Irigaray, Luce. (2002). *Between East and West: From Singularity to Community*. New Delhi: New Age Books.

Janes, Dominic. (2015). *Visions of Queer Martyrdom from John Henry Newman to Derek Jarman*. Chicago: University of Chicago Press.

Kane, Nina. (2004–18). 'A Theatre Project of Life-Models, Street-Performers and Itinerant Artists'. [Blog] *Cast-Off Drama*. Available online: www. castoffdrama.blogspot.com (accessed 5 Jan. 2018).

Kane, Nina. (2016). *Sisters of Perpetual Indulgence – Novice Sister Polly's Vestition*. [online video] Available online: https://youtu.be/PNwLUX2r5Zo (accessed 5 Jan. 2018).

Kane, Nina. (2017a). *Cast-Off Drama on BBC Look North East*. [online video] Available online: https://youtu.be/9UCEyusRPmY (accessed 5 Jan. 2018).

Kane, Nina. (2017b). 'Trans*tastic Morphologies: Life-Modelling Theatre and *The Lady of Shalott*'. In Kane, N. and Woods, J. (eds) *Reflections of Female and Trans* Masculinities and Other Queer Crossings*, Newcastle: Cambridge Scholars Publishing, pp. 112–64.

Kane, Nina and Woods, Jude. (2017). 'Introduction'. In Kane, N. and Woods, J. (eds), *Reflections of Female and Trans* Masculinities and Other Queer Crossings*. Newcastle: Cambridge Scholars Publishing, pp. 1–10.

King James Bible Online. (2018). Song of Solomon and Proverbs. Available online: https://www.kingjamesbibleonline.org/(accessed 5 Jan. 2018).

Koosed, Jennifer L. (2006). 'Ecclesiastes/Qohelet'. In Guest, D., Goss, R. E., West, M., and Bohache, T. (eds), *The Queer Bible Commentary*. London: SCM Press, pp. 338–55.

Lorenz, Renate. (2012). *Queer Art: A Freak Theory*. Bielefeld: transcript Verlag.

Lundy, Craig. (2012). *History and Becoming: Delueze's Philosophy of Creativity*. Edinburgh: Edinburgh University Press.

The Manchester Sisters. (2015–17). *21st Century Nuns*. Available online: https://www.themanchestersisters.org/ (accessed 5 Jan. 2018).

McCune Jr., Jeffrey Q. (2004). 'Transformance'. *Journal of Homosexuality*, vol. 46, nos 3–4, pp. 151–67.

Norton, Rictor. (1992). *Mother Clap's Molly House: The Gay Subculture in England 1700–1830*. London: GMP Publishing.

Nosferatu: Phantom der Nacht, 1979. [Film]. Directed by Werner Herzog. Germany: Twentieth Century Fox.

Peter Fuller's Vision Thing. (2010). *Saint Derek*. Available online: https://youtu. be/YcessfaJW0M (accessed 5 Jan. 2018).

Rope Wolf Photography. (2016). *La Voix – Total Eclipse of the Heart – Manchester Pride 2016*. Available online: https://youtu.be/7jDNA6sNHcg (accessed 5 Jan. 2018).

Stanton, Helen (ed.). (1997 [1990]). *Mary and Human Liberation: The Story and Text – Fr. Tissa Balasuriya*. London: Mowbray.

Starhawk (1989 [1979]). *The Spiral Dance: A Rebirth of the Ancient Religion of the Great Goddess*. 10th Anniversary ed. San Francisco: Harper and Row Publishers.

Stepto, Michele and Stepto, Gabriel (trans.). (1996). *Memoir of a Basque Lieutenant Nun, Transvestite in the New World: Catalina De Erauso*. Boston: Beacon Press.

Stuart, Elizabeth. (1992). *Daring to Speak Love's Name*. London: Hamish Hamilton.

Stuart, Elizabeth. (1995). *Just Good Friends: Towards a Lesbian and Gay Theology of Relationships*. London: Mowbrays.

Stuart, Elizabeth. (1997). *Religion is a Queer Thing*. London: Cassell.

Sullivan-Blum, Constance R. (2004). 'Balancing Acts'. *Journal of Homosexuality*, vol. 46, pp. 3–4, 195–209.

We Are Here (2019) [Short Film]. Directed by Ellie Hodgetts, UK: Northern Film School.

Wilcox, Melissa M. (2012). 'Spirituality, Activism, and the "Postsecular"'. In 'The Sisters of Perpetual Indulence' In Nynäs, P. and Yip, A. K. T. (eds), *Religion, Gender and Sexuality in Everyday Life*. Farnham: Ashgate, pp. 37–50.

Wilcox, Melissa M. (2018). *Queer Nuns: Religion, Activism, and Serious Parody*. New York: NYU Press.

Yip, Andrew K. T. (1998). 'Gay Male Christians' Perceptions of the Christian Community in Relation to their Sexuality'. *Theology and Sexuality*, vol 8, pp. 40–51.

Yip, Andrew K. T. (2002). 'The Persistence of Faith Among Nonheterosexual Christians: Evidence for the Neosecularization Thesis of Religious Transformation'. *Journal for the Scientific Study of Religion*, vol. 41, no. 2, pp. 199–212.

Yip, Andrew K. T. (2003a). 'Spirituality and Sexuality: An Exploration of the Religious Beliefs of Non-Heterosexual Christians in Great Britain'. *Theology and Sexuality*, vol. 9, no. 2, pp. 137–54.

Yip, Andrew K. T. (2003b). 'The Self as the Basis of Religious Faith: Spirituality of Gay, Lesbian and Bisexual Christians'. In Davie, G., Heelas, P., and Woodhead, L. (eds), *Predicting Religion: Christian, Secular and Alternative Futures*. Hampshire: Ashgate, pp. 135–46.

York Museums and Gallery Trust. (2018). *Flesh*. Available online: https://www.yorkartgallery.org.uk/exhibition/flesh/ (accessed 5 Jan. 2018).

Index